Bobbie

I love this guy for two reasons.

First, he was a great President,
the right man at the right time
Second (or first?), he'd drive the
liberals nuts!

DEAR
AMERICANS

DOUBLEDAY

New York • London • Toronto

Sydney • Auckland

DEAR AMERICANS

Letters from the Desk of President Ronald Reagan

Edited, with Introduction and Commentary, by

RALPH E. WEBER

Editor

RALPH A. WEBER

Associate Editor

PUBLISHED BY DOUBLEDAY
A division of Random House, Inc.

DOUBLEDAY and the portrayal of an anchor with a dolphin are trademarks
of Random House, Inc.

Photographs courtesy of The Ronald Reagan Presidential Library

Book design by Judith Abbate/Abbate Design

The cataloging-in-publication data is on file with the Library of Congress

ISBN 0-385-50756-9

PRINTED IN THE UNITED STATES OF AMERICA

November 2003

First Edition

1   3   5   7   9   10   8   6   4   2

For Rosemarie and Patti

Contents

—

DEAR
AMERICANS

Introduction

—

RONALD Reagan's critics deride his abilities and presidency, referring to him as a "cue card" president who did little more than read lines written by others. Such persons see only Reagan the actor and assume that advisors actually masterminded the domestic and foreign policy accomplishments of 1981 to 1989.

The letters that follow put these misconceptions to rest. While researching at the Ronald Reagan Presidential Library in Simi Valley, California, the senior editor discovered a remarkable collection of over 3,500 letters in Reagan's handwriting. Popularly known as the Great Communicator, he should also be recognized as the Great Correspondent. These fascinating letters written to lifelong friends and ordinary citizens who corresponded with the President reflect an engaged mind focused on policy issues and keenly sensitive to government's impact on American society. The Handwriting File letters likewise reveal a person with a strong, self-deprecating sense of humor who had seen all aspects of the human condition over his eight decades, or as he might put it, the four decades after his thirty-ninth birthday.

Dated 1981 to 1989, the letters went to a diverse number of American citizens, such as indigent persons who lost their jobs, parents of service members killed in Lebanon, African Americans wounded by racial discrimination, angry critics of the "Star Wars" missile defense system, senior citizens worried about the viability of Social Security, political supporters of his domestic programs, grade school students with questions about the presidency, and friends who encouraged him to continue his domestic and foreign policy initiatives. Reagan's replies show his optimism about the American economy, his frequent frustration with the print and television media, his determination to halt Soviet expansion (especially into Central America), and his hopes for securing a missile shield over the United States. They also reflect his decades-long crusade to lower taxes, reduce federal expenditures, and rebuild the American military.

Anne V. Higgins served as director of Presidential Correspondence with her office in Room 94 of the Executive Office Building next to the White House. In our interview with her, she related how she had gone to Washington, D.C., from New York originally to manage President Richard Nixon's presidential correspondence. On her first day working for President Reagan, a thoughtful Nixon phoned her at 7:30 A.M., congratulated her, and told her to continue the fine work she had done in his administration. For both presidents, staff members typed selected incoming handwritten letters before being given to the presidents; for President Nixon, a synopsis of the letter was also prepared. Higgins recounted that President Reagan asked on one of the first days of his presidency whether the staff wanted him to dictate replies or write them out. Surprised, the staff said it was his choice. In his first months in office and before his personal secretary, Kathy Osborne, rejoined his staff in October 1981, Reagan dictated several dozen replies; however, he also wrote out several hundred before the year ended. "He was a secretary's dream," Higgins related, "because he wrote out the recipients' addresses at the top of his handwritten letters."

All of the mail to the White House—according to Osborne, some 300,000 pieces of mail each month—passed through a fluoroscope and through X-ray machines. Higgins had a staff of almost 60 full-time analysts, 30 part-timers, and 500 volunteers who processed the letters. They were sorted according to subject matter: children's letters; hardship inquiries; requests for birthday and anniversary congratulations from the president; and job inquiries were just a few of the categories. After sorting, some went to specific federal agencies for answers and replies. Others went to a special staff who assisted with Social Security and Internal Revenue Service questions and problems. Envelopes from correspondents with the code number "16691" or "Attention: Kathy Osborne" on the front went directly to the President's office.

Higgins selected the sample of thirty or so incoming letters that the President received each week. These letters might be critical of a key cabinet member, or in praise of the defense budget, or bitterly opposed to American foreign policies regarding the Middle East, or vehemently angry about the President's upcoming trip to Bitburg cemetery, or confused by the Iran-Contra arms sales. She included other letters—for example, those complaining that the President was an actor playing president, that he did not understand the problems of the poor and unemployed because he was wealthy and surrounded by rich friends. Also common were accusations that too many dollars were poured into the defense budget instead of education and welfare. Letters from farm families told of low crop prices and high bank loans; one tragic account told of financial collapse and a despondent father who committed suicide.

Complimentary letters also reached the President's folder. Messages from African Americans who praised him for his help to the community especially pleased President Reagan. Letters from personal friends in Illinois and Iowa recalled his years in the town of Dixon and at Eureka College, when he was known as Dutch, and he signed his replies with that nickname. Some personal correspondents included clippings of positive newspaper or magazine columns that, as he replied, "brightened my day." Some conservative supporters, deeply anxious about unemployment and the weak domestic economy, or Soviet threats, or sometimes both, encouraged the President to continue his budget blueprint and foreign policy principles despite opposition from Democrats in Congress. In his replies, Reagan acknowledged their kind support and urged patience until his full economic program, delayed by inflation and the recession, could begin. Several conservative correspondents criticized Reagan's tax program and his failure to push all of it through Congress. The President wrote in anger to one conservative editor and called his July journal "one of the most dishonest and unfair bits of journalism I have ever seen." Osborne said that often his handwritten replies did not go to the staff for review before being typed.

President Reagan especially enjoyed writing letters to grade and high school students who asked him about the presidency, the White House, his hobbies, and his daily schedule. His special young pen pal, Rudolph, in Washington, D.C., received individual attention with letters, birthday gifts, and encouragement. The President also visited him at his home. Anne Higgins said the President gave Ruddy distinctive photographs of the presidential trip to China and labeled each with a description.

This sensitive President found it difficult to reply to letters from parents, wives, and children of those who died in the Beirut bombing, the liberation of Grenada, and the *Challenger* explosion. Sometimes he would write on the top of these incoming letters "Phoned, no reply" or "I phoned her instead of writing—it's lump in the throat time. RR." Also painful for him to read were the sad letters from welfare parents and/or their children. One of these writers revealed a tragic story about an abandoned mother whose two husbands deserted her and their young children. Hunger and despair filled their days; they became gypsies when they couldn't pay the rent. She described coldhearted welfare staff members who did not truly care about the family. Instead, she believed, they protected the welfare system in order to keep their jobs. Reagan's reply promised more welfare reform and, he hoped, more caring caseworkers. Sometimes he sent a personal check to ease the poverty of a family. One Indiana recipient prized the $100 check and planned to frame it instead of cashing it. When Reagan learned this, he told her to cash it and his accountant would return it for framing. Higgins related that the President read some pro-life letters aloud during cabinet meetings and said he realized that not all agreed. One woman wrote about being pregnant decades ago and that she considered an abortion but opened the Bible to the page where it said "Thou shalt not kill" and decided to have the baby. That baby was now caring for her in Arizona.

Osborne gave the President the weekly batch of letters from Higgins. Osborne read one of the incoming letters from a young woman whose father, an Army private, went ashore at Omaha Beach in World War II and had hoped to return to see the beach and the graves. He had died of cancer before realizing his dream, and his daughter had promised to return for him and put flowers on the graves. With a lump in her throat, Osborne gave the letter to a sympathetic president, who honored this soldier and the caring daughter who was present during his beautiful speech at Omaha Beach in June 1984.

Osborne explained to us that when the President was traveling, all letters to him offered by visitors or bystanders were given to the Secret Service agents who in turn gave them to the staff to process. She also added that frequently she got the letters to his office on Friday so he could take them to Camp David, and sometimes he began writing as the helicopter lifted off. Most of his handwritten letters were signed "Ron" or "Ronald," or "RR"; to childhood and college friends he often signed as "Dutch."

His handwritten letters had few words crossed out: they were typed by secretaries in the White House, signed by hand or machine, and mailed out. The presidential stationery was off-white bond paper with the White House letterhead printed in royal blue. The incoming letter and his handwritten and typed copy were then filed together in the archives.

In several instances White House officials, including James Baker, Dick Darman, and Ed Meese, reviewed his handwritten letters when they contained statistics. Rarely were inaccuracies found. In one of his letters written during the Iran-Contra furor, staff wrote in unclassified CIA figures concerning military exports to Iran from the Soviet Union in place of the figures written by the President. In another rare instance, Reagan wrote that the House of Representatives had been under Democratic control for sixty years except for four years; staff changed the sixty to fifty. In several cases, State Department officials counseled the President and his advisors about the method of contacting high-level foreign government officials. Some of the incoming and outgoing letters were reviewed by various offices, such as Domestic Affairs, Office of Legal Affairs, Office of Management and Budget, as well as Justice.

Osborne said that when President Reagan arrived in California after leaving the presidency, there were forty thousand letters awaiting him. In Washington, Higgins noted that for days after his departure, letters continued to pour in and were answered by a special card and a photograph of the President and Mrs. Reagan. January 1989 marked the end of a remarkable presidency. During his last days in the White House, President Reagan may have recalled the words he wrote for his inaugural in 1981: "We shall reflect the compassion that is so much a part of your makeup. How can we love our country & not love our countrymen? And loving them reach out a hand when they fall, heal them when they are sick and provide opportunity to make them self-sufficient so they will be equal in fact & not just in theory?" This president did indeed reflect that compassion, did reflect that love of country and its citizens, and sought equality for all regardless of race, creed, and gender.

Editorial Notes

—

LL the letters from the Handwritten File at the Ronald Reagan Presidential Library and published in this volume were handwritten by President Reagan, typed by secretaries, and mailed to correspondents. There are typed letters in the file for which there are no handwritten attachments; their rhetoric is different from Reagan's, and they were prepared by staff members. These letters are not included. Reagan's letters to the General Secretary of the Soviet Union are located in the Executive Secretariat, National Security Council, Head of State Records file at the library.

In his pen-and-ink letters, the sentences flow smoothly, with few crossed-out words or phrases. Very few spelling errors were found in the letters he wrote. We have compared his handwritten letters with the typed letters, and for ease of reading, we have printed the typed rather than the handwritten letters, which often contained abbreviations. In a few cases, we have printed directly from his handwritten letters (and added dates in brackets) because typed copies were not available in the file. He often omitted apostrophes in his handwritten letters and we added them. Also he or the typist would vary the spacing of "a while" and "awhile," and we have consistently added a space between the two words. He did not date the handwritten letters when he wrote them in the White House, Camp David, or Air Force One, and therefore the dates on the correspondence in this volume are those from the typed letters prepared by his staff secretaries soon after he composed the letters. We have excluded street addresses from the letters and, in a few instances, names and cities. Because Reagan's handwriting was so clear, White House secretaries had no problems reading his letters nor did the editors. After the typed letters were mailed, Reagan's handwritten copy, a typed copy, and the correspondent's letter sent to the White House were filed and later moved to the library in Simi Valley, California. Library staff members removed family and other personal letters before the files were opened to the public. The correspondence selected for this book was chosen from over 3,500 letters located in the Handwriting File. They truly reflect President Reagan's character, compassion, insights, humor, wisdom, and American optimism.

1981

Let me say I'm very lucky and the Lord really had his
hand on my shoulder. Literally, a sequence of minor
miracles strung together to help me have a recovery that
is complete . . .

·*Letter of June 15, 1981*·

O n Tuesday morning, January 20, 1981, in a sun-filled
ceremony on the west side of the Capitol, Chief Justice
Warren E. Berger swore in Ronald Reagan as the fortieth
President of the United States. Nancy Reagan held the
Bible used formerly by the President's mother, Nelle.
Wearing a charcoal-gray coat, striped trousers, gray vest and tie, Reagan,
called by some columnists the "Cowboy Hero," became at age sixty-nine
the oldest man to assume the presidency. Thousands of invited guests, including columnist William F. Buckley, Jr., and singer Pat Boone, along
with 150,000 citizens witnessed the start of the Reagan presidency and
joined in singing "America the Beautiful."

Brimming with optimism, the Reagans welcomed the opportunity to begin an era of national renewal and religious dedication. Earlier that morning they had gone to St. John's Episcopal Church near Lafayette Square and listened to sermons by the Reverend Donn Moomaw, their pastor at the Bel Air Presbyterian Church in Los Angeles, and another favorite minister, the Reverend Billy Graham.

Time magazine's "Man of the Year" entered the presidency at a time of intense national frustration. For fourteen months, American hostages (President Reagan called them prisoners of war) had been held in Iran; the American economy was depressed and unstable, with high unemployment, numerous business bankruptcies, and a national debt exceeding $900 billion and climbing. Reagan enjoyed the boost in national optimism soon after his inauguration when the Iran hostages were released.

During the first ten weeks of his presidency, Reagan began deciphering the codes and intricacies of Washington's power structure. He told *Time* reporter Laurence I. Barrett in early February that White House business was not that much different from Sacramento's business. Maybe his early estimate was a hope rather than a reality, for the President had not yet experienced many of the complex machinations in the district. He also told Barrett he did not have a moment for pleasure reading, that he dreaded the uproar of complaints about budget cuts, and that he found that complex issues had positive values on both sides.

Each weekday morning he went to the Oval Office at 9 A.M. and gave his secretary, Helene van Damm, a folder of papers he had read and signed the night before. During Cabinet Room meetings, with treasury secretary Donald Regan and budget director David Stockman, he discussed various ways to lower federal spending and methods for reducing taxes. Other Oval Office meetings with National Security Advisor Richard Allen, White House Counsel Edwin Meese, and Chief of Staff James Baker, reporters, and occasionally foreign ministers filled the afternoons until 5 P.M.

During the early months of his administration, Reagan answered many of the letters from correspondents with a recording machine rather than handwritten letters. In the twelve months after mid-February 1981, he filled twenty-five minicassettes. As the year unfolded he gradually shifted to handwritten replies. He had various staff members, such as Mike Deaver, Deputy Chief of Staff, check complex questions posed by writers and also answer ordinary requests and invitations. Reagan's dictated replies

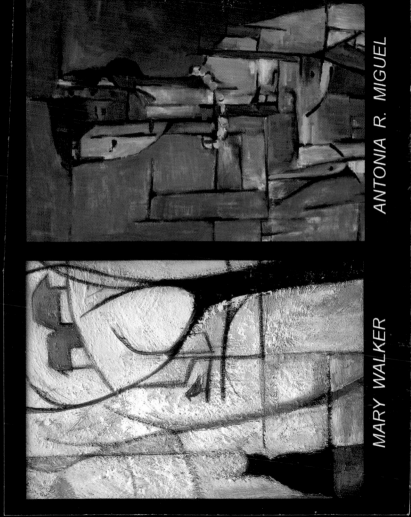

ANTONIA R. MIGUEL

MARY WALKER

JULIE HELLER EAST
465 Commercial Street
Provincetown, MA 02657

MARY WALKER
ANTONIA R. MIGUEL
CONNECTIONS

JULIE HELLER EAST
(across from PAAM)
July 16 - 29, 2010

-- Opening Reception --
Friday, July 16, 7:30 - 10 pm

Open 10:30 am - 11 pm daily
508 487-2166 / 508 487-2169
www.juliehellergallery.com

STEFANI
PO BOX 189
WELLFLEET, MA 02667-0189

Presorted
First-Class Mail
US Postage
PAID
VistaPrint
48174

11101 Metro Airport Ctr Dr, Ste 105
Romulus, MI 48174

during the early months thanked writers for their encouragement and support: the President's favorite phrase was "your letter brightened the day for many of us." To his friend and astute columnist Lieutenant General Victor "Brute" Krulak, Reagan dictated that he was battling those who forget the last forty years and seem to think that all troubles came about in the last four months. Moreover, he promised the general that he would not whittle back defense and would fight to the "last pop gun" before giving in: "In fact, I won't give in. They'll have to do it over my carcass if that's possible." To another writer he replied that the President did not cause inflation, it was started by Washington, D.C. And the person who sent a shamrock from County Tipperary received a grateful dictated acknowledgment.

As in every first One Hundred Days, Washington welcomed the new President; and he, like his predecessors, basked in the friendly reception. An astute politician, Reagan quickly selected the right invitations. In late January, on a Saturday afternoon, he went to the Alibi Club on I Street and visited with fifty of the district's power brokers. That evening he joined six hundred members of the Alfalfa Club, and after speeches by Senator John Glenn and Henry Kissinger, he spoke briefly and included jokes about his age. In his first press conference on January 29, he promised to lower the inflation rate, set a sixty-day freeze on government regulations, restrict federal hiring, and to eliminate all price controls on domestic oil. On national television on February 5, he spoke to the nation about the economy, announcing sobering numbers: 7 million persons unemployed; double-digit inflation back to back for the first time since World War I; a national debt of $934 billion. He predicted that unless taxes and spending were reduced, the nation faced a huge economic calamity.

On February 18, in his State of the Union Address to Congress, Reagan spoke for thirty-four minutes about his economic program and called for $467 billion less federal spending together with $709 billion in reduced taxes. He believed the federal government must make over $41 billion worth of budget cuts in fiscal 1982 and $123.8 billion in cuts by fiscal 1986. His blueprint for economic recovery numbered 281 pages; only defense spending escaped cuts; rather, it would be increased. Eighty-three federal programs would have their budgets reduced; states and cities would have more control over federal allotments. Although his remarks were greeted with numerous standing ovations, critics soon tore into his speech. Eighteen members of the Congressional Black Caucus accused the administration of making the poor "hungrier, colder, and sicker." Democrat congressman Tip O'Neill of Massachusetts promised "We're not going to let him tear asunder programs we've built." Congressional and public debates quickly focused on Reagan's national renewal program: A *Washington Post* survey reported in early March that Americans favored the program to cut taxes and slash the budget three to one. Although those statistics encouraged the President, difficult months lay ahead.

Also during these first months, Reagan welcomed to Washington Prime Minister Margaret Thatcher from Great Britain, Foreign Minister Jean François-Poncet from France, and Foreign Minister Yitzhak Shamir from Israel. Thatcher became his favorite foreign leader, and she, along with her husband, Denis, were guests of honor at the first State Dinner during the Reagan presidency. The Soviet threat continued as the primary foreign policy issue. On the day of Reagan's inauguration, Leonid Brezhnev, president of the Soviet Union, in a broadcast over Moscow Radio, called for improved relations between the Soviet Union and America. However, in an early February press conference, Reagan said he knew of no Soviet leader since the Russian Revolution who did not pursue the goal of world revolution. Moreover, the Soviet leaders lie, cheat, and commit any crime during their pursuit. Despite Reagan's rhetoric, in a speech to the Soviet Communist Party Congress several weeks later, Brezhnev suggested a summit meeting between Reagan and himself. He also expressed a willingness to talk about arms control and about notifications by Warsaw Pact countries and North Atlantic Treaty countries on military maneuvers and troop moves. Reagan's response called on the Soviets to halt arms shipments to leftist guerrillas in El Salvador before a summit could be considered. The March assassination attempt on the President in Washington, D.C., halted all progress for improved relations with the Soviet Union.

In the midafternoon of March 30, John W. Hinckley, Jr., shot President Reagan as he was entering the presidential limousine outside the Hilton Hotel in Washington. The bullet tore into his lung and lodged within an inch of his heart. The limousine sped to nearby George Washington Hospital in less than four minutes. Reagan, determined to walk into the emergency room, collapsed as he entered. The medical staff, at first puzzled by the President's fragile condition and thinking he had had a heart attack in addition to being shot, finally found a narrow bullet wound below the left armpit. The wound caused the loss of half of Reagan's blood volume.

A shocked nation followed the televised medical bulletins. As his recovery grew stronger, newspapers reported he quipped to doctors before his surgery "I just hope you're Republicans"; and in the recovery room he repeated heavyweight boxer Jack Dempsey's comment to his wife after he lost the championship fight to Gene Tunney: "Honey, I forgot to duck." He also told one of the nurses the old comic W. C. Fields's lines: "All in all, I'd rather be in Philadelphia." On April 11 a pale Reagan, showing typical determination, rejected the offer of a wheelchair and walked slowly and stiffly out of the hospital.

During the two months before the shooting he wrote more than eighteen letters to friends and the general public, but during his recovery in April he wrote only four. Among the most important handwritten letters during 1981 were the ones addressed to the Soviet president, Leonid Brezhnev. Both were classified top secret and not declassified until 2000.

A defense buildup required frequent decisions and analysis from President Reagan during 1981. During President Jimmy Carter's administration, designing the MX missile program had proven to be a sensitive problem for the President and his military advisors. President Reagan also faced complicated questions about implementing this costly defense weapon. A column by syndicated advice columnist Ann Landers produced thousands of letters calling for reevaluating the needs and design for this venture.

The Middle East troubled Reagan, as it had his predecessors. In mid-August two carrier-based F-14s shot down two Libyan SU-22s that had challenged them over the Gulf of Sidra. The assassination of President Anwar el-Sadat of Egypt during a military parade in Cairo shocked Reagan and his cabinet. Only two months earlier Sadat and his wife had been welcomed warmly at a state dinner in the White House. The Senate approval of the Airborne Warning and Control System aircraft (AWACS) sale to Saudi Arabia, which was opposed by Israel, required considerable presidential pressure on certain senators.

Often notice of domestic problems were conveyed in the mail pouches arriving at the White House. Letters from American citizens described bitter unemployment problems, business bankruptcies, and depressing economic statistics. A few correspondents complained that Reagan had only rich friends; none recognized that most of those friends used their wealth to endow universities, hospitals, and other charitable organizations. Some letter writers accused him of robbing the poor and giving to the rich. Others questioned why he fired the air traffic controllers. His replies explained his actions and perspectives on these topics. His projected tax bill won congressional approval with its provision that individual tax rates would decline by 25 percent over three years. Sobering, however, during his first year was the fact that the annual deficit would run to almost $79 billion.

The President's foreign and domestic travel schedule, though reduced somewhat after April to ensure complete recovery from the shooting, proved formidable. In early March the President traveled to Ottawa and addressed the Parliament. He returned to Canada for the Economic Summit in July, and in his address he noted that the seven countries attending the conference accounted for more than 80 percent of the gross national product of the industrialized world. He attended the North-South Summit in Cancún, Mexico, in late October. His rigorous domestic travel schedule included over twenty trips, including New York, Los Angeles, Chicago, and San Antonio. He returned to the locale of the Knute Rockne film, a 1940 movie about the famous Notre Dame football coach: Reagan played George Gipp, Rockne's star player. At the University on May 17 he received an honorary doctorate. There were also nineteen visits to Camp David, where he wrote many of his letters; critical correspondents never knew about his handwritten letters to former Dixon, Illinois, neighbors, classmates at Eureka College, young students, Vietnam and Lebanon veterans and their families, and disabled citizens.

Embedded in the year 1981 and in each of the following years was the President's dedication, expressed in his diary on his return to the White House after the shooting and revealed in his autobiography: "Whatever happens now I owe my life to God and will try to serve him in every way I can." Restoring the domestic economy and rebuilding confidence in foreign affairs would require much of this dedication.

Before his presidency, Reagan visited in England with Margaret Thatcher, the first woman to lead the British Conservative Party, and he was deeply impressed with her strong determination to reduce "wall-to-wall government." In her London address to the Pilgrim Club, Prime Minister Thatcher praised the Pilgrim Fathers and their followers who came to America because they rejected tyranny and loved freedom.

WASHINGTON

February 2, 1981

Dear Madame Prime Minister:

I have read the initial news reports of your speech to the Pilgrims' Dinner on January 29, and I wanted to convey my thanks and good wishes for your kind words.

You are indeed right that we share a very special concern for democracy and for liberty. That is the essence of the special relationship between our two countries, and it is similarly an excellent basis for inaugurating an extended period of cooperation and close consultation between your government and my administration.

It is with greatest anticipation that I look forward to your arrival here and to the opportunity for extensive discussions on the broad range of world issues with which we must deal in partnership.

Sincerely,

Ronald Reagan

The Right Honorable
Margaret Thatcher, M.P.
Prime Minister
London

Pat Boone, singer, movie and television star, was a family friend. One day in Reagan's second term as Governor of California, Boone brought several Evangelical ministers to Reagan's residence in Sacramento for a prayer service.

WASHINGTON

March 18, 1981

Dear Pat:

Thank you so much for your thoughtful letter. Unfortunately, because of the transition, I just recently received it and hope you will excuse my delay in answering.

I appreciate your suggestion about Herb Ellingwood and will give it careful consideration. I know I will need the support of Christian leaders to deal with the problems facing our nation. But, more importantly, I will need their prayers.

Again, thank you for writing, and you and Shirley have my best wishes.

Sincerely,

Ronald Reagan

Mr. Pat Boone
Los Angeles, California

President Reagan began writing the following letter to Leonid Brezhnev, president of the Soviet Union (1960–64, 1977–82) during his recovery in the White House after the assassination attempt.

[April 24, 1981]

My Dear Mr. President:

In writing the attached letter I am reminded of our meeting in San Clemente a decade or so ago. I was Governor of California at the time and you were concluding a series of meetings with President Nixon. Those meetings had captured the imagination of all the world. Never had peace and goodwill among men seemed closer at hand.

When we met I asked if you were aware that the hopes and aspirations of millions and millions of people throughout the world were dependent on the decisions that would be reached in your meetings.

You took my hand in both of yours and assured me that you were aware of that and that you were dedicated with all your heart and mind to fulfilling those hopes and dreams.

The people of the world still share that hope. Indeed the peoples of the world, despite differences in racial and ethnic origin, have very much in common. They want the dignity of having some control over their individual destiny. They want to work at the craft or trade of their own choosing and to be fairly rewarded. They want to raise their families in peace without harming anyone or suffering harm themselves. Government exists for their convenience, not the other way around.

If they are incapable, as some would have us believe, of self-government, then where among them do we find any who are capable of governing others?

Is it possible that we have permitted ideology, political and economic philosophies, and governmental policies to keep us from considering the very real, everyday problems of our peoples? Will the average Soviet family be better off or even aware that the Soviet Union has imposed a government of its own choice on the people of Afghanistan? Is life better for the people of Cuba because the Cuban military dictate who shall govern the people of Angola?

It is often implied that such things have been made necessary because of territorial ambitions of the United States; that we have imperialistic designs and thus constitute a threat to your own security and that of the newly emerging nations. There not only is no evidence to support such a charge, there is solid evidence that the United States, when it could have dominated the world with no risk to itself, made no effort whatsoever to do so.

When World War II ended, the United States had the only undamaged industrial power in the world. Our military might was at its peak—and we alone had the ultimate weapon, the nuclear weapon, with the unquestioned ability to deliver it anywhere in the world. If we had sought world domination then, who could have opposed us?

But the United States followed a different course—one unique in all the history of mankind. We used our power and wealth to rebuild the war-ravaged economies of the world, including those nations who had been our enemies. May I say there is absolutely no substance to charges that the United States is guilty of imperialism or attempts to impose its will on other countries by use of force.

Mr. President, should we not be concerned with eliminating the obstacles which prevent our people—those we represent—from achieving their most cherished goals? And isn't it possible some of those obstacles are born of government objectives which have little to do with the real needs and desires of our people?

It is in this spirit, in the spirit of helping the people of both our nations, that I have lifted the grain embargo. Perhaps this decision will contribute to creating the circumstances which will lead to the meaningful and constructive dialogue which will assist us in fulfilling our joint obligation to find lasting peace.

Sincerely,

Ronald Reagan

An old Eureka friend wrote to thank President Reagan for his phone call on March 25, the day her husband, Sam, died.

June 15, 1981

Dear Mrs. S. G. Harrod, Jr.:

It was good to hear from you and I appreciate your concern about me. Let me say I'm very lucky and the Lord really had his hand on my shoulder. Literally, a sequence of minor miracles strung together to help me have a recovery that is complete—and even the doctors say that it is.

To begin with, when [March 30, 1981] I walked into the emergency entrance the entire surgical staff of George Washington Hospital were just concluding a meeting. I had the top medicos by my side in half a minute. Then the bullet, which had glanced off the side of the car, hit a rib before entering the lung which helped stop it about one inch from my heart.

But most important, I had the prayers of a lot of people and for that I'm most grateful.

That's enough about me and my operation. I know these are not easy times for you. And I know words can't be of much help. We just have to believe in God's wisdom and mercy. You are in our prayers.

Nancy sends her best.

Sincerely,

Dutch

Mrs. S. G. Harrod, Jr.
Eureka, Illinois

Reagan wrote to President Brezhnev to pardon Anatolii Scharansky and Pentecostal Christians, a religious community that seeks to be filled with the Holy Spirit as were the disciples at Pentecost. Scharansky, accused of treason and spying for the United States, had been in a Soviet prison since 1977. After his release in 1986, he went to Israel. The Pentecostal Christians were permitted to leave the U.S. embassy and emigrate in 1983.

WASHINGTON

[July 1981]

My Dear Mr. President:

I'm sorry to be so long in answering your letter to me and can only offer as an excuse the problems of settling into a routine after my hospitalization. I ask your pardon.

I won't attempt a point-by-point response to your letter because I agree with your observation that these matters are better discussed in person than in writing. Needless to say, we are not in agreement on a number of points raised in both my letter and yours.

There is one matter, however, which I feel I must bring to your attention. All information having to do with my Government's practices and policies, past and present, is available to me now that I hold this office. I have thoroughly investigated the matter of the man Scharansky, an inmate in one of your prisons. I can assure you he was never involved in any way with any agency of the United States Government. I have seen news stories in the Soviet press suggesting that he was engaged in espionage for our country. Let me assure you this is absolutely false.

Recently his wife called upon me. They were married and spent one day together before she emigrated to Israel [1974], assuming that he would follow shortly thereafter. I believe true justice would be done if he were released and allowed to join her.

If you could find it in your heart to do this, the matter would be strictly between us, which is why I'm writing this letter by hand.

While on this subject, may I also enter a plea on behalf of the two families [sic] who have been living in most uncomfortable circumstances in our embassy in Moscow for three years. The [Vaschenko] family and the [Chmykhalov family] are Pentecostal Christians who feared possible persecution because of their religion. Members of that church in America would, I know, provide for them here if they were allowed to come to the U.S.

Again, as in the case of Scharansky, this is between the two of us, and I will not reveal that I made any such requests. I'm sure, however, you understand that such actions on your part would lessen my problems in future negotiations between our two countries.

Sincerely,

Ronald Reagan

WASHINGTON

August 3, 1981

Dear General Pattison:

Thank you very much for writing as you did and for giving me an opportunity to comment with regard to your concern. I appreciate your generous words and the support that you are giving to the party.

I have to say I believe our positions with regard to conservation have been wildly distorted and exaggerated. I do think there are some conservationists who have been rather extreme and would prevent us from meeting any of our needs for minerals, energy, etc. However, I, too, am a conservationist and a lover of the beauty of this country, and I assure you we are not going to allow it to be de-spoiled. I know Secretary of Interior [James] Watt is a conservationist, and much of what he's supposed to have said or what he's doing is being quoted out of context and distorted. Please rest assured we will not return to poisoned air or water nor will we wipe out the beauty of this land.

Again, my thanks.

Best regards,

Ronald Reagan

Mr. Hal C. Pattison
Brigadier General, USA (Ret)
Fairfax, Virginia

Under President Carter, a plan was advanced for building 200 MX missiles and moving them back and forth between 4,600 shelters in Utah and Nevada. Carter abandoned this "racetrack" plan eight months before leaving office. Esther "Eppie" Lederer (1918–2002) wrote the Ann Landers advice column. She was the most widely syndicated columnist in the world, with over 70 million readers in 1981. She wrote an insightful letter to Reagan and urged him to put the MX missile on the "back burner" because of cost and obsolescence.

October 5, 1981

Dear Eppie:

By the time you get this, you'll already know of our plans regarding the MX. I appreciate your letter and your concern very much. I assume part of your feeling about the MX was due to the ridiculous idea of running it around a track with 4600 silos. I've always been opposed to that. Our use for it will be to replace the aging Titans and some of the Minuteman missiles. The MX is a much more accurate missile with 10 warheads instead of 3.

Again, thanks for writing. Nancy sends her love.

Sincerely,

Ron

Ann Landers
Field Newspaper Syndicate
Chicago Sun-Times Building
Chicago, Illinois

President Carter had promised AWACS to Saudi Arabia; however, Israel and the Israeli lobby in Congress opposed the sale. Five aircraft were finally approved by the Senate in late October after personal intervention by President Reagan. Reagan's friendship with the Reverend Graham had begun decades earlier, and as governor of California Reagan appreciated Graham's spiritual guidance. Graham's letters to Reagan did not mention military weapons; rather Graham wrote that God spared the President's life to help lead the nation in a spiritual renewal.

WASHINGTON

October 5, 1981

Dear Billy:

I'm so sorry to hear about Ruth. Please know that you are both in our thoughts and prayers. We hope that her health is much improved by the time you receive this.

Thank you very much for your statements about unilateral disarmament. I'm happy to have them on hand. They will be most useful in the days ahead for anything from AWACS [Airborne Warning and Control System aircraft] to our disarmament talks with the Soviets.

I don't know how the AWACS matter will come out with the Senate, but I do know that a refusal to allow the sale will set us back perhaps irretrievably in our Middle East peacemaking effort.

This is a very late reply to your good letter, and I apologize. Nancy and I are so grateful for your prayers and your readiness to be of help. Please believe we offer that in return.

Give our love to Ruth, and we hope we'll see you both soon.

Sincerely,

Ron

The Reverend Billy Graham
Montreat, North Carolina

In early August Anwar el-Sadat, president of the Arab Republic of Egypt, and his wife, Jihan, were honored at a White House reception. Sadat's remarks at the dinner called for Reagan's recognition of the Palestinian Arabs. On October 6 Egyptian extremists assassinated Sadat in the reviewing stand during a military parade in Cairo. The picture President Reagan mentions is an official White House photograph taken of Sadat on August 5.

WASHINGTON

October 7, 1981

Dear Jihan:

We know there are no words that can ease the burden of grief you bear. How we wish there were. Just know that we share your sorrow and pain.

True, our meeting was brief. But in that short time, we came to feel a deep and abiding friendship for you both. That is not surprising because the world had already found a place in its heart for Anwar and all that he represented. A statesman, yes, but also a warm, kindly man of courage and vision.

We can only trust in God's infinite mercy and wisdom as he did and pray for understanding and healing.

We will try to carry on the great effort for peace Anwar so nobly began, but we shall miss him more than words can say.

Please know how deep is our sympathy for you and your family and know that you are in our thoughts and prayers.

We are sending the album of your visit here, but also this picture which shows, we believe, his very soul.

God bless you and keep you.

Nancy and Ronald

Mrs. Sadat
Office of the President
Cairo, Egypt

Reminded that former football star, the Reverend Donn Moomaw, his pastor at the Bel Air Presbyterian Church, would celebrate his fiftieth birthday on October 16, President Reagan sent a Western Union telegram to a mutual friend for inclusion in an album of congratulations.

WASHINGTON

October 11, 1981

Dear Donn,

Happy Birthday! We know very well you are having trouble thinking of it as a happy occasion hence this message of understanding and encouragement. Also some tips.

Never use the term, "half a century," that only accentuates the pain, wear your monogram sweater while puttering in the yard. Unless, of course it's totally out of style. But even that is no cause for worry. Like Victorian houses they come back in style—mine has.

And that brings me to the real point of all this. You'd be surprised how good 50 looks from where I sit. Pretty soon you'll find this is just part of your youth.

You'll also find that age is not a matter of chronological statistics so stop counting. There are any number of people who haven't reached 50 who are twice your real age.

In our book you are our first choice for linebacker, physically and more important spiritually.

Again—happy birthday! And we mean it.

Love,

Nancy & Ronald Reagan

c/o Lois Knighton
Sherman Oaks, California

Alan Brown, a family friend who lived in Spain, described left-wing influences on King Juan Carlos.

WASHINGTON

October 12, 1981

Dear Allen:

I hope you won't mind my answering your most informative letter to Nancy. I've finally gotten around to this on the day before the King's [of Spain] arrival. Your information will be most helpful in tomorrow's meeting.

One wonders at times if some of our friends and allies haven't taken a narcotic that keeps them smiling vacantly while termites eat away the timbers supporting the ivory towers in which they live.

I'll do my best in the upcoming meetings but will of course have to be subtle and look for an opening. For one thing I'm going to do my best to extol the virtues of joining NATO.

Nancy sends her very best—as do I. Thanks again.

Sincerely,

Ron

Mr. Alan Brown
New York, New York

Chester Gould drew comic strips for Hearst's Chicago–American Newspaper *and then for the* Chicago Tribune, *where he created Dick Tracy. Gould sent an original framed 13 x 11–inch cartoon of the President shaking Dick Tracy's hand. The cartoon is on file in the Reagan Library.*

WASHINGTON

October 16, 1981

Dear Mr. Gould:

Thank you very much for my "original Dick Tracy" cartoon. Thank you more however for your words (via Dick) of encouragement. They mean a great deal to me when there are so many Monday-morning quarterbacks sounding off on Friday night.

You should know that Dick Tracy and I are old friends. I am a comic strip reader from way back and still consider it a major crisis if I have to start a day without them. I rarely do.

Again my heartfelt thanks. I won't weaken any more than Dick would turn crooked.

Best regards,

Sincerely,

Ronald Reagan

Mr. Chester Gould
Woodstock, Illinois

Thomas Reed, Air Force missile officer in the 1950s, became Governor Reagan's appointments secretary and secretary of the Air Force from 1976 to 1977. He joined the National Security Council in Reagan's first term. The decision concerns the MX missile program.

WASHINGTON

October 19, 1981

Dear Tom:

It was good to hear from you, and I appreciate your generous words. Both Cap [Casper Weinberger, Secretary of Defense] and I did some real soul-searching before the decisions were reached, and we both felt secure in them.

You are right, though, about the flack. The Monday-morning quarterbacks started on Friday. But, I'm still sleeping well and reading the comics.

Again, my thanks and best regards.

Sincerely,

Ronald Reagan

Mr. Thomas C. Reed
San Rafael, California

George Eccles, a prominent Utah and Idaho banker, also served as a financial consultant to the Marshall Plan. The Senate rejected a resolution stopping the sale of AWACS by a vote of 52 to 48. Five AWACS were approved in the $8.5 billion sale.

October 28, 1981

Dear George and Lolie:

I learned from Doug [Morrow] about the unfortunate illness that kept you from making the China trip and I'm truly sorry and hope there will be another opportunity. Above all I hope that you are recovered and feeling fit—that's more important than any trip.

I'm sitting here waiting out the long afternoon till 5 p.m. when the Senate votes on the AWACS sale to Saudi Arabia. At the moment the count looks about even. One undecided Senator told me he was going to pray for guidance. I told him if he got a busy signal it was me in there ahead of him with my own prayer.

Well—again I hope and yes, pray, that you are once again enjoying good health.

Best regards,

Ron

Mr. and Mrs. George Eccles
Salt Lake City, Utah

[October 1981]

Dear Mrs. Porter:

Thank you for giving me the opportunity to address myself to your concerns. Your letter of October 1st has just reached my desk. You specified that you wanted to hear from me personally, so here I am.

You asked how we could balance the budget by robbing the poor and giving to the rich. Well, that isn't what we're doing. We are trying to reduce the cost of government and have already obtained consent of Congress to reduce the budget by more than 35 billion dollars.

We are reducing tax rates *across the board.* This will give 74 percent of the relief to those who are presently paying 72 percent of the total tax, the average middle-class Americans.

We are trying to do what you suggested—make able-bodied welfare recipients work at useful community jobs in return for their welfare grants. As Governor of California I did this and it worked very well. So far, Congress doesn't like the idea.

We have not suggested reducing Social Security. We are trying to do what you suggested—removing those who are not disabled or deserving of grants they are presently getting.

We are not cutting back on school lunches for the needy. We are trying to quit providing them for those who aren't needy.

Now, as to the White House, we aren't spending a penny of tax money. The government provides $50,000 for an incoming President to do what he will to the White House. We gave that money back to the government. We found, however, that the White House was badly in need of painting inside, and the plumbing was so old there was danger of it giving way. Drapes and much of the upholstery was in need of recovering and replacing. Friends started a campaign to get donations to have this work done. It has all been completed without spending a single tax dollar.

The dishes were a donation by a trust and the company making them did so at cost. This is the way the White House has always been furnished. Beautiful antiques, etc., have been gifts to the government. The last new china was in Harry Truman's time. There is a certain amount of breakage over the years. We're talking about china for state dinners when heads of government visit the United States and more than 100 people must be served. That is not the china we use for family meals.

Now, for your other concerns; we are not going to increase the risk to miners and, yes, I've been down in a mine. As for Black Lung, we are only trying to eliminate those cases where people who don't have Black Lung are getting benefits.

Selling planes to Saudi Arabia will run no risk of giving secrets away and it will provide thousands of jobs for American workers.

We don't take Air Force One to Camp David. The Camp is only twenty minutes from the White House by helicopter. The helicopters have to fly a required number of hours each week to keep crew and machine in shape.

I hope this answers your concerns and I assure you this Captain isn't in his tent when the fight is going on.

Sincerely,

Ronald Reagan

Mrs. Bonnie M. Porter
Central City, Kentucky

[October 1981]

Dear Miss Walton:

I'm glad you provided me with a return address so I can respond to your letter of September 2nd. Incidentally, forgive me for being so late in answering. With the hundreds of thousands of letters that come in each month, it takes a while for one to reach my desk.

You expressed worry about "supply side" economics. I don't know who gave it that title but we're really talking about common sense. Runaway inflation, high interest rates and unemployment didn't start with this Administration. They are the result of almost forty years of deficit spending and excessive taxation. Our national debt has now reached a trillion dollars.

I know we can't cure all that at once, but we have to start and that means reducing taxes that are stifling the economy and cutting back on government spending. Our program just went into effect October 1st so it can hardly be blamed for our troubles. The truth is inflation is falling and so are interest rates. I believe our program will work.

Now with regard to my working habits, I can understand why you would have some wrong ideas in view of some of the ridiculous falsehoods that pop up in the news.

This President doesn't have a nine-to-five or nine-to-three schedule, nor does he have a five-day week. I take the elevator up to the living quarters in the White House with reports, briefings, and memoranda for which there is no reading time during the day. I spend my time until "lights out" trying to absorb all of that. The same is true of the weekends—when I'm not attending a Summit Conference or making a speech somewhere.

The air controllers were warned well in advance that the law specifically prohibits Federal employees from striking. In addition, they had each signed a written oath that they would not strike. May I remind you that F.D.R. (whom I supported) declared that public employees could not be allowed to strike.

Now it is true I went to California for roughly three weeks, but the Congress had gone home as they always do at that time of year. I was still President, however, and there was never a day that I did not have meetings with Cabinet members or staff and, of course, the reading went on as usual.

You referred to the incident of the planes* and my not being awakened. That isn't exactly correct. I was awakened at 4:30 a.m. when full information had finally been received. I wasn't awakened earlier because early bulletins were too sketchy and provided no information that might require a decision by me. But being called at 4:30 a.m. is hardly a case of letting me sleep the night through for fear of disturbing me.

I assure you I am not the head of a "royal family." Our program and my efforts are aimed at helping the poor because they are hit hardest by inflation.

Thanks again for letting me respond.

Sincerely,

Ronald Reagan

Miss Dorothy Walton
New York, New York

* On August 19 two Navy jet aircraft were attacked by two Libyan fighters over the Gulf of Sidra, an area claimed by the Libyan government. Reagan was in California when the attack occurred at 10:20 P.M. National Security Advisor Richard Allen told Ed Meese forty-five minutes later; however, Meese delayed telling the President, who had retired for the night, until early the next morning. This public relations mistake became the focus of Reagan media critics' columns and cartoons.

October 28, 1981

Dear Ella:

Forgive me for being so late in telling you how grateful Nancy and I are for the wonderful evening you gave to all of us at the White House. We know the demands that are made on your time and talent. You were more than kind.

The King [Juan Carlos] and Queen [Sophia] are both fans of American music and they were still talking about you when we put them in their car to return to Spain.

And why not—Nancy and I are still talking about you. Nancy sends her love and again from both of us a heartfelt thanks.

Sincerely,

Ron

Miss Ella Fitzgerald
Beverly Hills, California

Dick Crane and Reagan were classmates at Eureka College, and both attended a reunion at the college in May. A family friend wrote to the President and asked him to send a personal note to Crane, who had had surgery.

November 19, 1981

Dear Dick:

I've just learned of your recent surgery—Garth let me know. Take care of yourself, and please know you will be in my thoughts and prayers.

Tell Monta [Mrs. Crane] to remind you, if you get rambunctious, that "a surgeon's scalpel is five months long." And, while you're about it, give her my love.

It's a long way back to Eureka days, but I have to say those days are as fresh in my memory as if they happened last week.

Again, the very best to you both.

Yours in the Bond,

Dutch

Mr. Richard Crane
Pompano Beach, Florida

December 1, 1981

Dear Mrs. Casey:

Thank you very much for writing as you did and giving me a chance to answer. Forgive me for being so late in responding but it does take time for mail to get through the mill and to my desk. Your letter has just reached me.

Mrs. Casey, having a ranch of my own, I do have some understanding of the problems you're talking about. I don't know of anyone who has been caught harder in the cost price squeeze than the American farmer. You asked what is inflation—it really is just a plain case of our money becoming less and less because, over the years, they've turned on the printing presses at the mint and printed more money while we haven't made an increase in the things to buy with that money.

Our whole program is aimed at reducing that inflation which has caused the problems your son faces. We have made gains, we've reduced inflation by several percentage points in these ten or eleven months that we've been here. But, we have much farther to go. We have to bring inflation down to the point that interest rates also will come down, and we can do this by reducing government spending and reducing taxes, which we have just started to do.

The Congress is working on a farm bill. I have not seen it as yet, but I hope that it will offer some help in this situation.

Again, thank you for writing and best regards.

Sincerely,

Ronald Reagan

Mrs. Bill Casey
Anna, Illinois

Tony Dorsett played for the Dallas Cowboys under Coach Tom Landry from 1977 to 1988. In 1981 he hoped to be an actor or a sportscaster after his football career.

December 7, 1981

Dear Tony Dorsett:

Thank you very much for the gift of your game jersey. I'm deeply grateful and more proud than I can say.

I'm delighted to hear that you feel the number 33 might have something to do with the season you've had. I've developed quite an attachment for it. Yes, it was my football number, and then I became the 33rd Governor of California. During that time, we discovered the beautiful property that is now our ranch, and went through a lengthy negotiation to buy it. The phone rang one day and it was a call telling me escrow has closed at 3:33 p.m. on the 3rd day of the month.

I know that neither of us is going to start planning our lives around numbers, still it's kind of fun to think you might have a lucky one.

Congratulations on being team captain and on the season you've been having. Please give my best regards to your teammates and to Coach Tom Landry.

Again, a heartfelt thanks.

Sincerely,

Ronald Reagan

Mr. Tony Dorsett
Dallas Cowboys Football Club
Dallas, Texas

In early August Reagan fired twelve thousand federal air traffic controllers who had been on strike for three days despite federal judge Harold Greene's back-to-work order. Patco, the union representing the controllers, wanted a shorter workweek, higher pay, and retirement after twenty years.

December 11, 1981

Dear Mrs. Browning:

I can understand your concern and your heartache. I can only hope that you will understand why it isn't possible for me to re-instate all those who went on strike. The law specifically prohibits public employees from striking. As you say striking "is an inalienable right"—but not for government employees.

There is a difference. I was an officer of my union for some 25 years—President of that union for six terms. I led the union in the first strike it had ever engaged in. But even then I had to agree with F.D.R. who proclaimed that public employment was different and that strikes against the people could not be tolerated.

When public employees began unionizing, organized labor at the highest levels supported their efforts only on the condition that they provide in their constitutions they would not strike. A strike is an economic contract between labor and management when negotiations have failed to resolve an issue. But government can't shut down the assembly line. The services provided to the people, who in this case are the employees of all of us in government, must be continued.

Mrs. Browning, there are more than two million Federal employees. What message would we be sending to all of them if we allowed a strike by one group or gave amnesty to them if they did strike? Believe me there is no thought of punishment in what we are doing. There just is no way I can avoid enforcing the law. Let me recap what took place prior to the strike. I ordered our negotiators to point out to the "Patco" representatives that a strike would mean the union members had quit their jobs and we would have no alternative but to replace them. Concerned that the union officials had not notified the members of this I withheld enforcement for 48 hours for the word to get around. Some controllers did report back for work in those 48 hours and in fact we kept the door open longer than that to make certain everyone had gotten the word.

The black listing you mentioned is a law that says Federal employees who leave the government in this manner cannot re-apply for Federal employment for three years. I am trying to arrange a waiver of that law so that all the 12,000 can apply for whatever government jobs are available without waiting.

We have an obligation to those who did stay on duty and who have maintained flying schedules up to 75 or 80% of normal. At the same time however I do feel a very real sorrow for those who followed the union leadership at such a sacrifice. This is especially true of someone like your son who served our country in uniform. Please believe the plight of families such as that of your son is of great concern to me.

Sincerely,

Ronald Reagan

Ms. June Browning
Wyandotte, Michigan

[December 1981]

Dear Cousin Bess:

I've just been reminded of your birthday by Anabel. I hope this arrives by the 15th.

But whether on time or late please accept my best wishes on this 47th anniversary of your 39th birthday. Just between us I've been using that system of counting for some time now. It makes me feel better.

Happy birthday.

Love,

Ronald

Mrs. Bess Dillon
Estes Park, Colorado

1982

~

> . . . while I was on the phone to Prime Minister
> [Menachem] Begin and he was telling me I was the best
> friend Israel ever had, a group of Jewish demonstrators
> were out in front of the White House protesting my
> anti-Israel attitude. I know they were sincere—they just
> were uninformed.
>
> *·Letter of April 26, 1982·*

FOREIGN policy issues and misunderstandings involving the
Middle East continued to frustrate President Reagan as military tensions increased when Israeli forces battled Syrian and
Palestinian forces in southern Lebanon in June. Also as 1982
unfolded, depressing economic statistics continued to pour in
to Treasury and White House offices. The number of Americans without
jobs would soon match the unemployment rate for 1975, another recession year. Although Reagan would emphasize in his correspondence that
the largest percentage of Americans were employed, his upbeat assertions
gave small comfort to distressed business leaders, building contractors,
farmers, and auto dealers on the edge of financial ruin. Business failures approached the Great Depression rate of the 1930s. Some Reagan critics, es-

pecially those in the opposition party with eyes on the congressional elections in November, called him "President Hoover," in reference to Herbert Hoover, the president at the beginning of the Great Depression in 1929. Representative Tip O'Neill, Democrat from Massachusetts, more cleverly referred to Reagan as "Hoover with a smile." Undaunted publicly, Reagan explained that his economic program had not really begun; moreover, Congress had to cooperate in slowing the rate of federal expenditures.

Reagan's replies to senior citizens anxious about Social Security, younger workers worried about the future, worried writers who inquired about taxes, and parents troubled by the status of public education were sensitive and supporting. His word portraits of talented actresses Shirley Temple and Helen Hayes reveal his admiration and thoughtful evaluation of their professional abilities. His descriptions captured their unique qualities. Similarly his defense of James Baker, a very able advisor in the White House, accentuated Baker's contributions to the nation.

Foreign trips during this year took him to nations as close as Canada and Mexico and as distant as Brazil and West Germany. Jamaica, Barbados, France, the United Kingdom, Vatican City, Colombia, Costa Rica, and Honduras also welcomed the Reagans. The June Group of Seven Economic Summit in Versailles was followed by his visit to Pope John Paul II in Vatican City. Several days later in London, President Reagan became the first U.S. president to address Parliament. Thirty-two domestic trips to the West Coast, Middle West, and the South, together with two visits to the United Nations, and five trips to his Rancho del Cielo near Santa Barbara completed his travel schedule.

Secretary of State Alexander Haig resigned in late June because of differences over the conduct of foreign policy. George Shultz, a former secretary of the treasury and Nixon aide, became secretary in July. Correspondents continued to question Reagan about this transfer of power and the nuclear freeze movement. In his Eureka College address on May 9, the President urged the superpowers to reduce their strategic nuclear weapons. This prompted some members of the press to hope that the upward spiral of nuclear weapons would now stop. Reagan worried that the nuclear freeze movement was directed only at the United States rather than all superpowers, especially the Soviet Union. During these months Reagan continued his personal crusade to reduce all nuclear weapons and cancel the policy of Mutual Assured Destruction (MAD). He believed the "evil empire" was centered in the Soviet Union and that the United States must negotiate with it. Reagan's attitude toward such negotiations was best captured in his phrase "trust but verify."

American defense expenditures climbed during 1982. Soviet forces continued fighting in Afghanistan. Brezhnev's death in November would open opportunities for Secretary Shultz to negotiate with the new Soviet government. Brutal warfare between Israelis and Arabs in Lebanon heightened anxieties and foreign policy debates in Reagan's cabinet. Reagan's reluctant decision to send a small contingent of troops as a part of a multinational peacekeeping operation to Lebanon as a buffer between Israeli and Palestinian liberation forces began a painful chapter in the history of the U.S. Marine Corps. Still, this humanitarian mission to prevent innocent civilian casualties, especially in and around Beirut, lessened the number of civilian dead and wounded in the months after the Marines arrived.

Every president in the twentieth century complained privately and sometimes publicly about newspaper articles, editorials, and television commentaries that distorted foreign and domestic policy decisions made in the Oval Office. Ronald Reagan was no different from the other seven presidents since World War II, complaining to his correspondents about this media treatment, especially with regard to racial discrimination issues. The bitter political campaigns for Congress together with the slowing economy brought the President's approval rating with the public down to 41 percent. The Democrats gained twenty-six House seats and a majority role. Nevertheless, Reagan remained confident that the nation was reducing inflation, lowering interest rates, and rebuilding the defense establishment. His letters continued to reflect his optimism and encouragement.

Arthur Burns was an economic advisor to President Dwight Eisenhower, and a professor at Rutgers, Columbia, and Georgetown Universities. He later served as chairman of the Federal Reserve Board, 1970–1978, and was U.S. ambassador to the Federal Republic of Germany, 1981–1985.

WASHINGTON

January 4, 1982

Dear Arthur:

Thanks very much for sending me a copy of your speech. As the young people you were talking about say, "it was right on."

I'm convinced we must give them a legitimate cause to serve and one that will not require them to bleed their lives away on a battlefield. At the same time, however, maybe making them understand that being willing to die for something could be the best guarantee they won't have to make that sacrifice.

Thanks again and best regards.

Sincerely,

Ron

The Honorable Arthur F. Burns
American Ambassador
Bonn

Bill Keane developed the cartoon panel "The Family Circus" in 1960. He was named "Cartoonist of the Year" in 1982.

January 11, 1982

Dear Mr. Keane:

Thank you very much for your letter and for your kind treatment in the newsletter. I make no claim to deserving acceptance by you and your associates—I am strictly a doodler. Now President Lopez Portillo is another matter. I've seen some of his work, and he is an artist. Indeed, that's what he intends to do when his term in office expires.

Let me, however, express my gratitude to all of you. I am a dedicated, committed reader of the comic strips, and consider the day lost if for some reason I'm deprived of them. They truly start my day served up with breakfast. And, I treasure the collection of originals wishing me well after the episode of last March 30th.

Again, thanks and best regards.

Sincerely,

Ronald Reagan

Mr. Bill Keane
Paradise Valley, Arizona

January 11, 1982

Dear Mr. Rieb:

Thanks for your letter and most interesting account of your travels through Russia. You confirm what I've always felt—that we and the Russian people could be the best of friends if it weren't for the godless tyranny and imperialistic ambitions of their leaders. I said as much in a handwritten letter to Brezhnev last April while I was in the hospital. His reply was most disappointing.

Thank you again for writing and for your generous words.

Sincerely,

Ronald Reagan

Mr. Bill Rieb
Rapid City, South Dakota

January 11, 1982

Dear Mike*:

You didn't take up my time, and I'm glad you wrote. You must be very proud of your father and you have every right to be. And, I'll keep on trying to rebuild our defense strength to what it should be.

You asked about Air Force One. It really is a great plane equipped for comfort on flights of any length and manned by a magnificent crew.

With regard to Iran, I have always felt we could have done more to prevent the revolution there, and that the hostage matter was badly handled. We should have brought our people home when the revolution took place without waiting for them to be taken hostage.

I am in full support of the space shuttle and feel we must continue our exploration of outer space.

Again, thanks for writing and best regards.

Sincerely,

Ronald Reagan

Mr. Mike Schaefer
Quantico, Virginia

* The son of a serviceman killed in the April 1980 hostage rescue attempt.

Reagan's friend General Victor Krulak served in China before and during World War II and then in Korea. Before his retirement from military service in 1968, this highly decorated officer served as commanding general of the Fleet Marine Force Pacific. In his syndicated newspaper columns he praised Reagan for his courageous defense policies.

WASHINGTON

February 2, 1982

Dear Brute:

Thanks very much for your letter but, again—as I do so often, I thank you for that column—the open letter that you addressed to me but sent to the people. You said a lot of things that made me feel just fine.

Back here I'm still battling, of course, against those who would have us forget the forty years, and think that all the troubles came about in the last four months. You set them straight in a masterful way and I'm most grateful.

There's going to be an effort, I know, to whittle back national defense, but I will fight to the last pop gun before I give in on that. In fact, I won't give in—they'll have to do it over my carcass if that's possible.

Thanks again.

Best regards,

Ronald Reagan

Lt. Gen. V. H. Krulak, USMC (Ret.)
San Diego, California

Laurence W. Beilenson and Samuel T. Cohen (the father of the neutron bomb)
wrote "A New Nuclear Strategy," which was published in the New York
Times *on January 24, 1982. Beilenson, a military historian, attorney for the*
Screen Actors Guild, and former advisor to Reagan, urged the United States
to halt the attempt to match the Soviets in conventional weapons and instead
build security through "overwhelming nuclear armaments."

WASHINGTON

February 5, 1982

Dear Larry:

Thanks for sending the "Times" [the *New York Times* magazine] article. I
had not seen it. It's most interesting and I'm giving it circulation starting
with our National Security Council.

Larry, I must confess that while we are moving to upgrade civil defense, at
long last, I can't accept the doctrine of ignoring conventional weapons. It
seems to me this leaves only Armageddon as a response to all the brush-
fire wars in existence. Can we resolve Afghanistan, El Salvador or even
Cuba, to say nothing of Poland with just a threat of the bomb? I know you
probably have an answer to this, but I have to ask.

Thanks again and best always.

Sincerely,

Ron

Mr. Laurence W. Beilenson
Los Angeles, California

The Reverend Daugherty received a three-page printed letter with President Reagan's signature requesting $120 as a contribution to keep Republican senators in office. Daugherty was quoted in the newspaper story as saying he would offer a little prayer that Reagan policies are processed better than his computer mailings.

WASHINGTON

March 11, 1982

Dear Reverend Daugherty:

I've just received a newsclipping regarding the campaign solicitation you received addressed to Mr. God. I thought perhaps I should offer an explanation to you. I've already spoken to God about it.

I hope both He and you will understand that, while the letter bore my signature, such letters are the product of a computer. The Senate Campaign Committee has permission to use my name in its fundraising, so I hadn't seen or known of this letter until the clipping arrived.

Reverend Daugherty, I've asked God for a great many things—particularly since getting this job—but never for a campaign contribution. Maybe I'll ask for help in correcting a greedy computer. At least the computer has raised its sights considerably; the only other experience of this kind was hearing from a lady whose prize show horse had received such a letter.

I've already asked God's pardon—I hope I have yours.

Sincerely,

Ronald Reagan

Reverend Doyle Daugherty
Commack, New York

April 5, 1982

Dear Mrs. Meyer:

I'm sorry to be so late in answering your letter, but it takes a while before they reach my desk.

I appreciate your giving me a chance to reply and, hopefully, clear up a misconception about our approach to the medical situation and to senior citizens. I'm sorry you feel that I have not been truthful regarding Social Security recipients. I can understand your thinking that because of the political attacks on me which were totally based on lies, but which were widely carried by the press.

I can assure you, there has been *no* action by our Administration hurtful to the elderly, poor, and blind. My proposed budget for the coming fiscal year contains $8.9 billion—a $1 billion increase—for Supplemental Security Income payments to individuals facing these hardships. Social Security in 1980 was $122 billion—next year it will be $175 billion.

What you evidently read or heard about Medicare is a plan we are considering as a proposal to the Congress. There would be no way you could face a $10,000 doctor or hospital bill. We propose a program where you do pay a certain percentage, but the most you could ever pay would be $2500. At that point, you would be fully insured for *all* additional costs. What we are offering is protection against catastrophic illnesses. In other words, that $103,286.00 bill would be paid by Medicare. What you suggested in the final words of your letter is exactly what we are trying to do—without the costly faults of socialized medicine.

One last thing in my own defense. Yes, I do know what it is like to live on little or no income and to worry about medical bills. I was raised in poverty and entered the job market in 1932 in the depths of the great depression.

Again, thanks for giving me a chance to explain.

Sincerely,

Ronald Reagan

Mrs. Helen G. Meyer
Gulfport, Florida

Shirley Temple Black, born in 1928, became the most successful child star in film history. She retired from acting in 1949 and served the State Department as chief of protocol after being a delegate to the United Nations in 1969. She also served as Ambassador to Ghana and to the Czech and Slovak Federal Republic.

WASHINGTON

April 12, 1982

Dear Mr. and Mrs. David:

As per our phone conversation, here is the letter about Shirley Temple. I won't repeat the story about her dramatic scene as a child and then her composed curtsy to the director and crew on the set, and her line—next week—"East Lynne." (This is just a reminder in case it's useful.)

Like everyone else in America, I loved Shirley Temple in those days when a depression-haunted world forgot the drab dreariness for a few hours in a neighborhood movie house, especially when a tiny golden-haired girl named Shirley Temple was on the screen. Her talent and ability were such that at one time rumors went around that she was much older than she was said to be, and was somehow stunted in her growth. This was so patently ridiculous that little credence was given to it. But affection for her probably helped, too. She was a beloved American institution, and people wouldn't hold still for any attempt to deprecate her.

I never knew her in those years when she was a child star. We became acquainted when she was borrowed by Warner Brothers and we co-starred in a picture called "That Hagen Girl," somewhere around 1947.

It was a story of an older man and a younger girl. But I believe you are interested in her as a person. Let me just say that she was totally unspoiled, with a delightful sense of humor. She was most likeable and in theatre language a real pro. She was also intelligent, well informed, and with an interest in a wide range of subjects.

She was conscious of the fact that audiences were unwilling to let her grow up. She wanted very much to be accepted as an adult actress carrying on in the profession which had been hers for so long. I never let her know that having been a part of that audience, I wasn't quite ready either, and not so sure I wanted to be a party to presenting her to America for the first time as a young lady. But she was just that—a lady in every sense of the word.

I hope this is of some help.

Best regards,

Ronald Reagan

Mr. & Mrs. Lester David
Woodmere, New York

Young Mark, suffering from muscular dystrophy, made several eighteenth- and nineteenth-century soldier figures for President Reagan for Christmas 1981. Mark died before presenting them. His sister planned to leave them with the President's staff, but Reagan insisted on seeing her personally.

WASHINGTON

April 21, 1982

Dear Mr. and Mrs. Retter:

Denise has delivered the figure created so beautifully by your son Mark. Thank you so very much. Please know that I'm very proud that Mark wanted to do this for me and I shall treasure it always.

It is hard at times to understand the why of things and yet I've always believed there is a divine plan for us. I'm sure Mark realized this and thus was able to bring so much comfort and joy to others. Brief as it was, his was truly a full life. Many who have lived to their three score and ten have failed to bring as much love to others as Mark apparently did in his brief span.

Thank you for letting me share a little of his generous warmth.

Sincerely,

Ronald Reagan

Mr. & Mrs. Fred Retter
(Hand Delivered)

President of the Adolph Coors Company in Colorado, the fifth largest brewery in the United States, Joseph Coors was a member of President Reagan's "Kitchen Cabinet" [policy advisors] and financial supporter of conservative foundations. The letter from nuclear physicist Dr. Edward Teller, who helped develop the hydrogen bomb, to author Irving Kristol recommended that the United States should pledge not to be the first to use nuclear weapons on enemy territory.

WASHINGTON

April 22, 1982

Dear Joe:

Help! You didn't enclose the [Edward] Teller letter. However, you and I are on the same track with regard to the points you raised. There is no way we could assure the Soviets or our allies that we'd never make the first strike, even though we know in our hearts we wouldn't.

I agree with you also about the "neutron bomb." I've tried using "warhead," and perhaps "weapon" is better, but it isn't a bomb and that word does have a wrong connotation.

Incidentally, rest easy about all the furor over a freeze. We can't go for that until there is a verifiable reduction to equality. I think the Soviets would be delighted with a freeze at the present levels.

It was good to hear from you. Give my regards to that lovely lady—my chairman. [Mrs. Coors chaired the Colorado Republican Reagan-Bush presidential organization.] Nancy sends her best to you both.

Sincerely,

Ron

Mr. Joseph Coors
Adolph Coors Company
Golden, Colorado

April 26, 1982

Dear Mr. Harris:

Thanks very much for your letter, which has reached me by way of V.P. Bush, and thanks for your generous words. I am most grateful.

In reply to your position paper let me say your suggestions are sound and we are proceeding along the lines of several of them. We are for example moving toward a summit meeting with Leonid Brezhnev and our team is in Geneva trying to negotiate a zero base in Europe for intermediate large nuclear missiles. You are right about their SS 20's. Even behind the Urals they could reach every target area of Europe and the Middle East. If they dismantle we'll cancel the Pershings and Cruise missile deployment.

The on-sight [*sic*] inspection will prevent a problem as will any method of verification. Since WW II our country has proposed arms reductions and even total elimination of nuclear weapons nineteen times. Always the Soviet Union stopped short of agreement and in practically every instance verification was the stumbling block.

Your idea for helping the underdeveloped nations was the issue on the table at the Cancun, Mexico, conference. Some pretty good headway was made. Our Caribbean initiative embodies that same idea. Mexico, Canada, Venezuela and Colombia have joined me in that.

So far the Soviet Union has not joined in any of these undertakings. In all fairness it could be inability on their part. They are up against the wall economically, more so than at any previous time. It is my hope that this may make them more reasonable about arms reductions because their military buildup is the cause of their depression.

Again my thanks to you and best regards.

Sincerely,

Ronald Reagan

Mr. Jay Harris
Lubbock Avalanche Journal
Lubbock, Texas

Douglas Morrow, Hollywood screenwriter for the 1949 award-winning movie
The Stratton Story *and other movies and television shows such as "77 Sun-*
set Strip," Mister Roberts, *and "The Lucy Show," was a family friend who*
offered considerable support to the President.

WASHINGTON

April 26, 1982

Dear Doug:

Thanks for your letter and your concern and offer of help. Believe me, we
are not unaware of the perceptions and the image building that have gone
on. I have to say it can't be entirely laid to inattention on our part. You'd
have to live here to appreciate the extent of our frustration. Having determined the perception of me that they want to create, the media by and
large will not accept anything that does not add to it. Let me give you a
couple of "for instances." Some time ago, a press conference was followed
by stories having to do with supposed errors on my part. The bulk of them
had six items and all in the same order. My own staff researched for themselves (wouldn't take my word for it) and found I was correct on five and
half correct on the sixth (a technicality).

On checking one, they called some county officials in Arizona who were
part of one of my answers. The officials confirmed my answer and then
added that NBC had already been out to see them, but apparently didn't
want any answer unless "it proved the President was wrong."

More recently—yesterday in fact—on the day of the Sinai return, while I
was on the phone to Prime Minister Begin and he was telling me I was the
best friend Israel ever had, a group of Jewish demonstrators were out in
front of the White House protesting my anti-Israel attitude. I know they
were sincere—they just were uninformed. On that same day, Prime Minister Begin was on "Meet the Press" from Tel Aviv. He said in answer to a
question what he said to me on the phone. That evening, virtually every
newscast on TV showed excerpts of the Prime Minister on that program.
Not one used his lines about the United States.

It goes without saying that Bill Moyers on the CBS special presented a totally dishonest report on poverty. We can refute every heartrending experience he portrayed as being the result of our economic program—they weren't.

Doug, I'll show your letter to Mike Deaver, but I hate to think of you coming all the way here for a short meeting. I appreciate your willingness to do that, but the conservative in me rebels. Anyway, I'll see what Mike comes up with since he's the timer on my activities.

In the meantime, a heartfelt thanks.

Warm regards,

Ron

Mr. Douglas Morrow
Glendale, California

Dr. Spock's letter to Reagan called for an immediate nuclear freeze before the United States spent hundreds of billions more, which would be matched by the Soviet Union. Spock, a vocal opponent to the Vietnam War and nuclear weapons, ran for president against Richard Nixon and George McGovern in 1972.

May 7, 1982

Dear Dr. Spock:

I'm afraid the experts you mention are not all that expert. We do not have Strategic parity. In throw weight—meaning destructive power—the Soviets are far superior. They also are technologically superior in a number of other features.

We are going to engage them in negotiations to reduce nuclear weapons. This will be the 20th attempt by the United States to get such a reduction since WW II. Always the Soviets refuse. I believe our intention to build the MX might offer an incentive to them to think of a mutual reduction in nuclear weapons.

Sincerely,

Ronald Reagan

Dr. Benjamin Spock
Rogers, Arkansas

WASHINGTON

May 11, 1982

Dear Mr. Eldredge:

I'm sorry to be so late in writing you but want to thank you for the information you provided. I want to assure you I'll continue on course. While my experience is nothing as compared to yours, I went through the period following WW II when the attempt was made to take over the Motion Picture Industry. I went from a naïve liberal unbelieving in the communist threat to number one on their hate list. I'm proud to say I earned that latter rating.

Believe me I share your concern and, as I say, will stay the course. Thanks again.

Sincerely,

Ronald Reagan

Mr. Ronald S. Eldredge
Portland, Oregon

May 11, 1982

Dear Mr. Matzger:

Thank you very much for your letter and for your generous words about our Economic Recovery Program. I'm most grateful.

With regard to the arms situation, let me clarify something. I agree with you that it wouldn't make sense to build up a parity with the Soviets and then propose a mutual reduction. I've studied the nineteen previous efforts we've made since WW II to persuade them to join us in reducing nuclear weapons. I don't believe there will be a move on their part, however, so long as they have superiority and we are continuing to disarm unilaterally.

I'm sure you know that we are in negotiations now with them in Geneva regarding their intermediate range nuclear missiles targeted on Europe. The negotiations were agreed to when we announced we would place Pershing missiles in Europe as a counter to their SS 20's.

Tomorrow I am announcing our invitation to the Soviets to join us in strategic nuclear arms reduction talks. I believe such talks will take place if they are convinced that the alternative is an arms race. A cartoon recently said it all; Brezhnev was speaking to a Russian General. He said, "I liked the arms race better when we were the only ones in it."

Again thank you for your good letter and sound suggestions.

Sincerely,

Ronald Reagan

Mr. John Matzger
San Leandro, California

WASHINGTON

May 11, 1982

Dear Mrs. Brady:

I'm sorry to be so late in answering your letter but it takes a while for mail to reach my desk. I can well understand the bitterness you feel. I hope and pray your husband will soon find a market for his skills.

In reading your letter I gathered that you felt my criticism of the press indicated a lack of understanding or sympathy for those who through no fault of their own are victims of this recession. Nothing could be further from the truth. I saw my father get word that he no longer had a job when he opened an envelope on Christmas Eve during the great depression of the 30's.

Mrs. Brady, a conversation I had with a newspaper publisher, which I did not know would be the subject of a story, has been somewhat distorted by the press. We were talking about the psychological contribution a constant barrage of downbeat recession stories might make to worsening the recession or delaying recovery. That isn't exactly the way the story came out.

Please believe everything we are doing here is aimed at ending this recession. A key factor must be reducing interest rates and to that end we've at least succeeded in bringing down inflation, but of course there is much more to be done.

Again, my very best wishes.

Sincerely,

Ronald Reagan

Mrs. Patricia Brady
Wadsworth, Ohio

WASHINGTON

May 17, 1982

Dear Mrs. Essary:

Forgive me for being so late in replying to your letter of March 6th. It takes a while for letters to reach my desk, so I've only received yours in the last several days.

Please know you have my deepest sympathy. I say that knowing such words are of little help in the face of your tragic loss.* I wish there were words that could ease the pain you feel, but there are none. I believe, however, that you have already found the only road to peace, and that is asking and trusting in God's help.

It isn't given to us to understand the why of tragedies such as you have known. We can only have faith in God's infinite wisdom and mercy, trusting that He does have a plan for each one of us.

I can remember my mother telling me many times that if we will accept God's will, understanding will, in time, come to us and we'll see a purpose in all that has happened. Such understanding has come to you. Yes, the pain remains, but you have come to know that Bob was part of God's plan as you are, and He intended that you should not take that plane. Take comfort from knowing that having fulfilled his part in God's plan, Bob is with God.

Nancy joins me in wishing you the very best. You are in our thoughts and prayers.

God bless you,

Ronald Reagan

Mrs. Jackie Essary
Gaithersburg, Maryland

* Her husband was among the seventy-eight persons who died when his plane crashed after takeoff from Washington National Airport, on January 13, 1982, in a snowstorm.

Dr. Walter H. Judd served as a physician and missionary in China from 1925 to 1931 and from 1934 to 1938. From 1943 to 1962 he served in Congress as a representative from Minnesota. He received the Presidential Medal of Freedom in 1981.

WASHINGTON

May 18, 1982

Dear Walter:

Thank you very much for your letter and for sending me the messages from the retired Ambassadors. I'm happy to hear that you are on the mend.

I hope you know that, regardless of the press stories, I have not and will not change my position on our longtime friend Taiwan. It is true there are those in certain circles who think we must trade one China for another, but I don't subscribe to that. I'll be tactful and try to improve and maintain the relations with the People's Republic of China started by President Nixon, but there will be no lessening of our relationship with our friends on Taiwan.

I'm dropping a line to each of the Ambassadors to that effect. Take care of yourself and, again, thanks.

Sincerely,

Ronald Reagan

The Honorable Walter H. Judd
Washington, D.C.

Clymer Wright served as finance chairman in the Reagan for President campaign in Texas. In his letter he enclosed articles from the December New York Post *and an Evans/Novak column in the April 23* Washington Post. *The clippings targeted Chief of Staff James Baker as one of the White House leaders damaging Reagan's leadership.* U.S. News & World Report *carried an interview with Reagan's close friend, Senator Paul Laxalt of Nevada, who praised Baker and also reported the President was bearing up well.*

WASHINGTON

May 18, 1982

Dear Clymer:

I've just received a copy of your letter with the attached news articles and must tell you I'm very distressed. Yes, there is undermining of my efforts going on and, yes, there is sabotage of all I'm trying to accomplish. But it's being done by the people who write these articles and columns, not by any White House staff member and certainly not by Jim Baker.

Some in the media delight in trying to portray me as being manipulated and led around by the nose. They do so because they are opposed to everything this administration represents. I could show you similar stories with only the name changed—stories in which other staff or cabinet members are named instead of Jim Baker. Don't join that group, Clymer—you are helping them with their sabotage.

Clymer, I'm in charge and my people are helping to carry out the policies I set. No, we don't get everything we want and, yes, we have to compromise to get 75% or 80% of our programs. We try to see that the 75% or 80% is more than worth the compromise we have to accept. So far it has been.

There has not been one single instance of Jim Baker doing anything but what I've settled on as our policy. He goes all out to help bring that about. I'm enclosing an article in this week's *U.S. News & World Report*. It is an interview with Paul Laxalt who remains as solid in his convictions as he has always been. Please note his comment regarding Jim Baker.

Sincerely,

Ronald Reagan

Mr. Clymer L. Wright, Jr.
Houston, Texas

Ann Landers' column on May 17, 1982, included a letter from "Terrified in D.C.," which said that talk and plans for a limited nuclear war were insane. Landers agreed and noted that a nuclear attack on the United States could kill 150 million Americans. Landers urged her readers to sign their names to the column and send it to President Reagan. As of May 24, 80,183 letters and/or columns were received at the White House. Reagan's handwritten reply is noted below; however, a different letter was sent to Landers after National Security Advisor William P. Clark moderated Reagan's reply.
    The President also enclosed his handwritten note:

Dear Eppie

Hope you'll forgive me but I had to write a Dear Ann letter. Nancy sends her best.

Sincerely,

Ron

May 24, 1982

Dear Ann Landers:

I'm writing about your column of May 17 regarding the letter from "Terrified in D.C." I've had a few scares myself since I've been here but none of them radioactive.

Don't get me wrong, I'll take second to no one in my concern over the nuclear weapon threat—Such a war is unthinkable. That is why I've called for negotiations leading to reduction—not limitation of nuclear weapons. Under the so-called limitation terms of "SALT II" both the United States and the Soviet Union could go on adding to the nuclear arsenals. We must have a true verifiable reduction leading to an eventual elimination of all such weapons.

We have to prove to the Soviet Union we are prepared to match them in such weapons or they won't even negotiate. Pretend to negotiate—yes. Make any headway—no. They have such an edge on us now we have no choice but to rearm. As their superiority grows, so does the danger of confrontation.

Ann, we've tried 19 times since WW II to persuade them to join us in reducing or even eliminating nuclear weapons with no success. Wouldn't it be better if your readers sent that May 17 column to President Brezhnev?

Sincerely,

Ronald Reagan

Ann Landers
Field Newspaper Syndicate
Chicago Sun-Times Building
Chicago, Illinois

June 24, 1982

Dear Mr. Loebker:

Thank you very much for your wire of June 14 and for giving me a chance to reply. I can understand the perception you have of me in view of the image-building done by so much of the press—false image-building I might add.

You say I'm so far removed from the average family that I can't understand your problems. Mr. Loebker, I read about myself and the stories that somehow I only like, understand and tolerate rich people and I get pretty frustrated.

I'm one of a family of four. My brother and I are all that are left—our parents died before any of this happened. We were poor and lived in a small town in Illinois. I worked my way through a small college in Illinois with a little help for playing football. In those days that meant they saw that you got a job, washing dishes in the dining hall.

I've kept contact with all the friends I knew in those days. And now, though it may be hard to understand, I'm surrounded more on a daily basis with the same kind of people I always knew than I am with the so-called rich. The security detail, aides and staff and, to tell you the truth, our friends though successful now had backgrounds like my own.

You ask if there is some way that you and others could unite behind our programs—that you feel left out. I'm not sure I understand exactly what you mean. Believe me I want and need your support to get measures through Congress to reduce spending and taxes, to help in the battle to get inflation and interest rates down. I'd like to hear from you and have your suggestions. To get a letter to me quickly, address it to Mrs. Kathy Osborne here at the White House.

Again, thanks.

Sincerely,

Ronald Reagan

Mr. Kenneth Loebker
Lawrenceville, Georgia

Nackey Scripps Gallowhur, the granddaughter of newspaper publisher E. W. Scripps, married William Loeb III in 1952 and continued publishing the conservative and nationally influential newspaper Manchester Union Leader *after her husband's death in 1981.*

WASHINGTON

June 28, 1982

Dear Nackey:

How good it was to hear from you even if you did give me a polite spanking. From you I'll take it and like it.

Nackey, my old friend Jeffrey Hart based his column on some misinformation plus the image that is being created of me as being packaged and delivered by staff and aides who won't let me think for myself. First, let me clear up the "misinformation." Solzhenitsyn was definitely invited to the luncheon but didn't want to be a part of the group we'd invited. For what reason I don't know. As for the "off the record" ruling on my remarks, our guests had asked that our discussion be off the record—no press coverage.

Now, back to the image-making, that seems to be not only a theme of the liberal pundits, but of the so-called "new conservatives" including some of my old friends from *Human Events,* etc. It just isn't true. I'm not turning my back on Taiwan and, other than a few State Department types, no one is trying to push me that way. Maybe my speech at the United Nations will also indicate I'm not soft on Russia. And none of our gang tried to talk me into giving up our tax cuts even though for a time half the columnists were saying they were doing so on a nearly daily basis.

Maybe a few events in the last couple of days will further substantiate my claim that I'm being me. I just hope being me can accomplish all that needs to be done.

I tried a meeting with some of those conservatives I mentioned: John Lofton, Stan Evans, Alan Ryskind, et al. and gave them chapter and verse on what the actual record is, but it didn't do much good.

Again, it was good hearing from you and I thank you for sending Jeffrey's column. I hadn't seen it.

Sincerely,

~~Ronald Reagan~~

Ron

P.S. I just signed that 1st time out of routine habit—forgive me.

Mrs. William Loeb
Union Leader Cororation
Manchester, New Hampshire

WASHINGTON

June 28, 1982

Dear Rob Iosue:

Thanks very much for your letter and your kind words. I'm happy if my remarks were of help to you.

As I look back on those college days I find the entire experience contributed to my education. It's true I was caught up in a number of extra-curricular activities besides football. There was the drama club, and that certainly contributed to my earlier career in Hollywood. In fact, that was the only formal training in acting I ever had. But I got involved in student government, also, as well as staging homecoming and putting out the yearbook. Again, as I say, looking back I realize all these things were part of my education.

Best of luck to you and hang in there.

Sincerely,

Ronald Reagan

Mr. Robert V. Iosue, II
Gettysburg, Pennsylvania

July 16, 1982

Dear Private Tzapp:

I read about you in the *New York Post* of June 25th and what you had to say about this country. I'm afraid many of us who were born here take our blessings and our freedom too much for granted. Now and then it takes someone like you to remind us of all that we have to be thankful for. Thank you.

I just wanted to let you know how very welcome you are and how proud I am that you are a Marine.

Please give my regards to your family and, again, my thanks. God bless you.

Sincerely,

Ronald Reagan

Private First Class Vladimir Tzapp
Brooklyn, New York

July 21, 1982

Dear Mr. Ruble:

I'm sure you must realize how sorry I am to learn of what the recession is doing to your business and to you. I wish I could promise some miracle cure for our economic problems but we both know that is impossible. Indeed, our problems have been brought on by more than two decades of government intervention in the economy featuring quick fixes and artificial stimulation of the market. The result has been the longest sustained period of inflation in history—8 recessions since WW II and each one worse than the other before.

In your letter you indicated you hold me to blame for this one. I don't suppose you'll be surprised if I defend myself against that charge. When I took office we had interest rates of 21½%, inflation had been at double digit rates for two years in a row, and unemployment had been increasing since 1979. I campaigned in areas where it had reached 20%. The overall average was almost 8%. Yes, it is 9½% now but interest rates are 16 and inflation has been more than cut in half.

I realize interest rates are still too high particularly with regard to the housing industry. They are higher than can be justified by the reduced inflation. Today the Federal Reserve dropped the discount rate half a point and hinted at another drop soon.

I believe we are beginning a recovery, and this time one based on sensible economics. It will be slow for a time and employment will be the last to recover but the recovery won't be a temporary pause between recessions.

We have more than cut the rate of Federal spending growth in half and we've offset the gigantic (biggest in history) tax increases of the previous administration with an incentive type tax cut. We could have done better, but to get what we have we had to compromise with Democratic leadership in the House which resisted our spending cuts and our tax reductions.

In short, I think we are on the right course to cure a mess that was not of our making.

I hope you'll hang on and that you'll make it through, and I wish you the very best.

Sincerely,

Ronald Reagan

Mr. David F. Ruble
Chicago, Illinois

A mother in modest circumstances, confined to a wheelchair with spina bi-fida, wrote President Reagan and praised her children, especially her teenage son, a senior in high school who was also enrolled in a technical college. In answer to Reagan's July 26 letter, she wrote again and with gratitude asked if it would be all right to save the check rather than cash it. Reagan wrote at the top of this letter: "I phoned her instead of writing—It's lump in throat time."

WASHINGTON

July 26, 1982

Dear Mrs. . . . :*

Forgive me for being so late in answering your letter, but now and then things just pile up in the Oval Office. . . . you were more than kind to write as you did. Your letter has reinforced my faith and overcome the effect of some editorials that evidently were written by journalists who don't know Americans like you and your son. You must be very proud of . . . and with complete justification.

I know you didn't write with anything other in mind than expressing support for what I'm trying to do, and I hope you won't be offended by the enclosed [President Reagan's check for $100]. I worked my way through

70

school many years ago and someone did a little something one day to help. Maybe I can show my appreciation by doing a little something for someone the same age as I was at the time. It isn't much, but please accept it as a thank-you for lifting my morale. God bless you.

Sincerely,

Ronald Reagan

* Name and address withheld.

July 30, 1982

Dear John:

I'll be happy to answer your question although the answer seems so obvious I'm surprised that I have to.

If you don't mind, I'll use the three-year projection figures which seem to be the ones being discussed on the Hill and in the press. Besides, I haven't much confidence, if any, in economic projections as far out as 1987.

Over the three years the increased revenue from the Senate Bill will total roughly $99 billion. Of that amount, $31 billion is not additional tax. It is tax owed under the present laws but not now being collected. The remaining $68 billion is from shutting off unintended tax advantages such as the estimated 60% tax cut from insurance corporations received as the result of faulty legislation a few years ago and some new taxes.

I point this out as a preface to refuting the common practice of calling this the biggest single tax increase in history. It is no such thing. Even if you take the entire $99 billion for '83 through '85 that is less than the $112 billion increase in the Social Security Tax for the same period. There are other equally valid examples.

Now, to answer your question of "why?" It's very simple. This was the price we had to pay to get a reduction of outlays which amount to three dollars for every one dollar of increased revenue.

Leaders of the opposition were determined to cancel the remaining tax cuts passed last year and which come into place beginning in 1983. (The tax cuts from our 1981 bill total $408 billion for '83 through '85.) We found we could not put last year's coalition together unless we agreed to some increases in revenue. The defectors were on both sides of the aisle.

Personally, I had to swallow very hard. I believe in "supply side," and that tax increases slow the recovery. I'm also determined that we haven't had all the spending or tax cuts we're going to get. However, I could not stand by and see the further cuts in spending go down the drain when the price, distasteful as it is, gave us the biggest share of what we are seeking.

John, I can't conclude this letter without telling you I believe the July *Conservative Digest* is one of the most dishonest and unfair bits of journalism I have ever seen.

Sincerely,

Ronald Reagan

Mr. John Lofton
Conservative Digest
Falls Church, Virginia

September 13, 1982

Dear Miss Porter:

I'm sorry to be so late in answering your letter of July 12, but it takes a while before mail reaches my desk. This time it reached my desk while I was in California—so more delay.

I can't tell you how much I appreciate your letter and how much I'm in agreement with you about some of our so-called leaders. For some time now I've wondered whether many of those who've made a career of heading organizations, whatever the cause, would prefer to see the problems remain unsolved because their jobs would otherwise be gone.

In those tough '30's you mentioned I wasn't too far from you. I was washing dishes in the girls' dormitory of a small college in Illinois to get an education. I worked and played football beside a young black man from Greenfield, Illinois—Franklin Burghardt. We remained close friends throughout the years until his death a year ago. He had gone on to be the Athletic Director of Morgan State University in Baltimore.

Bless you and thank you for writing me as you did. Believe me, your letter continues to make me feel good because I read it over again every once in a while—especially when I've been raked over the coals by Carl T. Rowan.*

Sincerely,

Ronald Reagan

Miss Effie Porter
Chicago, Illinois

* In her letter to Reagan, the African American writer mentioned a recent Carl T. Rowan newspaper column, "Blacks See Red Over Reagan."

President Reagan met the Sisco sisters and their brother, Buzzy, when he pur-chased some leather goods at their shop. They wrote to him about the tame and wild animals around their ranch seventy-five miles north of San Francisco.

October 15, 1982

Dear Miss Sam, Miss Bertha and Buzzy:

Your Grass Valley land and lake sound wonderful. I can understand why you are anxious to move.

For a time our ranch was evidently on the circuit of a bear. We never got a glimpse but would find evidence, tracks, etc. The periods in between such visits indicated it covered quite a large territory. Now we haven't seen any tracks and, by coincidence, a bear was shot in Goleta when it began coming into the town raiding garbage cans about a year and a half ago.

About your walnuts—do you still have a horse? Our horses eat acorns, shells and all. I can offer a handful and they eat them like sugar lumps.

All the best to all of you, and I hope your move comes soon.

Sincerely,

Ronald

Miss Sam, Miss Bertha and Buzzy Sisco
Healdsburg, California

October 25, 1982

Dear Mrs. Conway:

Thank you very much for your letter of September 21. I know you will be pleased to learn that we are proceeding along the very lines you proposed in our effort to make world peace a reality.

I am encouraged by my recent meeting with President Gemayel [of Lebanon] and King Hassan [of Morocco] and the representatives of the Arab nations. While it won't be easy, a foundation has been laid that can lead to real negotiations in the Middle East.

I share your conviction that an answer must be found to the nuclear threat and am glad you support our effort to get mutual reduction of nuclear weapons. Our teams in Geneva are working very hard but I fear their efforts have been impeded by the nuclear freeze movement. Their Soviet counterparts have made no secret of their pleasure at the idea of unilateral restrictions on our part.

I am convinced that our own buildup is necessary if they are to continue to bargain in good faith. But, let me assure you, I share your view that our ultimate goal must be the elimination of nuclear weapons. We are also proceeding with plans along the line you proposed for increasing cooperation among the peoples of the world and greater understanding of man's potential for progress.

Again, thank you.

Sincerely,

Ronald Reagan

Mrs. Jill Conway
President
Smith College
Northampton, Massachusetts

Buddy Ebsen, Hollywood western actor, dancer, and TV star of "The Beverly Hillbillies," which drew an average viewing audience of 60 million in the 1960s, was active in Reagan's campaign for public office. In his letter, Ebsen praised the President for the "magnificent job" he was doing.

December 8, 1982

Dear Buddy:

Received your letter and just wanted you to know how great an example of voluntarism I think your arson watch is.

Also thanks for your generous words—they make the job a little easier. I must say bad reviews of a picture only came along a few times a year. On this job you read them every morning in the *Washington Post* and *New York Times* to say nothing of the CBS evening news.

Nancy sends her best and again thanks.

Sincerely,

Ron

Mr. Buddy Ebsen
Marina del Rey, California

December 9, 1982

Dear Mr. Lachowicz:

Forgive me for being so late in answering you letter of November 11, but it arrived while I was away from Washington. I am just now catching up with my mail.

Let me assure you that I feel as deeply as you do about the abuse of human rights of the people in the countries you mentioned. We are engaged in actions as a result that are hurtful to the Soviets. I lifted the grain embargo [April 1, 1981] because no other free world nations would join us and we were, therefore, hurting only our own farmers. We did have another thought in mind; the Soviets are facing grave economic problems—our sale of grain further drains them of hard cash.

We have also finally succeeded in getting our allies to join in an agreement that denies credit to the Soviet Union and restricts trade in high technology.

In the meantime we maintain contact and seek, through quiet diplomacy, to bring about changes. And, of course, we are negotiating with the hope of reducing the arsenal of nuclear weapons.

Our goal is peace and freedom for the enslaved people behind the "iron curtain."

Sincerely,

Ronald Reagan

Mr. Franciszek Lachowicz
Bridgeport, Connecticut

December 20, 1982

Dear Mr. Barrow:

I don't know if I have the words to do justice to Helen Hayes or to make a contribution worthy of your [. . . forthcoming official biography of the actress].

No, I never had the experience of working with her on stage or screen— I'm sorry to say. Yes, I was acquainted with her as we all knew each other in that Hollywood of the Golden Era. I have come to know her better in these later years when we are both somewhat removed from that time and place.

She is ever and always a lady; a lady of warmth and kindliness, as eternally feminine as she was when she captured the hearts of all who saw her on stage or screen.

What was her secret? Certainly it wasn't just theatrical artistry although she was a superb actress. There was more to it than that. There was beauty and an inner light that was Helen Hayes herself shining through every role she played.

Many, many years ago an American patriotic poem was set to music to the noble strains of your anthem "God Save the Queen." Our American poem, however, lost much in the transposition because in order to fit the music it had to be badly phrased.

During World War II a great ceremony was held in Soldiers Field Stadium in Chicago. Helen Hayes was introduced to a crowd of 125,000. Looking so tiny down on the floor of that great stadium she recited that poem, the words that everyone in that crowd had sung hundreds of times. I think it was the first time we had ever heard the beauty of those words. The silence when she finished was, I'm sure, a greater ovation than any she had every received.

Perhaps others could be effective in reading that poem, but would anyone else think of it?

If anyone is looking for sheer enchantment, tell them to run a Helen Hayes picture.

Sincerely,

Ronald Reagan

Mr. Kenneth Barrow
London
England

December 22, 1982

Dear John:

I just received your good letter and the report on your trip. I'm happy to know that President Chiang Ching-Kuo has confidence in my friendship for him and for Taiwan, and that he feels friendship for me as well. Please thank him for his message to me.

I remember with great pleasure our meeting and, before that, being guests in his father's home in 1972. Please assure President Chiang that my feeling for the Republic of China remains unchanged and, while we will continue to seek accord with the People's Republic of China, it will not be at the expense of our friends in Taiwan.

I'd appreciate it also if you would deliver the attached photo to him on your next visit.

Sincerely,

Ron

Mr. John Morley
Laguna Hills, California

December 27, 1982

Dear Ms. Masin:

Thank you very much for your kind and, may I say, informative letter. I agree with you about the importance of the Spanish language. I am of the generation that had to take a couple of years of French in high school because it was the official language of diplomacy. But here we are in the Western hemisphere where Spanish is the language of all but three countries.

I am determined to develop a relationship between ourselves and our neighbors to the South. On my recent trip I made very sure that I didn't appear to be proposing a plan—we've done that before. I asked them what our differences were and how they thought we might resolve those differences. I received some sound answers.

These two great continents have known more peace than any other area of the world and from pole to pole we worship the same God. Believe me I won't let up on this task.

Thank you again for your letter and your prayers.

Sincerely,

Ronald Reagan

Ms. Mary Louise F. Masin
Temple Hills, Maryland

December 27, 1982

Dear Mr. Lowenburg:

Let me assure you the press has a way of leaving out more than they include in their reports. All of us here are on the same course and it is one directed toward persuading Jordan to take the lead among the Arab States in coming to the negotiating table. It is true that publicly we at times have to say things to meet the other person's political needs at home. But first and foremost in all we do is concern for the security of Israel. Believe me, we've made great progress and while there is still much to do our goal remains a just and fair peace.

Best regards.

Sincerely,

Ronald Reagan

Mr. William J. Lowenberg
San Francisco, California

December 27, 1982

Dear Ms. Herrin:

I hadn't heard about the suit* so don't know whether there really is one or not. But let me assure you I will not back away from what I have done.

When I took the oath of office I did so with my hand on my mother's Bible. It was opened to Second Chronicles 7:14. "If my people who are called by my name humble themselves and pray and seek my face, and turn from their wicked ways, then will I hear from heaven and will forgive their sin and heal their land." And yes, we'll continue to try and get prayer restored to our schools.

Thank you for your generous and kind words. God bless you.

Sincerely,

Ronald Reagan

Ms. Barbara G. Herrin
Gainesville, Florida

* The writer reported she had heard on TV that a lawsuit had been filed against the President because he proposed to designate 1983 as the Year of the Bible.

December 27, 1982

Dear Mr. Frey:

May I take issue with you on your suggestion that I'm beginning to think like a Democrat? I guess I've probably—in years passed [*sic*] made more speeches than anyone about extravagances in foreign aid. But that was when we were buying Haile Selassie [the Emperor of Ethiopia, 1930–1974] a million-dollar yacht, sawmills for a country that had no trees, and paving a highway in a land where there were no automobiles.

Let me assure you foreign aid as we are handling it today is very much in line with our national security needs. In some instances it substitutes for a military presence we would have to otherwise maintain.

As for the highway tax—we had put that off for more than a year now but finally could not wait any longer. We have an emergency situation with regard to our national highway system and a great many bridges, any one of which has the potential for a tragic disaster. We feel that a gas tax as a user fee to fund necessary repairs was a fair way to solve the problem. I assure you I will never approve such a tax as just a part of general revenue raising.

Thanks for writing and giving me a chance to respond.

Sincerely,

Ronald Reagan

Mr. Lyle V. Frey
Mitchell, South Dakota

1983

—

Prejudice is not a failing peculiar to one race, it can and
does exist in people of every race and ethnic
background. It takes individual effort to root it out of
one's heart. In my case my father and mother saw that
it never got a start.

·Letter of January 19, 1983·

O F all the private and public accusations against President
Reagan, few were more hurtful to him personally than
his supposed disregard of the aspirations and rights of
African Americans. Common during and after the presidential campaigns were complaints by African Ameri-
can leaders in the Democratic Party regarding his lack of support for civil
rights. These complaints were silenced for a time after he signed the bill
in November making Martin Luther King's birthday a national holiday.
Hostile letters from liberal critics who wrote that Reagan had no sympathy for the economically distressed and jobless also crossed his desk.
From the other side of the political spectrum were letters from ultra-
conservatives who complained that the Reagan they voted for had

changed. The President read with appreciation letters from optimistic Americans, some of whom had lost their jobs or houses or medical care but still endorsed Reagan's tax cuts, his defense rebuilding, and his calls for reduced federal spending. Reagan answered these hostile and friendly letters: the former with careful arguments and the latter with grateful humility.

Letters from correspondents who questioned the wisdom of Reagan's foreign relations policies increased in volume during 1983. Violence raged in Central America as leftist-led rebels in Nicaragua sought to expand their power into El Salvador and Guatemala, where they faced armed forces operating out of Honduras and supported by the United States. This conflict, which began four years earlier during the overthrow of Nicaragua's Somoza regime by Marxist leader Daniel Ortega Saavedra and supported by Cuba and the Soviet Union, soon spread well beyond Nicaragua. Early in March, in an address to the National Association of Evangelicals, the President termed the Soviet Union the "evil empire." Presidential addresses on Central America and El Salvador in later March and April described these more immediate communist threats to the United States. The Commission on Central America, created in July and headed by Henry Kissinger, sought answers to the economic and political questions troubling that region. In early 1984 the commission sought over $8 billion in economic aid over five years for Central America.

On September 1 Korean Airlines Flight 007 strayed into Soviet airspace on its route from Anchorage to Seoul and was shot down by a Soviet pilot following military orders. Two hundred and sixty-nine passengers and crew died. Only weeks later did the Soviet government take responsibility for this disaster, called by President Reagan in a television address on September 5 a "crime against humanity." Some correspondents called for the United States to punish the Soviets for this crime.

A remarkable potential answer to the Soviet missile threat came with President Reagan's proposal for building a missile shield, the Strategic Defense Initiative (SDI), which he hoped would be in place before century's end. In October the military operation to rescue eight hundred students attending a medical school on the island of Grenada, located in the West Indies, brought letters of gratitude to the White House from these students. The force of two thousand Marines removed the Cuban and Marxist forces and made it possible for democratic institutions to begin again on the island. However, the rescue also produced negative media accounts as reporters complained about tight military censorship.

Almost two months after the Korean Air tragedy, terrorists struck U.S. forces in Beirut. On Sunday, October 23, shortly after 6 A.M. Beirut time, a truck driven by a young Shiite fundamentalist crashed through several barriers and guard posts into the four-story concrete-and-steel Marine headquarters building. Its explosives caused the building to collapse into rubble: 241 Marines died, and over 100 were wounded. Minutes later another suicide bomber drove into the French peacekeeping headquarters, destroying that eight-story building and killing over 50 soldiers. Especially sensitive to military casualties, President Reagan considered that Sunday the saddest day of his presidential life because he had insisted on sending the Marines to Lebanon as peacekeepers. He explained to the American parents and public that a peaceful Middle East was vital to the United States, Western Europe, and Israel. He also took full responsibility for the lack of security at the Marine headquarters. Moreover, during the following weeks, he wrote and talked to the parents and other relatives of those who died.

Secretary of the Interior James G. Watt faced increasingly hostile criticism from environmental groups such as the Sierra Club and the National Audubon Society for his attempts to open more public lands and resources to private development. Some writers also chastised Watt for his supposed criticism of American Indians. Watt resigned in October 1983, and William Clark left his post as National Security Advisor to become the new secretary.

A gentle promise for Social Security to be available for his longtime friend actor George Burns together with other letters regarding Taiwan, Israel, CCC [Civilian Conservation Corps camps, established for unemployed persons during President Franklin Roosevelt's administration], and alcohol abuse were answered on White House stationery as Reagan caught up with his correspondence. This year his foreign travel schedule was modest. A one-day visit to Mexico in August was followed by a weeklong trip in November to Japan and Korea. In Japan Reagan visited his friend Prime Minister Yasuhiro Nakasone and gave an address to the Diet, the first address by an American president to the Japanese Parliament, where he was warmly praised for his statement that a nuclear war must never be fought and that nuclear weapons must be banished from the face of the earth. Then Reagan visited Korea and the Korean Demilitarized Zone, an area he called freedom's front lines. Thirty-eight domestic trips completed his travel year as he considered the prospects for running for reelection in 1984.

January 13, 1983

Dear Larry:

It was good to hear from you as always, but please not to worry. I must confess I didn't see the NBC interview, but am grateful for the kind things you said even if they didn't use them. Believe me, I'm familiar with that technique. In fact, I've come to believe there is little, if any, honesty in the media, and ethic is a word they are totally unfamiliar with. Barbara Walters gave the best advice I've ever heard with regard to TV interviews—they should be live—no tape, and limited to the exact time that will appear on the air.

Larry, in a press conference some time ago, I told of a county in Arizona that had gone volunteer on a program which had been run by government. The reduction in cost and the increase in effectiveness was my reason for telling the story. The people I was talking about told me later that NBC had interviewed them but was not interested in their answers unless they could prove me wrong.

Thanks for the job rating—and, again, it was good hearing from you.

Nancy sends her warm regards.

Sincerely,

Ron

Mr. Laurence W. Beilenson
Los Angeles, California

President Reagan wrote this personal letter to Benjamin Hooks, executive director of the National Association for the Advancement of Colored People (NAACP). After White House staff members reviewed the statistics in this letter, a revised letter was signed and sent to Hooks.

WASHINGTON

[January 19, 1983]

Dear Ben:

A short time ago you were quoted as having told the press that no administration in 30 years has "demonstrated as much determination as President Reagan to roll back hard-won gains of black Americans." You then described 1982 as the worst year in recent memory for blacks because of my budget policies.

Ben, there are no facts to substantiate such charges and they are a distortion of the actual record as well as of my own position on these matters. The number of cases involving civil rights litigation were 753 for only 9 months of 1982 as against 656 for all of 1980. In just 8 months of '82, $9.7 million in back pay and other monetary benefits was collected compared again to the full year 1980 when the figure was less than half that, $4.6 million.

The results of complaint processing for victims of discrimination show appreciable gains. The number of persons benefiting from E.E.O.C.'s [Equal Employment Opportunity Commission] voluntary complaint settlements was 32,790 in the 1st six months of '82, a 53% increase over fiscal 1981 which includes 3 months of the Carter administration. The figures for investigations, settlements, etc. show similar gains for our nearly two years here.

As for our budget cuts, economic policy, etc., hasn't the lowering of inflation by almost two-thirds been of help to blacks as well as to all others? Even people on welfare or at the poverty level of earnings have several hundred dollars more in purchasing power than they would have had if inflation had remained at the 1980 level. Yes, I know there is economic distress in the land and that black unemployment is exceptionally high. But all the political demagoguery in the land can't hide the fact that this recession was caused by the high interest rates (the result of inflation) which prevailed in 1980 and much of '81. Our program was not yet in place when the bottom fell out. Now there are signs of recovery and I'm determined it will benefit everyone across the board. I hope that political prejudice will not keep you from really looking at our record and learning how unjustified your attack was.

Ben, if only it were possible to look into each other's hearts and minds, you would find no trace of prejudice or bigotry in mine. I know that's hard for you to believe and that's too bad because together we could do more for the people you represent that either of us can do alone.

Prejudice is not a failing peculiar to one race, it can and does exist in people of every race and ethnic background. It takes individual effort to root it out of one's heart. In my case, my father and mother saw that it never got a start. I shall be forever grateful to them.

Sincerely,

Ronald Reagan

Mr. Benjamin Hooks
President, NAACP
New York, New York

Arthur Laffer, considered the father of supply-side economics, was a member of Reagan's Economic Advisory Board. He believed that tax revenues rise along with tax rates only to a certain point, and then higher rates result in lower production and government tax revenues.

January 24 1983

Dear Art:

In trying to cover the range of subjects this morning in our meeting I left one out. You had mentioned the five-cent gasoline tax in discussing our tax increase. I intended and then overlooked commenting on that. I realize it is a tax and yet I would never have held still for that as a part of a tax package simply to raise revenues.

Here is a brief history of how it came about. More than a year ago Drew Lewis came to Cabinet with a very disturbing rundown on our deteriorating highways and bridges. He had some frightening figures on bridges that school buses refused to cross without making the children walk across, etc.

I was concerned but faced with our budget battle and asked him to wait a year—which he did.

As you can imagine, when he came back a year later his report was even more frightening. I agreed to the tax as purely a user fee for the purpose of restoring the system and that it would expire once that was done. If I'm still around, I'll see that it does. I'm not only against taxes—I never want to see a gasoline tax used for general revenue.

It was good to see you.

Best regards,

Ron

Professor Arthur Laffer
Rolling Hill Estates, California

February 3, 1983

Dear Light:

I've written to Virginia Hughes, but I'm afraid I can't use a mule.* I have several hundred up on Capitol Hill.

I've signed the enclosed pamphlet [for a dairy farmer in Ogle County, Illinois].

All the best,

Dutch

Mr. Light Thompson
Princeton, Illinois

* His friend, Light, who lived forty miles south of Dixon, Illinois, asked the President if he would like a small mule for his ranch: he also asked the President to send a note to Virginia Hughes, a loyal supporter of the President.

February 8, 1983

Dear Mr. Robinson:

I appreciate your letter and am grateful for having had your support. I believe, however, there may be some misunderstanding about the Social Security taxes.

In legislation adopted during the previous administration (1977) a package of Social Security payroll tax increases was adopted. It amounts to the biggest tax increase in our history and calls for further increases from 1985 to 1990. At the time the President said we had solved the fiscal problem of Social Security to at least 2015. If you'll recall in late 1981 I called attention to the fact that Social Security would be broke by July 1983 unless some action was taken. No action was taken—the temptation to use Social Security as a political football in the '82 election was too great.

I called for a bipartisan task force to present a plan aimed at restoring the fiscal integrity of Social Security. I believe the tax increase you referred to in your letter is the schedule of tax increases between 1985 and 1990 which were passed in 1977. It is true that we acceded to moving them up to 1984. In return for that one year acceleration, however, an income tax credit will be given for that first year.

No one is truly happy with the compromise solution but compromise was the only alternative with the "House" in Democratic hands.

There are two other tax changes in the package but I must confess I don't feel as bad about those. Present Social Security recipients are receiving much more than they ever paid in. We are asking that single individuals who have $20,000 income, not including Social Security benefits, and couples with $25,000 income be required to pay income tax on their Social Security benefits. I see this as a step at least toward correcting a mistake in the program. There should have been a means test from the beginning. I find that I am eligible for Social Security and I am refusing to take it.

The other tax change has to do with the self-employed. They presently pay 75% of the total payroll tax of employee and employer. They will be asked to pay 100% but will get an income tax deduction for the employer half just as employers do now.

I hope you can understand the necessity of compromise in this highly politicized issue. I assure you, my basic goals have not changed. Right now I'm faced with a Democratic effort to cancel the 10% income tax cut scheduled for July 1st, and the indexing of that tax beginning in 1985. I shall fight to the end to prevent that happening, and can use all the support I can get.

Best regards,

Ronald Reagan

Mr. Philip N. Robinson
Pacific Palisades, California

George Burns (1896–1996) became a famous motion picture, radio, and TV performer. He wrote to the President and Mrs. Reagan, thanking them for the birthday greeting, and added his hopes that Social Security problems would be solved because with his luck there would be nothing left when he got old. He would live to be one hundred.

February 9, 1983

Dear George:

I just had to answer your letter knowing how concerned you are about Social Security. Now that I've reached the age of eligibility you can rest assured I've done something about it. I've made sure it will be on a solid basis for all you young fellows when your turn comes.

February 6 was my birthday—I finally made PAR-72—the hard way.

Nancy sends her love and so do I.

Sincerely,

Ron

Mr. George Burns
Hollywood, California

John Morley, planning a news trip to the Far East, had received a phone call from Taiwan inviting him to visit with President Chiang Ching-Kuo. Morley planned to present Reagan's autographed photo to President Chiang and wondered if the President wanted to provide a letter of support for the Republic of China.

February 10, 1983

Dear John:

Thank you for all three letters and for your masterful essays. I was especially taken by the ones on women. Did you know that Will Rogers once commented that if women kept on trying to be more and more like men—pretty soon they wouldn't know any more than the men do. You've caused me to wonder what the result might be if we turned our arms reduction negotiations over to women—both sides of course.

John, I've decided against a separate letter. I would greatly appreciate it if you would convey my warmest regards to President Chiang. I still recall our meeting with great pleasure. I'm sure he understands that we must continue to seek better relations with the Chinese on the mainland but we will never do so at the expense of our friends on Taiwan. Secretary Schultz on my direct order made this completely clear on his recent visit to Peking. He informed them we would continue to abide by the Taiwan Relations Act.

Please, if you will, tell my friend President Chiang Ching-Kuo that I asked you to assure him of my continued friendship for him and his people and that we shall not waiver in that friendship.

All the best to you on your trip and God be with you.

Sincerely,

Ron

Mr. John Morley
Laguna Hills, California

In the 1930s George Murphy began his film career in Hollywood. During his career he appeared in over forty films. A founding member of the Screen Actors Guild, he, like his friend Reagan, fought against Communist Party influences in the guild during the 1940s. Active in state politics, he won election as a Republican to the U.S. Senate from California for one term in 1964.

WASHINGTON

February 14, 1983

Dear Murph:

I turned to Don Regan on the idea about household help and making them tax deductible. He had the Treasury boys and girls get into it. They found it attractive in many respects—the private sector keeping records on possible illegals, tax payments, etc. But then they came down on the politics of it—a tax break for those who could afford such help, denied to those who did the work themselves.

There is no question but that we're vulnerable on that one. They've done quite a job on me as "favoring the rich" in our tax policies. They also reminded me that in the tax package we passed last year we built in some techniques for getting at the underground economy. They felt we should give them a chance to work.

I'll go along, but I won't forget the idea because, tax issues aside, it could possibly increase employment in the household field, aid the working wives and even lift the pay scale for that type of work.

Nancy sends her love.

Sincerely,

Ron

The Honorable George Murphy
West Palm Beach, Florida

February 22, 1983

Dear Father Bill:

I hope you won't mind my answering your letter to Nancy. She passed the information to me about the two parishes and their employment program. I, in turn, am telling our "Private Initiatives" group. They have, in a year's time, created a computer bank with information on more than 2500 private programs which are treating a variety of problems very successfully. I know they'll be interested in this one.

You know, Father Bill, I find myself wondering at times if maybe the Lord didn't let our present troubles come upon us so we could find our way back to the values we once knew. It is almost as if the people were hungry to get back to neighbor helping neighbor. For too long we have let government take over what was once accepted as our personal responsibilities. Now I'm constantly learning of things the people are doing through their churches, organizations, neighborhoods and communities.

Thank you very much for sending this information and thank you for your prayers. Nancy and I are both truly grateful. If now and then when you are praying you get a busy signal it's probably me in there ahead of you. I seem to be doing a great deal of praying myself these days. But, please, rest assured, I need all the help I can get.

All the best,

Ron

Father Bill Kenny
Los Angeles, California

According to the New York Times, *January 19, 1983, Interior Secretary James Watt, in an interview to be broadcast on the Satellite Program Network on January 20, criticized the federal government for ruinous social programs in the Indian reservations. "If you want an example of the failure of socialism, don't go to Russia, come to America and go to the Indian reservations. . . ." Here, alcoholism, drug abuse, divorce, unemployment and venereal disease are experienced. "Every social problem is exaggerated because of socialistic policies." Watt was also highly critical of some tribal leaders who failed to help their people. Earlier and later criticism of Watt by environmentalists and many liberals led to the secretary's resignation in October. Ron Hendren, nationally acclaimed journalist and California radio and television commentator, broadcast his views about Watt in January. Reagan's friend, Ward Quaal, broadcast pioneer and innovator, was president of WGN Broadcasting Company in Chicago.*

WASHINGTON

February 25, 1983

Dear Ward:

Thanks very much for sending the Ron Hendren script. Maybe he means well but you know this is an example of how unsuccessful the media and groups with an axe to grind can be in image making. The actual record of the Department of Interior under Jim Watt is possibly if not probably better than it has been for many, many years.

I've obtained the transcript of what Jim Watt actually said regarding the Indians and he was actually pointing out government's faults. Indian leaders who sounded off on him after hearing the press version did an about-face when given his verbatim statement.

Thanks again and best regards.

Sincerely,

Ronald Reagan

Mr. Ward Quaal
Chicago, Illinois

March 14, 1983

Dear Tom:

Just a quick line to acknowledge your letter. . . .

As for our British cousins I must say Her Majesty is a real, down to earth, likable person. All in all despite the weather the trip was a great success and she made friends all the way.

About the Marines in Lebanon and pot: when we came to Washington there was a real problem in the military. I'm happy to say we have a program under way that has reduced the smokers by more than two-thirds. I think the Lebanon story could be a bit of press sensationalism.

Regards,

Ron

Mr. Thomas M. O'Brien
Scottsdale, Arizona

John Erickson, national president of the Fellowship of Christian Athletes, wrote to President Reagan and recalled their visit a year earlier and their discussions regarding drug abuse. He offered his help in winning the battle against drugs.

March 14, 1983

Dear Mr. Erickson:

I share your concern about the drug and alcohol problem among our young people and believe, as I'm sure you do, that the answer lies in taking the customers away from the drugs not the other way around. I'm old enough to recall when heavyweight champion, Jack Dempsey, refused to endorse a cigarette because of the effect it might have on youngsters. When I was sports announcing, no professional athlete would do a beer ad.

As you know, Nancy is very much involved in working with kids on the drug program. At the government level we are having some success in intercepting the peddlers and the drugs, but as I said, the more practical approach is to turn the customers off.

I wonder if any progress could be made with the team owners regarding commercial endorsements? I remember a time in Hollywood when there was a morals clause in every one of our contracts. The studio could cancel the contract of any performer who violated commonly accepted moral conduct standards. Maybe something like that could work in pro sports.

Well believe me I share your concern and appreciate your offer of help.

Sincerely,

Ronald Reagan

Mr. John Erickson
Kansas City, Missouri

Beginning in the 1930s, Mickey Rooney, actor, singer, and dancer would appear in over two hundred feature films. His Broadway musicals and traveling stage shows continue to delight audiences.

March 14, 1983

Dear Mickey:

I'm late in saying thanks for your warm birthday greeting. Forgive me. It was good to hear from you.

I appreciate your suggestion about the C.C.C. [Civilian Conservation Corps] camps project but we've come down on the side of a training program to catch particularly those younger people and bring them up to the new technology. Even with all our unemployment you'd be amazed at how many unfilled jobs there are in electronics and such simply because not enough people are trained for that work.

Nancy sends her love and give our very best to Jan. Again, thanks.

Sincerely,

Ron

Mr. Mickey Rooney
Los Angeles, California

March 15, 1983

Dear Mrs. Mize:

Thank you very much for your letter. I'm sure the drum beat of false propaganda must be even more frustrating to you and your husband than it is to me. May I just say that from getting around the country and from the mail I receive I know the overwhelming majority of Americans are as proud as I am of our military forces.

For the life of me I don't understand the voices raised in what I must call our liberal press whining about the defense budget and criticizing virtually every aspect of the military. They don't speak for the American people and they aren't going to have their way.

Please give your husband, the Major, my regards and my thanks for what he is doing for all of us.

Sincerely,

Ronald Reagan

Mrs. Donald T. Mize
Dale City, Virginia

March 15, 1983

Your Majesty:

We miss you. I know your visit to our West Coast became a harrowing, tempest-tossed experience but through it all your unfailing good humor and graciousness won the hearts of our people.*

In two weeks we'll be back at the ranch you only got to see for a few moments when temporarily the fog lifted. I'll be trying a new saddle for which I thank you. We are having our card from the Brittania [*sic*] crew framed. And we are hoping that one day in the not too distant future you'll return to our shores when the sun is shining and the skies are blue. In other words, in good riding weather.

Thank you again for your many kindnesses and for the most memorable experience. Please give our very best regards to His Royal Highness.

Sincerely,

Ronald Reagan

Her Majesty
Queen Elizabeth II
London

* In a California February rainstorm, Queen Elizabeth and Prince Philip began the drive to the Reagans' Rancho del Cielo near Santa Barbara. When their limousine became stuck on the seven-mile switchback road, Reagan staff members rescued them with four-wheel-drive cars.

March 16, 1983

Dear Mr. Roweau:

Thank you very much for your kind letter, and please extend my thanks to Miss Mahon and Mrs. Kolek and all your students for their generous words.

They also had some questions: Yes, I have plenty of jelly beans; my favorite sport now is riding but my real love is football which I played in high school and college. Heather, I do like my job. Angela and Maria, I like pork chops, too, but my real favorite is macaroni and cheese.

Thank you all again and best regards.

Sincerely,

Ronald Reagan

Mr. Ed Roweau
Woodridge, Illinois

March 28, 1983

Dear Larry:

It was good to hear from you and I appreciate your concern.* I think the press did some out-of-context quoting and some guessing. I will say however, there is a firm consensus that our country is and has been for a long time pledged to the continued existence of Israel as a Nation. I've heard no contradiction of this in the State Department, Defense Department, the Congress or for that matter—the press.

But with regard to what I said: I was talking about the Lebanon situation and our effort to persuade Israel, Syria, and the P.L.O. to get out and give the Lebanese a chance to re-establish sovereignty over their own land. Israel sees its northern border as vulnerable to forays by remnants of the P.L.O. and wants to retain a military presence on Lebanon's side of the border. We have expressed a willingness to help Lebanon with our multinational forces until such time as Lebanese forces can demonstrate they are capable of guarding the border.

We've made considerable progress but haven't been able to get a sign-off.

Things have looked better the last few days with the change in Defense Ministers in Israel. Nancy sends her best.

Sincerely,

Ron

Mr. Laurence W. Beilenson
Los Angeles, California

* Beilenson was worried about newspaper reports that President Reagan offered a guarantee of Israel's northern border.

Malcolm Muggeridge, a British journalist for Punch *magazine, the* Manchester Guardian, *and several other newspapers, also produced special programs for the British Broadcasting Company.*

April 18, 1983

Dear Mr. Muggeridge:

Thank you for your kind letter. I must confess I'm still not used to remarks or speeches of mine getting attention across the seas. I'm grateful for your words which I quoted; they were most effective and well received.

I share your thought about Christianity in Russia but I also believe we're seeing a renewal of faith generally. Certainly it is true here in the United States.

Thanks again and thank you for your good wishes. Nancy and I return them to you and Kitty.

Sincerely,

Ronald Reagan

Mr. Malcolm Muggeridge
Robertsbridge
Sussex, England

April 18, 1983

Dear Rev. Kent:

Thank you for writing and for giving me a chance to respond. First let me say there apparently isn't as much difference between us as you seem to think. I am totally dedicated to negotiations leading to legitimate and ver-

ifiable reduction of nuclear weapons by all nations and the two super powers in particular. I hope and pray that once such reductions begin we could
one day see an end to all such weapons.

Some things however have changed since you left the service. We do not
have parity—quite the contrary. And we no longer excel in accuracy. The
bulk of our weapons are more than 15 years old. The bulk of theirs are less
than 5 years old. They outweigh us in megatonnage 4 to 1.

I have stated many times the overwhelming majority of people in the nuclear freeze movement are sincerely motivated and want peace. I join them
in that. All I ask is that we negotiate a reduction first to where we do have
parity—then we freeze. To freeze now adds to the risk of war because we
are inferior to them in such weaponry. It is our willingness to modernize
our forces that has brought them to the negotiating table.

I'm sure you realize that in my present position I have access to all the information available on this subject, in fact more than is available to almost
anyone else. I make my judgments based on those facts. Again I assure you
I want peace. There have been four wars in my lifetime. I want also the
total elimination of all nuclear weapons.

Sincerely,

Ronald Reagan

Rev. Robert E. Kent
Independence, Missouri

WASHINGTON

April 26, 1983

Dear Mrs. Nuese:

It has been quite a while since you sat in that empty bedroom writing me
of your son's departure. I've often thought about him and you and wondered how he's getting along and if he's happy with the choice he made. I
hope he is. I don't know which branch he chose.

It is a gray rainy day here in Washington and I've been reading your letter again. I don't mean to impose but if you could find the time to write and let me know about your son I'd be most grateful. If you'd send the letter to me at the White House in care of Kathy Osborne (my secretary) I'd get it right away.

Best regards,

Ronald Reagan

Mrs. Dorothy Nuese
Laurel, Iowa

WASHINGTON

May 2, 1983

Dear Lt. Swanson:

Your mother has just left the Oval Office after presenting me with a plaque portraying George Washington kneeling in prayer at Valley Forge. Your mother and others also gave me a new Bible. She spoke of you and gave me a snapshot of you and your "voice of freedom," a Tomcat F-14.

I just wanted to check in with my thanks for what you and all your teammates are doing in behalf of freedom. There are no words to properly express my pride in all of you.

God bless you.

Sincerely,

Ronald Reagan

Lt. Dave C. Swanson
FPO New York, New York

Peter D. Hannaford, cofounder of Deaver and Hannaford public relations firm in 1975, served as director of public affairs in Governor Reagan's cabinet and became his communications advisor during the 1976 and 1980 presidential campaigns.

May 5, 1983

Dear Pete:

Thanks very much for your kind words about the speech.* The returns on it reflect a better reception than some of our columnists are willing to concede. Of course the real test will be in Congress.

Thanks too for sending me the Thatcher interview. She continues to be my favorite head of state. And you ran into Ed Reed. I haven't seen him in years.

Nancy sends her best and give our regards to Irene.

Sincerely,

Ron

Mr. Peter D. Hannaford
Washington, D.C.

* Address to Congress on El Salvador.

May 23, 1983

Dear Mrs. Nuese:

Thank you very much for your letter—correction—letters. I did enjoy both and appreciate your writing. I'm pleased to know Ted doesn't regret his decision. Your concern about a "militaristic point of view" is understandable but may I offer another view? The paradox of military training is that young men are taught a trade which we hope and pray they will never use. It is important that they take pride in what they are doing, the terms are esprit de corps and morale. Those things are very important. The better they know this trade, the higher their morale, the better are our chances of maintaining peace. They are truly the keepers of peace by virtue of their willingness to man the ramparts and by hard-won skills.

Well I didn't intend to write a lecture but I am so proud of all the young men like Ted and yes the young women in uniform. But rest assured with that pride goes increased determination to do everything I can to prevent their ever having to go to war.

I appreciate your concern and understanding with regard to the news media and what it is like on my side of their cameras and note pads. Sometimes it seems they are less interested in legitimate news than they are in proving their knowledge and wisdom is superior to ours. The most frustrating thing is when I have the facts to prove them wrong but cannot reveal those facts without endangering security or wrecking some plan we're engaged in.

Thank you again and I wish you every success in your writing. Give my regards to Ted.

Sincerely,

Ronald Reagan

Mrs. Dorothy J. Nuese
Laural, Iowa

June 6, 1983

Dear Scott:

Your father told me of your coming marriage.* I hope you won't mind my offering congratulations. Your father has been more than kind in his help-fulness to me. Thanks to him I'm still able to get in the saddle in these times when I can't get to our ranch.

I wish you a lifetime of happiness and can assure you marriage is the best way to achieve that. Thomas Jefferson said, "Happiness in the married state is a blessing to be desired above all others." Now I didn't hear Jeffer-son say that but I know he's right. Ignore all the cynical jokes about mar-riage, a man can't be complete without it. It's worth working at and the more you work at it the more happiness you'll have.

Congratulations and best wishes.

Sincerely,

Ronald Reagan

Mr. M. Scott Ayres
Roanoke, Virginia

* The President also wrote to Scott's fiancée and told her that his own life really began thirty-one years ago in a marriage ceremony.

June 6, 1983

Dear Brute:

As usual your column hit it right on the nose and the fuzzy-minded right on the head. . . .

By the way (and back to your column) you probably know this but just in case you don't, back in those days of Winston's [Churchill] ignored warnings he summed up appeasement with a masterful statement. He said, "If you will not fight when you can win without bloodshed, if you will not fight when your victory will be sure and not too costly, you may come to a time when you will have to fight with all the odds against you and only a precarious chance of victory. There may be a worse case; you may have to fight when there is no chance of victory because it is better to perish than to live as slaves."

Again thanks and best regards.

Sincerely,

Ron

Lt. General Victor H. Krulak, USMC (Ret.)
San Diego, California

June 20, 1983

Dear Miss Solorzano:

Thank you very much for your letter and for giving me an opportunity to correct what seem to be some misperceptions on the part of Mr. Valancy [her teacher]. The first one is that I said the people supporting the nuclear freeze movement are communists. What I did say was that millions of such people were undoubtedly sincere in their belief that a freeze could improve the chance for peace. I also said I was sure they weren't aware of the part the Soviet Union was playing in providing propaganda to keep the movement going.

Right now we are trying to persuade the Soviet Union to join us in reducing on both sides the number of nuclear weapons. Then a freeze would make some sense. But right now the Soviet Union is so far ahead of us in such weapons that a freeze would leave them dangerously more powerful and would increase the chance of war. If we were not going forward with the MX missile I doubt the Soviets would have agreed to meet with us in Geneva to discuss arms reductions.

Again, I thank you and I'm glad you have come to our country. I hope one day your homeland, Nicaragua, can be free. God bless you.

Sincerely,

Ronald Reagan

Miss Martha E. Solorzano
Miami, Florida

Patrick Mulvey, who had been totally blind all his life, also asked President Reagan to tell him what the Capitol looks like through Reagan's eyes.

WASHINGTON

June 20, 1983

Dear Mr. Mulvey:

Thank you very much for writing as you did. You brightened my day. I'm glad you are working as you are for our country.

With regard to a "Star Wars" defense system against nuclear weapons let me say the news media seems to be responsible for that descriptive term. Frankly I have no idea what the nature of such a defense might be. I simply asked our scientists to explore the possibility of developing such a defense. My thinking is that if such a defense can be found we could then move to get agreement on eliminating nuclear weapons completely. I agree with you that a so-called freeze at this time would certainly increase the chances of war.

You and I are in agreement also about our dependence on God. Without His help there is no way we can be successful. I have quoted those words from Second Chronicles many times.

You asked that I share with you what Washington looks like to me. My favorite view is from the so-called Truman balcony on the south side of the White House. You look down a vista of green lawn, then the park like expanse called the Ellipse. The Washington Monument stands against the sky and then at the very end of the vista is the gleaming white pillared Jefferson Memorial. It is truly inspiring.

Again my thanks to you and God bless you.

Sincerely,

Ronald Reagan

Mr. Patrick Mulvey
Whittier, California

June 20, 1983

Dear Mr. Welling:

Thank you for writing as you did. Yes your Uncle did give his life for his country and it was not in vain. It is up to all of us to be sure of that.

A number of years ago a President of this country declared that we have a rendezvous with destiny. In a world where terrorism spreads and the innocent die we must fulfill our destiny. If not us who? If not now when? Your Uncle understood that. I know what a tragedy this must be for all of you who knew and loved him and you have our deepest sympathy. You also have my pledge to do all I can to see that what he believed in is carried on.

Sincerely,

Ronald Reagan

Mr. John Welling
Wooster, Ohio

Roy Innis, National Chairman of the Congress of Racial Equality, praised Reagan's March 23 speech on high energy beam technology.

June 20, 1983

Dear Mr. Innis:

I'm sorry to be so late in answering your letter but it has only just reached my desk. Sometimes the wheels of bureaucracy can turn very slowly.

Thank you very much for your generous words. With regard to the idea of a defense against nuclear missiles I share your views of the mutual assured destruction policy; it makes no sense whatsoever. Hopefully a defense could result in real negotiations leading to the total elimination of nuclear weapons.

Mr. Innis, I would like very much to cooperate with you in the educational and technological developments that will help all our people get, as you say, a "running start into the 21st century." If you don't mind I'd like to put a member of my Administration in touch with you and again my thanks to you.

Sincerely,

Ronald Reagan

Mr. Roy Innis
C.O.R.E.
New York, New York

June 21, 1983

Dear Mr. Wright:

Unlike you I had never met Al Schaufelberger [a lieutenant commander in the SEALS, murdered in El Salvador] but I share your sorrow. I knew of him, of course, and his record—one of the best—and I feel a great sense of rage at the cowardly terrorists who took his life. You are right. Our way of life is under attack, and we cannot falter in the fight. But I bleed for those fine young Americans who man the ramparts.

I phoned Al's mother and father, and to you his friend I offer my heartfelt sympathy.

Sincerely,

Ronald Reagan

Mr. James F. Wright
Carmel, California

In his letter, Richard Marsh mentioned the grasshopper who told industrious ants that "the world owes me a living."

June 21, 1983

Dear Mr. Marsh:

Thank you for your letter and your generous words. I'd be very proud to have your support.

You'll be pleased to know that in resisting proposals for the usual kind of make-work government programs we did ask for and get a program to train people for the kind of jobs that are available. I believe at least half of today's unemployment is structural and cannot be attributed to the recession. I agree with you also that we've been less ant and too much grasshopper and we're going to have to change.

I have one confession to make; speechwriters were not responsible for the "trite" slogan, "Stay the Course." It happens to be an expression of my own. I used it in a major speech in '82 and it was picked up by the press and literally made into a slogan. Believe me I'll "hang in there."

Best regards,

Ronald Reagan

Mr. Richard P. Marsh
San Francisco, California

WASHINGTON

June 24, 1983

Dear Mr. Powell:

Thanks very much for your good letter. We have just had a gathering here of many of the children and young people who are participating in the Special Olympics for those with handicaps, both physical and mental. You, I know, would understand their evident happiness and agree they enjoy a worthwhile quality of life. Yet so many of them would, if born today, be threatened by those who have arrogantly taken it upon themselves to decide who should live and who should die.

I am supporting the legislation you mentioned and will not forget the cause.* We have a case in the news today which exposes the fallacy of the abortionists' case. A pregnant woman was shot, she survived the wound but her unborn child was killed. The assailant has been charged with murder. Yet she could have killed the unborn by abortion and that would have been legal.

Thanks again for your letter and best regards.

Sincerely,

Ronald Reagan

Mr. Robert G. B. Powell, Jr.
Galveston, Texas

* Respect for Human Life Act.

June 24, 1983

Dear Mr. Anderson:

Forgive me for being so late in answering your letter of April 7. Sometimes it takes quite a while before letters reach my desk. I hope you are still hanging in there because I have to disagree that our land is dying.

You are 38 years old. Just by coincidence when I was 38 years old at exactly this time of year I was lying in traction in a hospital with my thigh broken in six places. I had been scheduled to start a picture three days after I went in the hospital and being a freelance actor I was moaning about the loss of revenue because they put another actor in my part and went ahead without me. But my mother had always told me "everything happens for the best." The picture I didn't make was a colossal failure and my being in it wouldn't have changed that.

Mr. Anderson, I know you are in a particularly hard-hit area and it must be hard not to get discouraged when, as on your bicycle ride, you see so many signs of the recession. But by hanging on you've spared a half dozen families from disaster. I've been all over this country and you'd be surprised how many people are doing the same thing.

Now the signs of recovery are picking up, more so than in any other land. I know if you read the *Enquirer* you don't see much to cheer you up but frankly I don't believe some of the press is in tune with what is going on.

You say more laws and regulations are making it harder on business. I have to disagree. Yes, there are some guys in Congress who are trying to do that but there are a lot of us getting in their way. In these two and a half years we have reduced regulations to the point that American business has been saved 300 million man-hours of government-required paperwork and we're not through yet. July 1st you get another 10% cut in the income tax. Yes, Congress or some in Congress want to cancel that. Well, if they try I'll veto it and I know my veto will be upheld. We're going to have that tax cut.

I wish I could tell you all that is happening in the country with people banding together to do things we'd begun to think only government can do. All over there is the neighborly spirit we once knew years ago. I even had a class of fifth graders send me a letter with $187.00 they'd raised on their own to help reduce the national debt. More than 100 Marines stationed overseas wrote to tell me they'd go without a cost of living raise if it would help the country.

I pray things are better for you and I hope you will hang in there. As the song says "There's a great day coming."

Best regards,

Ronald Reagan

Mr. R. Richard Anderson
Oreland, Pennsylvania

June 24, 1983

Dear Mr. Anderson:

Thank you for your letter, your generous words and your suggestions. We see eye to eye on a number of issues. You'll be pleased to know that our Caribbean plan which we're waiting for Congress to pass is aimed at improving the economy and widening trade with 28 countries in the Caribbean and Central America. About ¾ of our help to El Salvador is non-military and aimed at helping improve the living standard of their people.

We are also engaged in a worldwide effort to teach the developing nations about democracy, how it works and to practice self-rule. We are also expanding an exchange system among students. I know many of these things don't get much press attention and that's too bad.

I'm very sorry to hear about your illness. You will be in my thoughts and prayers. Again my thanks for your letter and very best wishes. God bless you.

Sincerely,

Ronald Reagan

Mr. Gary A. Anderson
Chandler, Arizona

The Aid Association for Lutherans requested Reagan's response to the question "How do you cope with stress?" Reagan's handwritten response follows.

FROM THE DESK OF PRESIDENT RONALD REAGAN

[June 1983]

When I first became Governor of California the state was faced with what seemed insoluble economic problems. Each morning began with someone standing before my desk describing another newly discovered disaster.

The feeling of stress became unbearable. I had an uncontrollable urge to turn and look over my shoulder for someone I could pass the problem to.

Suddenly one day it came to me that I was looking in the wrong direction. I looked up instead of back. I'm still looking up. I couldn't face one day in this office if I didn't know I could ask God's help and it would be given.

Sincerely,

Ronald Reagan

On June 26 the Soviet government permitted five Pentecostals to leave the U.S. Embassy in Moscow and immigrate to Israel with other family members. President Reagan was pleased; his request in a letter two years earlier had been answered. His letter to Andropov reflected his new optimism. Andropov sent a cordial reply. However, relations with the Soviet leadership worsened with the shooting down of the Korean Airline passenger jet on September 1 and the failure of arms control talks in Geneva in November.

WASHINGTON

July 11, 1983

Dear General Secretary Andropov:

I appreciate very much your letter pledging an "unbending commitment of the Soviet leadership and the people of the Soviet Union to the course of peace, the elimination of the nuclear threat and the development of relations based on mutual benefit and equality with all nations."

Let me assure you the government and the people of the United States are dedicated to "the course of peace" and "the elimination of the nuclear threat." It goes without saying that we also seek relations with all nations based on "mutual benefit and equality." Our record since we were allied in WW II confirms that.

Mr. General Secretary, could we not begin to approach these goals in the meetings now going on in Geneva? You and I share an enormous responsibility for the preservation of stability in the world. I believe we can fulfill that mandate but to do so will require a more active level of exchange than we have heretofore been able to establish. We have much to talk about with regard to the situation in Eastern Europe, South Asia, and particularly this hemisphere as well as in such areas as arms control, trade between our two countries and other ways in which we can expand east-west contacts.

Historically our predecessors have made better progress when communicating has been private and candid. If you wish to engage in such communication you will find me ready. I await your reply.

Sincerely,

Ronald Reagan

Gene Autry, famous cowboy movie star and astute businessman, sent President Reagan a reprint of the American Observer *for July 6, 1933, which included General MacArthur's speech to West Point cadets on that date. Autry thought Reagan would be interested in light of his problems with Congress and defense budgets.*

WASHINGTON

July 21, 1983

Dear Gene:

Thank you very much for sending me the copy of the "Observer." That was my first year in radio and I had a lot of memories re-awakened. I read every page of it.

You were right about the MacArthur speech, we are hearing the same chorus today. We call them "Peaceniks," and he called them "Peace Cranks." They are kissing cousins.

Again, thanks and best wishes.

Sincerely,

Ron

Mr. Gene Autry
Chairman of the Board
Golden West Broadcasters
Los Angeles, California

Diana Evans served as Reagan's state chairman for the Republican Party in Oregon in 1980. The appointment of Henry Kissinger to the National Bipartisan Commission on Central America, also known as the Kissinger Commission was troubling to her Oregon party members.

August 4, 1983

Dear Diana:

Thanks for your letter and I appreciate very much your concern. I was aware when the appointment was made that flack would be flying. We didn't make the decision lightly. I say we, because all of us here including the Secretary of State, Judge Clark, Jeane Kirkpatrick and others really round-tabled this. A lot of attention was given to what the reception would be abroad as well as at home.

His Commission will not be involved in our Central American policy. Its mission is to come up with a long-range plan for our relations with our neighbors to the South and how we can help in eliminating the economic and social problems that contribute to their unrest. Considering all these things I believe we made the right choice.

Thank you for writing as you did. I'm truly grateful. I promise you we'll keep things in line.

Nancy sends her best.

Sincerely,

Ronald Reagan

Mrs. Diana Evans
Salem, Oregon

Ezra Taft Benson served as secretary of agriculture in President Dwight Eisenhower's cabinet and as the thirteenth president of the Church of Latter-day Saints from 1985 to 1994. Benson thanked President Reagan for his speech to the International Longshoremen's Association on July 18 in Hollywood, Florida, and his emphasis on the problems facing the United States in the Americas.

August 4, 1983

Dear Friend:

Thank you very much for your letter and for your generous words. I'm most grateful. Believe me, I keep very much in mind the memory of those days when so many were hailing Castro as a liberator. I sometimes wonder if powerful papers like the *New York Times* can ever find it within themselves to front page an admission that they made a tragic mistake. That, of course, brings up the question of whether it was a mistake in their eyes or whether they approve of the final result.

There is, however, one thing I must say to you with regard to the Monroe Doctrine. On my visit with the leaders of several South and Central American countries I eased into that subject somewhat gingerly. Without exception they rejected the use of the term. Apparently it is interpreted as "big brother" doing for them what they are unable to do for themselves. There is no question about their wanting help but it must come under a different title which recognizes them as partners, not dependents.

I'm encouraged by gains we've made in winning their confidence and friendship, and I intend to keep building on these gains. I, too, believe these continents stretching from the South Pole to the North Pole are Zion.

Thank you again for writing as you did.

Sincerely,

Ron

The Honorable Ezra Taft Benson
Salt Lake City, Utah

August 18, 1983

Dear Mr. Crovisier:

Thank you very much for sending me that fine article.* I had not seen it and am delighted to have it. I assure you, I'll make good use of it. Would that there were more women coming to the defense of wife and mother-hood as an honored social function to be cherished and not denigrated as it too often is in today's world.

You were kind to see that I obtained this. Thank you again.

Sincerely,

Ronald Reagan

Mr. Baird Malcom Crovisier
Tarzana, California

* Crovisier wrote that Mrs. Boersma, the subject of an article in *Family Circle* magazine, would be a good model for a Reagan story on the positive qualities of Americans.

September 6, 1983

Dear Mr. York:

You say you considered writing to me for two years before you finally did, thinking it would be a "worthless exercise." Well I've considered respond-ing for almost two months for the same reason. I doubt that any words of mine can change a mind so opinionated as yours.

You have never met me. You are in a position to have some knowledge of the media image-building that takes place in the world of politics and yet you are confident that you can understand my thinking or, as you put it, the thinking of those who tell me what to think. And all of this because I suggested that teachers in a classroom are possibly not the best way to cope with physical assault, mayhem and rape in the classroom.

Mr. York, I have the highest regard for the intelligence of the American people and have been most outspoken in my criticism of those in the entertainment field and politics who look down and talk down to them. A President is not as lonely and isolated as you are so sure he is, nor is he surrounded by inferiors as you suggest. He is, indeed, usually surrounded by dedicated and unselfish people who have made considerable personal sacrifice in order to be of service to their countrymen.

You say you did many of the things I did when you were young and became self-supporting at a relatively young age. Yes, I did all that—21 years before you did it and while a great, historic depression gripped the world. According to you, we differ in that I didn't benefit from my experience as you did and don't remember as much as I should or I remember it incorrectly.

I assure you I have lived in and not above the world for 72 years as you say you have for 51. I hope that in your present work you have more tolerance than you've revealed in your letter.

Sincerely,

Ronald Reagan

Mr. Byron W. York
Murphysboro, Illinois

September 19, 1983

Dear Dr. Lindon:

I hope you won't mind my answering your letter to Mrs. Reagan since it concerned my response to the Soviet Union.

I can understand the frustration of those who want some kind of punishment imposed on the perpetrators of the Korean airline massacre. No one is more frustrated than I am. Do you believe that I and my advisors from Secretaries of State and Defense, the Joint Chiefs of Staff and others in the National Security Council did not review every possibility? There were things that might have sounded good on the TV news but wouldn't have meant a thing in reality. Send their diplomatic people home? They would send ours home. And, believe me, this is no time for us to be without eyes and ears in Moscow.

I have great respect for George Will but I think his endorsement of Mr. Rohatyn's economic plan is unjustified.* Mr. Rohatyn would impose suffering on the Polish people with the assumption that the Russians would have come to their rescue. That assumes a generosity the Soviets do not have.

We have concluded agreements with our allies as of last summer to end their subsidizing of interest rates in trade with the Soviets. Last Spring we helped them escape total dependence on the Soviets for energy. We also, and at the same time, secured an agreement shutting off high technology sales to Russia. These are some of the things now being suggested we do but we did them without waiting for something like this recent atrocity.

In reality this is not purely them versus us. It is the Soviet Union against the world and we intend to keep it that way. I assure you we have overlooked nothing nor will we.

Sincerely,

Ronald Reagan

Mr. John A. Lindon
Los Angeles, California

* Will's column in the September 12, 1983, *Newsweek* said that Western governments should buy the loan contracts that Western banks had made with communist countries. Then they should declare that Poland is in default, which would lessen credit flow to it and all other Soviet satellites.

Meldrim Thomson, Jr., served as governor of New Hampshire from 1973 to '74 and urged strict fiscal discipline along with lower taxes. In his September letter, Thomson urged the President to turn from internationalism to Americanism and to restore conservative values.

October 3, 1983

Dear Mel:

You asked me to accept your letter in the spirit in which it was written. We've known each other too long for me to do anything but that. I was pleased to see you the other day and wish our meeting could have been long enough to take up and discuss all the issues raised in your letter. Since that wasn't possible I'll try to take them in the order you listed them.

First: The matter of so-called trilateralists: Mac Baldrige is as solid a conservative as anyone could find, as is George Shultz. Both were top recommendations of the talent hunters I put together during the transition, and that team had virtually every top backer of conservative causes in the history of the conservative movement—Holmes Tuttle, Jack Hume, Joe Coors, etc. Henry Kissinger has no permanent place in the Administration. He is chairing a bipartisan study group which meets a Congressional demand as a price for getting the support we must have for our effort in Central America.

Second: The Departments of Energy and Education. Mel, we have been absolutely unable to get Congressional support for their elimination—and that includes even our staunchest allies on the Hill. We intend to keep it on the agenda, but in the meantime we have made substantial improvements. Let me just touch on energy. Total energy efficiency has increased every year we've been here. Domestic oil production is a million barrels a day over the Carter Administration's estimates. In '77 we imported half our oil. It's now down to a quarter. We produce nearly 90% as much energy as we consume. Our strategic petroleum reserve has been tripled and we have minimized Federal control and involvement.

Third: We talked about China so I won't dwell on that except to say we have definite restrictions on the level of technology we make available. And as I said, we have not retreated one inch in our relationship with Taiwan.

Fourth: On the Panama Canal, I'm not aware of any legal ground on which we could base a claim to take it back. We have done much to improve the relationship there and eliminate the hostility that prevailed at the time of the negotiations.

Fifth: The balanced budget. Mel, deficits aren't made in the White House. They are made in the chambers of Congress. Have you thought of how big the deficit would be without our economic plan? I can tell you how much smaller it would be if Congress had given us all the spending reductions I tried for. This year's deficit alone would be $40 billion less. Each year I come back asking for more reductions in what they want to spend. What is needed more than anything else is what many of us had as Governors—line item veto. I intend to keep working at getting that, but in the meantime my '84 budget proposal would have put us on a solid road of declining deficits leading to a balance a few years down the road. I'm still battling for it, and I'm closer than I was a few months ago.

Sixth: I have reduced the taxes on the so-called poor as well as improved their lot by bringing down inflation from more than 12% to under 3%. As for I.M.F. [International Monetary Fund], Mel, you used the right word in our talk—"perception." The *perception* that I.M.F. is a giveaway or a bank bailout is totally false. The $8.4 billion contribution (so-called) is not a budget item nor does it add to the deficit. It's like a deposit in a bank and we have full drawing rights on it. In fact, the two largest users of I.M.F. funds have been England and the U.S. When money is loaned to other nations we get our share back plus interest. At the same time it is the only institution which can impose economic reforms on extravagant countries as a condition for borrowing.

Seventh: Mel, as I told you about the Korean plane massacre, there were grandstand plays we might have made such as Carter's grain embargo, but they wouldn't really punish the Soviets. And how would pushing Poland into bankruptcy, as some have suggested, hurt the Russians? It would actually hurt the Polish people, and they are as innocent as the victims in the plane. Believe me, we reviewed every option and are still doing so.

The other points you closed your letter with—immigration, for one. Mel, we have lost control of our borders. I don't know whether the legislation will pass or not, but I believe I should sign it if it does. It is a very complex issue with our agriculture dependent on migrants, several million people as residents undetected, and a dozen other facets.

As for the Monroe Doctrine—don't think that wasn't on my mind. But I've learned even our best friends in Central and South America would turn on us. It has too much of the gunboat diplomacy aura around it. We're making progress in the Hemisphere but it has to be on a partnership basis not the big "Colossus of the North" giving orders.

On the National holiday you mentioned, I have the reservations you have, but here the perception of too many people is based on an image, not reality. Indeed, to them the perception *is* reality. We hope some modifications might still take place in Congress.

Finally: As for Lebanon, that situation is only one facet of the whole Middle East problem. Mel, is there any way the U.S., or the Western World for that matter, can stand by and see the Middle East become a part of the communist bloc? Without it, our West European neighbors would inevitably become Finlandized and we'd be alone in the world. As it is, we're not alone in Lebanon. We are part of a multinational force because those nations also recognize their stake in the Middle East.

In the world today our security can be threatened in a number of places far distant from our own shorelines. I'm not trigger-happy and I don't want a war. Whatever I do, it is based on my belief that certain actions offer a chance to forestall war. And those beliefs are based on full access to all the intelligence information available.

Well—there it is. And I hope you'll take this in the spirit in which it is written. Nancy sends her best and from both of us to that lovely lady of yours.

Sincerely,

Ronald Reagan

The Honorable Meldrim Thomson, Jr.
Orford, New Hampshire

Two years after receiving his B.A. from Indiana University in 1965, Tyrrell established The American Spectator *and served as its editor-in-chief. In the next two decades he wrote several books on American politics and numerous nationally syndicated political columns in support of conservative values.*

October 6, 1983

Dear Bob:

Thanks for sending me the "preprint" and for your letter. I'm grateful for your kind words. I'm pleased too with the opinions of the "assembled sages."

You know, Bob, I'm not sure I really understood simon-pure "supply-side," or that I agree with every facet. It's always seemed to me that when government goes beyond a certain percentage of what it takes as its share of the people's earnings we have trouble. I guess a simple explanation of what I've been trying to do is peel government down to bare essentials— necessities if you will—and then set the tax revenues accordingly.

If we find then that we overdid it on the tax cuts—adjust. But it will take a lot more evidence than I've seen to convince me adjustment is needed.

When the income tax amendment was being debated back there in 1913, one of its advocates declared the tax was necessary not for government's needs but for government's wants. Well, I think we've learned that government's wants are limitless.

Again, thanks.

Sincerely,

Ron

Mr. R. Emmett Tyrrell, Jr.
Bloomington, Indiana

A student at the St. George University School of Medicine in Grenada, Rosemarie Classi, telegraphed President Reagan two days after her rescue and expressed her gratitude to him, the Rangers, and the 82nd Airborne troops.

October 31, 1983

Dear Miss Classi:

Thank you very much for your wire. I can't tell you how much it meant to me to learn of your willingness to endorse the action we have taken. There seems to be a concerted effort on the part of much of the media to downgrade the need for our rescue mission which they insist on calling an invasion.

I share your feeling about those young men of the 82nd Airborne and the 75th Rangers. Our country can be very proud. Let me tell you it was a long night here in Washington as we waited for word that you were all safe.

Again, thanks.

Sincerely,

Ronald Reagan

Miss Rosemarie Classi
Ozone Park, New York

WASHINGTON

November 1, 1983

Dear Tom:

Things did get a little hectic back here but the Marines and the Rangers and the 82nd Airborne with a bit of Navy and Air Force to transport them sure has the situation well in hand. Tom, I've never been so proud as I am of those wonderful young guys in uniform. What makes it so wonderful is they weren't drafted, they chose to wear those uniforms.

Bill [Clark] goes to the Senate committee for confirmation tomorrow.* I really think he'll do fine and won't have any trouble. Incidentally he really wants this job and no other. By the way, and I don't want to start an argument, but George B[ush]† is really doing a job. I've undergone quite a change of mind. He stands tall in all these things such as we've just gone through.

Thanks again for the kind words.

Sincerely,

Ron

Mr. Thomas M. O'Brien
Scottsdale, Arizona

* As secretary of the interior; it would be his third and final assignment in the Reagan administration. Robert C. (Bud) McFarlane was named to Clark's former position as National Security Advisor.
† Reagan had been reluctant to select Bush as his running mate in 1980; however, as president, he appreciated Bush's support, courage, and loyalty.

Barney Oldfield began his journalistic career as a stringer for Variety *magazine, and movie editor for the* Lincoln Star *in Nebraska. He moved to Hollywood in the 1930s and became a publicist for movie, radio, and television stars. He served as a war correspondent in World War II and Korea (Colonel USAF, Ret.), followed by twenty-seven years as a corporate publicist for Litton Industries. At the Green Room in Hollywood, Oldfield spoke to the Warner Brothers retirees; and it was the same room where Reagan, Oldfield, and Jack Warner held meetings decades earlier.*

November 7, 1983

Dear Barney:

I'm off to Japan and Korea in the morning so this will be brief. Tell your friend [Soviet Peace Committee president] to keep his trigger-happy air jockeys on the ground. So he doesn't want Litton to build any more submarines. Tell him if his self-declared aristocracy would quit trying to conquer the world, Litton would make busses to bring the troops out of Afghanistan.

I wish I could have been in the Green Room. Nancy sends her best and give our regards to Vada.

Sincerely,

Ron

Col. Barney Oldfield
Beverly Hills, California

November 7, 1983

Dear Miss Sam, Miss Bertha and Buzzy:

I'm glad your predator [opossum] was finally trapped. I know we have some but only because one of our dogs brought one in after a night's prowl. You asked about our other wildlife; well we're evidently on the travel path of a bear—it shows up periodically. One day one of our Secret Service agents was sitting up on a hill above our house and a mountain lion strolled by. The agent didn't know if that was commonplace or not, so he just sat there. We also have wildcats, now and then coyotes but not too often—we're at about 2400 feet altitude.

Now just writing about it has made me homesick for the ranch and here I am off to Japan and Korea instead.

Best regards,

Ronald Reagan

Miss Sam and Miss Bertha Sisco
Healdsburg, California

John Davis Lodge served in the U.S. Navy during World War II, and later as governor of Connecticut, member of Congress, ambassador to Spain, 1955–1961; to Argentina, 1969–1974; and Switzerland, 1983–1985.

WASHINGTON

November 17, 1983

Dear John:

It was good to hear from you and I'm most grateful for your generous words.

You are absolutely correct in what you are saying about Grenada. The people met our troops with open arms, flowers and fruit. We brought home a treasure trove of documents—Soviet, Cuban, Libyan and even North Korean plus enough Soviet and Cuban weapons to fill an airplane hangar at Andrews Air Force Base.

The people here have approved the operation by an overwhelming majority.

Nancy sends her best, and from both of us our love to Francesca.

Sincerely,

Ron

The Honorable John David [sic] Lodge
Ambassador
Bern, Switzerland

Roy Brewer served as president of the International Alliance of Theatrical Stage Employees, a Hollywood union, in the 1940s. On October 10 Richard Viguerie, publisher of the Conservative Digest, *released the text of a telegram Viguerie sent to President Reagan, which included a litany of complaints: James Watt did not receive presidential support; the Soviets were not punished for the Korean Air shootdown; too much U.S. funding for the United Nations and international banks; presidential approval of increased trade with the Soviets and Chinese communists; and support of a federal holiday honoring the Reverend Martin Luther King.*

WASHINGTON

November 17, 1983

Dear Roy:

Your letter was waiting for me when I returned. I appreciate your concern—(Nancy shared it) about security but, believe me, in both countries [Japan, Korea] they had really gone all out. I never saw so many uniforms in my life, outside of a war movie or parade. As a matter of fact, I was practically in a military parade wherever I went. I didn't complain.

Thank you for your response to [Richard] Viguerie—it was great. You know this so-called conservative has never been for me. Back in '76 he and a few of his ilk had me to a secret meeting in which they pushed for me running on a third party ticket. I told them I was going to run as a Republican and that what they proposed just didn't make sense. That did it for me—I became the enemy. In 1980 they were for Connolly. But you told him off in great style. Thanks.

Best regards,

Ron

Mr. Roy Brewer
Tarzana, California

November 23, 1983
Aboard Air Force One

Dear Mr. Banks:

God bless you for writing as you did. I can't tell you how grateful I am and how much you brightened my day.

Back here we'll keep battling for an amendment to the Constitution to prevent abortion unless it is necessary to save the mother's life. And we'll be back at Congress in January for the restoration of prayer in the school room.

Thank you again.

Sincerely,

Ronald Reagan

Mr. Ed Banks
Bakersfield, California

November 23, 1983
Aboard Air Force One

Dear Mr. Washington:

I'm sorry to be so late in answering your letter but it takes a while for mail to get sorted and letters to arrive at my desk. I can't tell you how much your letter means to me. I've been frustrated and angered by the attempts to paint me as a racist and as lacking in compassion for the poor. On the one subject, I was raised by a mother and father who instilled in me and my brother a hatred for bigotry and prejudice long before there was such a thing as a civil rights movement. As for the poor, we were poor in an era when there were no government programs to turn to. I'm well aware of how lucky I've been since and how good the Lord has been to me.

Forgive me for telling you all this but I want you to know and understand how very moved I was by your kind letter. Again, my heartfelt thanks.

Sincerely,

Ronald Reagan

Mr. Freddie Washington, Jr.
Moss Point, Mississippi

November 23, 1983
Aboard Air Force One

Dear Mr. Thompson:

Forgive my being late in answering your letter but it takes a while for mail to reach my desk.

First of all, congratulations on settling the mortgage—I know the feeling. It was a long time ago, and I was the first in our family in three genera-tions to ever own a piece of property. Paying off the debt was a milestone in my life.

You were kind to write as you did and to give some of the credit to our tax cuts, but the credit is yours. I'm sure there were other things you could have done with the money saved on taxes but you chose to make your family more secure. God bless you.

Again, thanks, and give my regards to Mrs. Thompson, Rebecca, Gretchen and Matthew.

Sincerely,

Ronald Reagan

Mr. Buddy Thompson
Kansas City, Missouri

November 25, 1983

Dear Mr. and Mrs. Meyung:

Thank you very much for your letter of October 27th and forgive me for being so late in answering. It takes a while for mail to reach my desk.

I know how happy you must be that your son is now on his way back to the States and I'm happy for you. This letter is much easier to write than the letters I've been writing these past few weeks.* With all the sorrow and sadness, though, there is a pride in these wonderful young men who have volunteered to serve their country. And, yes, a pride in Americans like yourselves who so unselfishly see the need for what they are doing.

God bless you and again my thanks. Please express my thanks also to Lance Corporal Robert Meyung.

Sincerely,

Ronald Reagan

Mr. and Mrs. Art Meyung
Norwood, Ohio

* To parents and widows of the servicemen killed in the Marine barracks bombing in Beirut.

November 28, 1983

Dear Mr. Seymour:

I'm sorry to be so late in answering your letter of October 27 but it takes a while for mail to reach my desk, particularly so when a trip to Asia is factored in. Thank you for giving me a chance to respond to the press criticism regarding our rescue mission in Grenada.

First let me say I have not retreated from my belief in a free press and I share your own view about its importance to our way of life. But let me point out a few facets of the Grenada operation that seem to have been overlooked. From the time I received word of the request from the six Caribbean nations* that we help them take action we gave our Military Chiefs only 48 hours to put a plan into action. We knew that with six other governments involved the risk of a leak was very great. There was the risk of Cuban action, Cuba being much closer, which could have left us with an outright invasion against a sizeable military force. Even short notice to the press regarding coverage would greatly increase the risk of a hostage situation. I gave no order regarding the press. My order was that there be no interference with the Commanders in the field. We had given them a hard task with only a scant measure of intelligence information. I understand that many of them have since stated, it was the first time in years that a campaign was carried out without civilian overview. And some added, "it was the first time in years we've been successful."

On the second day a press pool team was taken to Grenada from Barbados. This was enlarged on the third day and again on the fourth and then full press coverage was allowed with transportation provided by the military and permission given to those who wanted to provide their own. A top priority of the entire operation was to minimize casualties.

I hope this information reassures you about my position. If you have further questions I'd be pleased to answer them.

Sincerely,

Ronald Reagan

Mr. Bill Seymour
School of Journalism
West Virginia University
Morgantown, West Virginia

* Six former British colonies that established the Organization of Eastern Caribbean States.

November 28, 1983

Dear Mrs. Minutoli:

I'm sorry to be so late in answering your letter of October 31 but it takes a while for mail to reach my desk. I've been writing a great many letters these past few weeks to the parents and widows of the men who lost their lives in Beirut. One of those letters was to the parents of Joseph P. Milano.

Giving the order to send these splendid young Americans into situations where their lives may be forfeit is by far the hardest task associated with the job I hold. It isn't something I can do unless I am convinced it is essential and absolutely the last resort.

You asked about the Marines' presence in Lebanon. I have just received a letter from a young lady who enclosed a letter she had received from a friend in Beirut.* I've enclosed a copy of this letter which might answer your question. Our men are part of a multinational force whose mission is to help and maintain order in Beirut freeing the Lebanese Army to put down the forces that are seeking to destroy the government of Lebanon.

Thank you for writing.

Sincerely,

Ronald Reagan

Mrs. Francine Stone Minutoli
Oakdale, New York

* The Beirut letter praised the President and the Marines for protecting the Christians in Beirut from the Syrians and Palestinians.

November 28, 1983

Dear Mr. and Mrs. Kuharski:

Thank you very much for your letter, your kind words and your prayers. More than that, thank you for what you are doing with your lives and for so many others. I've had some contact with other families like yours and know the love that fills your home and surrounds you.

I'm enclosing a note to Vincent [twelve years old]. My ear problem is the result of a shooting accident—no wound—the gun just went off right by my ear. Over the years the nerves in the inner ear deteriorated with the re-sult—a loss of much of the hearing in that ear. I wanted you to know because it is my understanding that various types of hearing aids are de-signed for different types of deafness. Vincent would probably have to be examined to see if this inside the ear amplifier would solve his problem.

My note to him is aimed at encouraging him to accept his problem. I hope it will help. In the meantime, the name of the company which makes mine is: Starkey Labs, Inc., 6700 Washington Avenue South, Eden Prairie, Minnesota 55344.

Again, thanks and God bless you.

Sincerely,

Ronald Reagan

Mr. and Mrs. John Kuharski
Minneapolis, Minnesota

[November 28, 1983]

Dear Vincent:

I've sent the name and address of the hearing aid company to your parents. Those of us who have hearing problems sometimes have to have different types of aids depending on what causes our problem.

I know how you feel about the aids you wear behind your ears but if that's the kind you need, wear them and be happy they help you hear.

When I was your age I learned I couldn't see as well as other people, and had to have glasses. They weren't quite as common then as they've become in recent years. I was very self-conscious and embarrassed about wearing glasses but believe me I outgrew that and learned to be happy because with them I could see all the beauty I'd been missing. Now it's glasses and a hearing aid and I think I'm pretty lucky.

Best wishes to you and God bless you.

Sincerely,

Ronald Reagan

November 29, 1983

Dear Mrs. Straitiff:

Thank you for telling me about your [ninety-year-old] mother's plans to run for President. I've just written to her wishing her well.

I can't subscribe to all the planks in her platform but am in agreement with several. If my decision is to seek re-election, maybe we'll meet along the campaign trail. There is just one thing—I hope she won't make my youth an issue. I'll be 73 on February 6.

Best regards,

Ronald Reagan

Mrs. Beverly B. Straitiff
New Cumberland, Pennsylvania

November 29, 1983

Dear Tip:

It was good to hear from you and I enjoyed reading about the 25th.* That brought on some nostalgia. I was adjutant of the outfit that trained those combat camera crews. We had them with every outfit all over the world. I better stop or I'll be telling you war stories and mine can't match yours because I never got off the ground or out of California.

Now about those bumper stickers—I won't be announcing a decision until sometime after the first of the year. Thanks for your offer.

I'm sure happy with the business upturn and share your feeling about Lee Iacocca.

Best regards,

Dutch

Mr. Ralph Tipton
Sugar Grove, Illinois

* Bomb Group of the Eighth Air Force.

December 14, 1983

Dear Mrs. Clark:

I hope you won't mind my answering your letter to Maureen [Reagan's daughter]. She allowed me to do this because she thought I could better respond to the concerns you expressed. She asked that I tell you she remembers you very well and sends you her very best regards.

Mrs. Clark, I'm aware that a great deal of image-making has gone on about me. That is to be expected with regard to anyone in this position, but in my case, much of it has been entirely contrary to what I believe and to what my goals and purposes really are.

Would it surprise you to know I share your horror of nuclear weapons and am convinced there must never be a nuclear war? I know this brings up a question with regard to our problem of modernization of our nuclear forces. Very simply, the answer to that is for some years back the only defense against these weapons has been a deterrent. An earlier Democratic administration named it the M.A.D. policy—Mutual Assured Destruction. We must admit it has prevented a major war in Europe for some 40 years now but it is a terrible threat hanging over the world.

In recent years the Soviet Union has engaged in the biggest military build-up in history both in conventional forces and in nuclear weapons. They now have superiority and are continuing to increase their margin. We still have a deterrent capacity but must replace our aging missiles with some that are comparable to theirs or face the reality of getting in the near future a surrender-or-die ultimatum.

Because of our change in policy the Soviet Union has grudgingly joined in disarmament talks with us to a greater extent than at any time since W.W. II. My hope, indeed, my dream, is that if we can once start down the road of reducing the number of missiles on both sides, they will be convinced of the wisdom of eliminating all such weapons. The U.S. has tried to interest the Soviets in arms control some 19 times since W.W. II without success. I believe we've caught their attention this time because they are convinced we'll re-arm to match them if they don't consider joining in a planned reduction.

As for Central America, 75% of all our aid has been in economic and social reforms. Only 25¢ out of each dollar has gone to military aid. The great economic inequities in many of those countries have made them ripe for subversion. We want to help correct this but, I assure you, we are not planning any military actions there. A very definite planned assault by Cubans as proxies of the Soviet Union is aimed at the western hemisphere. It must be stopped if we are to have peace.

Forgive me for going on at such length. I hope I have eased some of your concerns.

Sincerely,

Ronald Reagan

Mrs. Laurence M. Clark
Redlands, California

Rick Eilert's book was published in 1983. Wounded in Vietnam, the author recounts his evacuation to the United States and his painful recovery.

December 23, 1983

Dear Cheryl and Rick:

I have finished the book and am sorry. I'm sorry because it has been a long time since a book has gripped and held me the way yours did. I was rushing home to continue reading it. Thank you for giving it to me but more important, thank you for writing it and both of you for living it and for bringing about a happy ending after so much pain and suffering.

I've talked so much about your story while I was reading it that a line has formed here in the "West Wing," waiting their turn to read it.

You strengthened my belief that it was a noble cause and all of you who suffered through it were betrayed by those (you described some of them in your book) who preferred to think of the enemy as "Agrarian reformers."

Again, thanks and God bless you.

Sincerely,

Ronald Reagan,

Mr. and Mrs. Rick Eilert
Lake Zurich, Illinois

1984

—

. . . the Middle East is a complicated place—well, not
really a place—it's more a state of mind. A
disordered mind.

·*Letter of January 5, 1984*·

ARLY in January, the U.S. Commission on Civil Rights canceled the practice of promoting African Americans in employment through the use of numerical quotas. Frustrated
critics complained that this latest decision once again re-
tarded the growth of civil rights in America. The President's
correspondence during 1984 reflected this serious and ongoing domestic
issue. His letters, especially to African American correspondents, expressed
his lifelong opposition to racial prejudice and bigotry.

Other domestic problems answered by his letters concerned the continuing tensions about deficit spending, vocal or silent prayers in public
schools, the ongoing debate about abortion, and Social Security. Continuing criticism by ultra-conservative writers troubled by Reagan's supposed

support of the Trilateral Union, and the sniping at Ed Meese by Democrats angered the President. Meese, a lawyer and Reagan's loyal friend, became White House Counselor in 1981 and served for four years before becoming Attorney General of the United States.

In late January, President Reagan finally announced that he and George Bush would stand for reelection in November. As he explained later in his autobiography, *An American Life*, "I regarded the 1984 presidential election as pivotal—not because I wanted to live in the White House for four more years, but because I believed the gains we'd make during the previous four years were in jeopardy" and should be preserved, along with other things still to be done.

The President, still suffering from the loss of the Marines in Beirut, continued to face U.S. responsibility and relations in foreign affairs, especially in the Middle East. The departure of U.S. forces from Beirut in late February signaled an end to Reagan's Lebanon policy, devised a year and a half earlier. In announcing the withdrawal, President Reagan said "hatreds centuries old were too much for all of us." In September, another Beirut car bomb exploded in front of the relocated U.S. Embassy, killing and wounding dozens of Lebanese and Americans. The nine-year-old struggle in Lebanon continued to rage as Beirut suffered more bombardment from opposing Muslim and Christian units. The situation in the Middle East remained complicated.

Central American anxieties, particularly regarding El Salvador, which held its first presidential election since 1977, became front-page headlines. Leftist guerrillas sought to intimidate voters and close down polling places. José Napoleon Duarte of the moderate Christian Democrats defeated Roberto d'Aubuisson of the extreme right Nationalist Republican Alliance and became president. Another harbinger of future tensions occurred in the Pacific region, when almost one million demonstrators rallied in Manila, the Philippine capital, to protest the government of President Ferdinand Marcos and his support by the U.S. Government. Corazon Aquino, widow of the slain opposition leader Benigno Aquino, led the crowd in calling for Marcos's resignation. American naval and air force bases in the Philippines also were targeted by dissident leaders.

The year 1984 would be another stressful one for U.S. relations with Western Europe, where the first American Pershing II missiles were being installed despite riots and violent opposition begun the year before. Peace advocates and others, especially in Germany, believed that installing these missiles escalated the arms race and would shatter peace and the Western Alliance. In February President Yuri Andropov of the Soviet Union died and was succeeded by Konstantin Chernenko, who continued the call for peaceful coexistence with the United States. Reagan would now negotiate with the third Soviet leader since he had taken office, a man only one year younger than he.

In late April the Reagans traveled to Beijing and Shanghai, China, for six days, where the President signed scientific and cultural accords as well as a tax agreement that prevented the double taxation of U.S. businesses in China. The issue of reducing American military support to Taiwan was not resolved. In mid-May doctors removed a small polyp from Reagan's colon, but the surgery did not interfere with his scheduled foreign travels. In early June the president addressed the Dail (parliament) in Dublin, Ireland, and visited Reagan family roots in Ballyporeen, Galway, and Shannon before going to France for the fortieth anniversary of the D-Day invasion on June 6. Reagan's brilliant Normandy address, written by White House speech-writer Peggy Noonan, recalled the courageous U.S. Army Rangers who scaled the cliffs despite withering machine-gun fire: "These are the heroes who helped end a war." That afternoon he and Nancy prayed at the Omaha Beach Chapel and toured the cemetery, walking along the rows of crosses and Stars of David. Later the President honored Allied soldiers at cere-monies at Omaha Beach. The Economic Summit meetings of the Group of Seven in London completed this European trip, and it marked the end of the President's foreign trips in 1984. Campaigning for the presidency dur-ing the summer and fall months kept him closer to Washington, D.C.

President Reagan's brief notes regarding the Olympics in July and his personal thoughts about his press secretary, Jim Brady, reveal his sensitive writing style. After the Republican Convention in Dallas in mid-Au-gust, Reagan and Bush carried on a relentless reelection campaign, which brought a stunning margin of victory by carrying forty-nine states: Dem-ocratic presidential candidate Walter Mondale carried his home state, Minnesota. At age seventy-three and the oldest man to become president, Reagan also became the most popular presidential candidate since Franklin D. Roosevelt.

Ronald Reagan was a regular reader of the National Review, *edited by William F. Buckley, Jr. Buckley's column covered the Lebanon troubles. Reagan mentioned Kabul because earlier he had offered Buckley a fictional position as ambassador to Afghanistan.*

January 5, 1984

Dear Bill:

I hope your holidays in the Caribbean were as pleasant as ours in California. We really lucked out weatherwise, warm sun and no before-dawn phone calls.

I assume you are back in New York—or did you go directly to Kabul? That would be above and beyond the call of duty.

I'm not going to attempt a reply (in this letter) to your column. That will have to wait for a conversation time—glass in hand. I do have a reply, may I hasten to say.

Bill, the Middle East is a complicated place—well, not really a place—it's more a state of mind. A disordered mind. But of course you know that without my telling you. I'm not being stubborn or too proud to admit to error. There has been progress precisely because the M.N.F. [multinational force] is there. There could be instant chaos if a wrong or precipitate move is made. Withdrawal would be such a move. I could use all the clichés—"walking a thin line," "juggling with too many balls in the air," and so on and so on. The truth is, most of the clichés would fit the situation. Let me just say, there is a reason why they are there.

Nancy sends her love and tell Pat we love her.

Sincerely,

Ron

Mr. William F. Buckley, Jr.
New York, New York

As president, Reagan wrote most of his own major speeches
in longhand on a yellow legal pad. Here, the President composes
his inaugural address in the White House residence in
mid-January, 1985.

THROUGHOUT his eight years in office, Reagan was rarely without pen in hand.
Above, President Reagan writes at his desk in the White House residence
in January 1987. Below, the President writes to his correspondents aboard Air
Force One, on the way to his favorite retreat, Rancho del Cielo near Santa Barbara,
California, in mid-February 1981.

SHOWN HERE, Anne Higgins, chief of correspondence, who handled
a wide variety of letters for President Reagan to read and answer during the eight
years of the Reagan presidency. Below, the President with his personal secretary,
Kathy Osbourne, soon after she rejoined his staff in the fall of 1981.

O<small>N</small> M<small>ARCH</small> 30, 1981,
Reagan was shot in an assassination
attempt by John W. Hinkley, Jr.
Seen here, just twelve days after the
assassination attempt, the Reagans
leave George Washington University
Hospital. A few months later,
the President is seen, at left, at his
ranch in November 1981,
clearing away tree limbs.

WHILE IN OFFICE, Reagan corresponded with many private citizens on a regular basis. Two of his favorite pen pals were Rudolph Hines, seen here in September 1984, receiving a jar of jelly beans at his house in Washington, D.C., and below, William F. Buckley, an old friend of Reagan's and founder of the *National Review*.

Here, the President
and Mikhail Gorbachev at
the Geneva Summit in
mid-November 1985;
at left, the White House
photograph of Anwar Sadat,
which the President sent to
Mrs. Sadat with his condolence
letter of October 7, 1981.

THE PRESIDENT praised his wife Nancy for her campaign against drug abuse and her phrase, "Just Say No." The photograph above was taken at the ranch in September 1986, one week before they addressed the nation from the White House on drug abuse. Below, three months before his presidency ended, the President and his wife pose for a photo.

Seen here with his grandson, Cameron Reagan, the President builds a snowman at the White House on the day before his second inauguration in January 1985.

In his letter to Reagan, Christopher Kilpatrick noted his current assignment of shore duty with Destroyer Squadron Six in Charleston. His daughter, Alina, had given Mrs. Reagan a copy of Kirkmouse, *and his wife, Gina, was expecting their third child.*

January 12, 1984

Dear Christopher (Altar Boy):

It was good to hear from you and I'm glad you are ashore and with your family. Tell Alina that Mrs. Reagan sends her warmest greetings. She's very happy with "Kirkmouse."

Give regards from both of us to Gina. We are happy to learn of the newest Kilpatrick on the way. We'll be waiting for the great day.

I appreciate your words about the Destroyer and Frigates. You couldn't know this but when I was a boy my most prized possession was a toy boat. It had a motor but, most important, it was a model of a W.W. I destroyer. When I didn't have it in the river it was displayed in my room.

As you know, my schedule is pretty much determined for me and well in advance. However, I'm going to lobby for what you have suggested [a visit to the destroyer squadron in Charleston] and I thank you for the suggestion.

Again, all the best to your family.

Sincerely,

Ronald Reagan

Mr. Christopher H. Kilpatrick
Charleston, South Carolina

February 14, 1984

Dear Dr. Lillien:

I'm sure you weren't expecting an answer to your wire but I couldn't resist.

With the constant drum beat of political demagoguery about "fairness" and the willingness of so much of the press to amplify it, your misconception about me is understandable. And it is a misconception. There has been no cut in overall Federal spending. There has been a reduction in the rate of increase. We are spending more on social programs and helping more people than ever before in history.

An average husband and wife on Social Security is receiving $170 a month more than they were before we came here. The government is providing 95 million meals a day in addition to more food stamps for more people and we are subsidizing housing for 10 million.

We have removed from the rolls people who were not properly eligible for support by their fellow citizens. But we have retargeted help to the truly needy.

Thanks for giving me a chance to reply.

Sincerely,

Ronald Reagan

Dr. L. Lillien
Cambridge, Massachusetts

Suzanne Massie, Russian historian, wrote Lady of the Firebird: The Beauty of Old Russia, *which reviewed Russian history from 987 to 1917.*

February 15, 1984

Dear Mrs. Massie:

I waited to answer your letter until after your return from the Soviet Union. In the meantime a great change occurred there. I dare to hope there might be a better chance for communication with the new leadership.

Watching scenes of the [Andropov] funeral on TV, I wondered what thoughts people must have at such a time when their belief in no God or immortality is faced with death. Like you, I continue to believe that the hunger for religion may yet be a major factor in bringing about a change in the present situation.

I hope your trip was all you wanted it to be.

Sincerely,

Ronald Reagan

Mrs. Suzanne Massie
Irvington, New York

February 16, 1984

Dear Mr. and Mrs. Staley, Wesley and Kevin:

I'm sorry to be so late in answering your letter of December 9, but sometimes it takes a while for letters to reach my desk.

I will try to answer your one-word question—"Why?" But first let me say

I do understand the "personal and private anxieties of a parent." You know of course that I am a parent myself, but more than that I have a personal feeling about those splendid young men in uniform, among them your son and brother. There is nothing in my job so difficult as issuing the order that sends those young men into situations where they are endangered. There is nothing so heartbreaking as the calls I've made to wives and parents who've lost husbands and sons.

As to your question, our national security is involved very directly in the Middle East. Indeed, the security of the free world is at stake there.

In September of 1982 I proposed a plan for peace in the entire area carrying on the process started at Camp David under the last administration. Before the negotiations could really get started, the blowup came in Lebanon. In reality the Arab world and Israel were all involved—the very nations we were trying to bring to the peace table.

It was essential that Lebanon be helped to regain control of its own territory and that the foreign forces fighting there be removed. We and our allies, the British, French and Italians, sent in a force to help preserve stability while a government was reestablished and a Lebanese military was organized.

For the better part of a year, this Multinational Force contributed to very real progress. I wish you could see letters of the kind I've received from Lebanese people blessing us for bringing order and normal living to their land. The PLO terrorists were removed. The Israelis' withdrawal was begun and meetings were started to bring about internal peace in Lebanon.

Because progress was being made, those who don't want a stable Lebanon began the terrorist attacks on the Multinational Force last fall. We know the tragedies that followed.

We immediately began studying how we could redeploy our forces and still help bring about peace. As you know now, we are placing our men on the vessels offshore, and I have authorized firing back when we are fired upon. While there is still a chance for peace we must not give up. Our presence there is necessary if there is to be such a chance. However, if your son and brother is in the replacement detachment, I'm sure he will remain on board ship and not be stationed in Beirut as before.

I realize this is not a detailed reply to your question, but I hope it gives you some understanding of the importance of our presence there.

Sincerely,

Ronald Reagan

Mr. and Mrs. John Staley and Family
Charlotte, North Carolina

WASHINGTON

February 20, 1984
Aboard Air Force One

Dear Ward:

It was good to get your letter and I thank you for your generous words about the speech.* I have to tell you I've faced a lot of audiences, as you know, but that "joint session" does make for a slight case of nerves before and after. This makes your words very welcome indeed.

I'm glad, too, that you approve my decision about running. Wasn't it Lincoln who said, "having put the hand to the plow, it's no time to turn back"?

Nancy sends her love and from both of us to Dorothy.

Best regards,

Ron

Mr. Ward L. Quaal
Chicago, Illinois

* President Reagan addressed a joint session of Congress the evening of January 25.

February 20, 1984
Aboard Air Force One

Dear Betty and Bob:

Thank you very much for my suede shirt [a birthday present]. It is very handsome and I'm happy to have it for that important part of my life outside the Oval Office.

Only one thing bothers me. You know I can recite "The Shooting of Dan McGrew"—but there is one line, "In a buckskin shirt that was glazed with dirt." I'm not about to let this get "glazed with dirt." So I can't wear it if I'm reciting.

Thank you both. Nancy sends her love and so do I.

Sincerely,

Ronald Reagan

Mr. and Mrs. Robert Adams
Valley Center, California

February 22, 1984

Dear Arthur:

I'm very late in getting back to you—please forgive me. I appreciate your sending me the roundup of views on deficits.

While I deplore the deficits and am determined to get a handle on them, I can't accept their views that deficits are the cause of high interest rates.

Just recently I've seen a breakdown on deficit spending of the other industrial states (including U.K., West German, Japan et al.), as a percentage of gross national product. In every instance their own deficits are above ours in such a percentage but their interest rates are lower. At the same time I note that while our deficits increased tremendously in the '82 and '83 years, our interest rates were cut in half. I, therefore, have to challenge the assumption that deficits and interest rates are linked.

I'm convinced our problem is government spending as a percent of our national earnings and we must cut spending further than we have so far.

I didn't mean to get on a soap box. Thanks again and all the best to you.

Sincerely,

Ronald Reagan

The Honorable Arthur Burns
American Ambassador
Bonn

A successful oil and communications executive, Frank Whetstone served as western states coordinator of the Reagan for President Committee. During the Reagan administration, he was a member of the International Boundary Commission which was established by treaty between Canada and the U.S. in 1908. It is responsible for clearing and maintaining a boundary of 5,500 miles across North America from the Atlantic to the Pacific Ocean. The U.S. appoints one of the two commissioners.

WASHINGTON

February 27, 1984

Dear Frank:

It was good to hear from you. I'm sorry about the delay in answering but it takes awhile before mail reaches my desk.

Frank, I'm not sure who is engineering this operation that subjects you and others to all the phone calls. I realize, of course, that people like yourself are sincerely concerned, but you shouldn't be.

I'm not replacing Ed [Meese] because he'll be as near at hand as he's always been. I have a Cabinet operating similar to the way we ran things in California and, as Attorney General, Ed will be in those meetings as he is now. His job has been one of counseling and advising when I need someone to bounce things off of. He'll still be doing that. We've worked together for too many years for me to change now.

Frank, I'm not being manipulated by people who are out to change my beliefs. If there were any such trying I'd kick their fannies out of here. I've lived too long with my beliefs to change now, and no matter what those hacks in the press say, I make the decisions and will continue to do so.

I appreciate your writing and your support. Give my best to your gal.

Sincerely,

Ronald Reagan

Mr. Frank A. Whetstone
Cutbank, Montana

Harold Bell Wright's first book, That Printer of Udell's, *published in 1903, came from his minisermons to his congregations in Missouri and Kansas. He wrote eighteen novels, which sold millions of copies and placed him among the bestselling novelists of the first decades of the twentieth century.*

WASHINGTON

March 13, 1984

Dear Mrs. Wright:

It is true that your father-in-law's book, indeed books, played a definite part in my growing-up years. When I was only ten or eleven years old, I picked up Harold Bell Wright's book, *That Printer of Udell's,* which I'd seen my mother reading, and read it from cover to cover. Perhaps I should tell you I became an avid reader at a very early age and had my own card for the Dixon, Illinois, Public Library. I made regular use of that card.

That book, *That Printer of Udell's,* had an impact I shall always remember. After reading it and thinking about it for a few days, I went to my mother and told her I wanted to declare my faith and be baptized. We attended the Christian Church in Dixon, and I was baptized several days after finishing the book.

The term, "role model," was not a familiar term in that time and place. But looking back I know I found a role model in that traveling printer Harold Bell Wright had brought to life. He set me on a course I've tried to follow even unto this day. I shall always be grateful.

Sincerely,

Ronald Reagan

Mrs. Jean B. Wright
Valley Center, California

March 14, 1984

Dear Miss Accaso:

Thank you for writing and giving me a chance to reply to the "S.T.O.P. News" [Student/Teacher Organization to Prevent Nuclear War] and its so-called fact sheet, which I found somewhat lacking in facts.

There is no question about the horror of nuclear war. I believe with all my heart that a nuclear war can never be won and must never be fought. The problem facing us is how to prevent such a thing from ever happening. In that regard, I have to point out that a President of the United States has access to more information than the authors of the fact sheet can possibly have, no matter how well intentioned they are.

Let me give you a fact: The Soviet Union has a definite superiority today in nuclear weapons. We have asked them to join us in talks to reduce the number of such weapons, and I've even offered to get rid of such weapons altogether. In the meantime we have had to modernize our own force to reduce the Soviets' superiority and thus give them some reason to talk to us. It is true they proposed the nuclear freeze, but that was to freeze us into a position of inferiority, making it possible for them to attack with no risk to themselves.

I won't try to correct every so-called fact in the paper you sent me, although I assure you I can. As an example, take the first two items—that beginning in December '83 we plan to deploy hundreds of nuclear missiles in Europe and that the world will be only six minutes from nuclear war.

It is true we are going to deploy Cruise and Pershing II missiles in Europe. In 1979 (before I was President) our NATO allies asked us to do this and we agreed. It has taken until now to have such missiles available. What the fact sheet didn't say was that the Soviets have about 1300 nuclear warheads targeted on all of Western Europe, all capable of hitting the European cities in six minutes or less. The missiles we are just beginning to put in place are a deterrent to indicate that a Soviet attack could result in great damage to them also. The paper also does not show that I have invited the Soviets to join in disarmament talks to get rid of such weapons or at least reduce the number. The Soviets so far have insisted that our NATO allies should have no missiles, but they are only willing to reduce their own warheads to somewhere between 800 and a thousand.

Another item as an example, we are building 100 MX missiles. The paper says the Soviets will try to catch up. We are the ones trying to catch up. The Soviets have hundreds and hundreds of new missiles bigger and more powerful than the MX. We at present have nothing to match them. Again, we are trying to build a deterrent.

I hope you will look further than S.T.O.P. for information to help you arrive at a decision. In the meantime, let me again say, my most cherished goal is peace and the elimination of the nuclear threat hanging over the world. I must be frank and say I am disappointed that teachers—no matter how well intentioned—would resort to such one-sided tactics and impose such misinformation on students.

Thank you again, and God bless you.

Sincerely,

Ronald Reagan

Miss Therese Accaso
Euclid, Ohio

March 28, 1984

Dear Tom:

Thanks for your letter and kind words. I don't intend to give up on school prayer and we'll be back again next year if not before.

Tom, the tragedy here was one of perception. Believe it or not, a number of Senators honestly believed they were voting against something that would have the government mandating that the schools had to have regular prayers. Actually, our amendment said nothing of the kind. It specifically said the Constitution *permitted* prayer in schools and that no official could concoct a prayer.

Somehow though (aided by the liberal press) the debate raged about who would write the prayers, should the Federal government have the right to order religion, etc. I can't tell you how many Senators—good guys—I tried to convince that they'd jumped to a false conclusion—with no success.

When we try again we're going to have to word the bill so it's completely clear—we mean the Constitution to be neutral.

Tom, on another point—Ed Meese; there is no doubt this is a lynching of the innocent.* The head lyncher is Senator [Howard] Metzenbaum of Ohio who openly declared he was after him even before he found any of the things now being talked about.

Tom, I want you to know the Vice President has been as staunch a supporter of the administration as you could want. He carries a tremendous work load and is truly straight arrow.

Again, thanks and best regards.

Sincerely,

Ron

Mr. Thomas M. O'Brien
Scottsdale, Arizona

* In January 1984 Reagan nominated Ed Meese as the new attorney general, and a bitter confirmation process began. Meese admitted that he failed to list on a financial disclosure form his receipt of an interest-free loan of $15,000 from a man who later received a government job, as did the man's wife and son. A special prosecutor found no wrongdoing, and the Senate confirmed Meese's appointment 63 to 31 in February 1985.

William Rusher, a leading American conservative, was publisher of the National Review *from 1957 to 1988.*

WASHINGTON

April 9, 1984

Dear Bill:

Month after month goes by and I gratefully accept and read cover to cover the issues of *National Review* you so kindly provide. And those months go by without a thank you from me I'm ashamed to say.

Please know I'm grateful and I thank you especially for this last one with the note re the editorial about Ed Meese.

He's taking a bum rap as so many others have at the hands of our permanent lynch mob. Now they list him as just one of a long list of culprits without ever acknowledging that virtually everyone on the list was cleared of any wrongdoing. To the lynchers accusations is proof of guilt.

In my nightly prayers I have to ask forgiveness for what I've been thinking about those villains all day. It's not an easy thing to do.

Nancy sends her best and her thanks too.

Sincerely,

Ron

Mr. William A. Rusher
National Review
New York, New York

WASHINGTON

[April 16, 1984]

P.S. Mr. Chairman*:

In thinking through this letter, I have reflected at some length on the tragedy of scale of Soviet losses in warfare through the ages. Surely those losses, which are beyond description, must affect your thinking today. I want you to know that neither I nor the American people hold any offensive intentions toward you or the Soviet people. The truth of that statement is underwritten by the history of our restraint at a time when our virtual monopoly on strategic power provided the means for expansion had we so chosen. We did not then nor shall we now. Our common and urgent purpose must be the translation of this reality into a lasting reduction of tensions between us. I pledge to you my profound commitment to that goal.

---

* President Reagan added in his own handwriting this postscript to an April 16 letter to Konstantin Chernenko. The top-secret letter was declassified in October 2000. The entire six-page letter is not reproduced here because it is not clear which parts were written by staff members rather than the President.

Andy was a seventh-grade student whose mother declared his bedroom a disaster area. He applied to President Reagan for federal funds to hire a crew to clean up the room. He said that he would provide initial funds if the President would provide matching funds.

May 11, 1984

Dear Andy:

I'm sorry to be so late in answering your letter but, as you know, I've been in China and found your letter here upon my return.

Your application for disaster relief has been duly noted but I must point out one technical problem: the authority declaring the disaster is supposed to make the request. In this case, your mother.

However, setting that aside, I'll have to point out the larger problem of available funds. This has been a year of disasters: 539 hurricanes as of May 4th and several more since, numerous floods, forest fires, drought in Texas and a number of earthquakes. What I'm getting at is that funds are dangerously low.

May I make a suggestion? This Administration, believing that government has done many things that could better be done by volunteers at the local level, has sponsored a Private Sector Initiatives Program, calling upon people to practice voluntarism in the solving of a number of local problems.

Your situation appears to be a natural. I'm sure your mother was fully justified in proclaiming your room a disaster. Therefore, you are in an excellent position to launch another volunteer program to go along with the more than 3000 already under way in our nation. Congratulations.

Give my best regards to your mother.

Sincerely,

Ronald Reagan

Andy Smith
Irmo, South Carolina

Paul Trousdale, a California real estate developer in the Palm Springs and Los Angeles areas, supported Reagan's political career.

May 17, 1984

Dear Paul:

It was good to hear from you. Thanks for writing. You are so right. The Soviets shoot down a plane, they walk out of the disarmament talks, boycott the Olympics and the press asks, "Why don't we do something?" Actually, we have done everything we could quietly to let them know the door is open. We do have one reservation. We won't make some offer that would look as if we were rewarding them for walking out. Just between us, I think they are going to be this way until after the election.

Again, thanks and best regards.

Sincerely,

Ron

Mr. Paul Trousdale
Los Angeles, California

May 31, 1984

Dear Mr. Swanson:

Thank you very much for your letter of April 23, and I'm sorry to be so late in answering.

Our problem with the Soviets and arms control is not a new one. Indeed our government has tried to involve the Soviet government in arms control talks 19 times between WW II and my taking office. In 1946 we pro pose putting all nuclear weapons and material under an international commission to prevent any nation from having such weapons. At that time we were the only nation with such an arsenal. The Soviets had not yet completed a so-called bomb. Even so, they rejected the proposal.

Over the years we let our defenses down in the hope that, as you suggested, they would be reassured and join us in reducing their military. Instead, they engage in the most massive military buildup in history.

Let me give you a clue to their thinking. When they had an ABM (anti-ballistic missile) and we didn't, we tried to get them into an agreement banning such weapons. They refused. Then our Congress authorized our building of such a missile. The Soviets almost instantly proposed an ABM treaty and it was signed. They respect our technological capacity.

In the present situation, they have had SS20 nuclear missiles—intermediate range with three warheads per missile targeted on all of Europe for quite a while. Our NATO allies had no deterrent against these missiles.

In 1979 NATO asked us to provide such a deterrent. President Carter agreed and manufacture of the Pershing II missiles began. Our Administration inherited this program and, of course, carried on.

Suddenly the Soviets began a propaganda campaign to scare our allies into changing their minds. In response, I proposed an arms reduction agreement calling for the total abolition of such intermediate range weapons. The Soviets agreed to negotiate but rejected the total ban. We said all right, let's see how far down we can reduce the numbers. The Soviets agreed to some reduction of their SS20s but only if we totally eliminated our Pershings. They had continued to build and deploy all the time the talks were going on. Under their terms they would have had about 800 warheads to zero for us. We refused and that's when they walked out of the negotiations. They now have almost 1350 warheads in place.

If we reward their walkout by not continuing our deployment, why should they ever give in on any curb of their buildup? We believe our only chance of getting a reduction in nuclear weapons, and I pray someday elimination of all such weapons, is to go forward 'til they realize they are in a race with our superior industrial ability unless they negotiate in good faith. Almost 40 years of trying the other way has failed.

Again, my thanks to you.

Sincerely,

Ronald Reagan

Mr. Vincent J. Swanson
Eagle Bridge, New York

WASHINGTON

May 31, 1984

Dear Mr. Ide:

There were no misrepresentations or half truths in my Central America policy speech. I can, however, understand why you might think so, since your letter reveals your acceptance of the worldwide propaganda put forth by the Cuban and Soviet disinformation network.

The radical right-wing forces in El Salvador, which admittedly would have a totalitarian government every bit as repressive as the one the guerrillas are fighting to have, do operate without government sanctions. Indeed, the only elected government—three elections in 26 months—has made tremendous strides in curbing their activities [Roberto] D'Aubuisson had his chance in a free and open election and he was rejected by the voters—more than 80% of the electorate voted even though the guerrillas had told them, "Vote today and die tonight." Were we a perfect democracy for all of our 200 years? What about lynchings with no arrests being made more than a 100 years after we had adopted our Constitution?

Why is it that every murder is purported to be the work of the so-called death squads? The guerrillas a couple of years ago boasted openly they had killed more than 10,000 of their countrymen.

In Nicaragua, I'm sure, some of the Contras are former members of the National Guard. They would be executed if they tried to live as citizens under the Sandinistas. Most of the leadership of the Contras is made up of men who were part of the revolution against [Anastasio] Somoza.

When victory came they were denied a place in government. The Sandinistas, who a few years ago joined the P.L.O. in declaration of war against Israel, seized total control and with Cuban and Soviet help established a totalitarian government on the Cuban and Soviet pattern. I think there are other reasons behind Mr. [Eden] Pastora's reluctance to align himself with the other freedom fighters.

Nicaragua now has a military more powerful than that of all Central American nations combined. The government has declared its revolution is not bound by any national boundaries.

We do support the Contadora process and its 21 points. There have been criticisms from time to time by some in that process, but still we have a good relationship. We continue to seek a negotiated peace and the government of El Salvador and the Contras support us in this. Only the guerrillas and the Sandinistas refuse. We were providing financial aid to the Sandinista government for some time after I took office as my predecessor had. Then it became clear the Sandinistas were supplying arms to help overthrow the government of El Salvador. In fact, the guerrillas' headquarters is in Nicaragua about 20 miles from the capital.

Incidentally, the persecution of the Miskito Indians has not ceased. Thousands upon thousands are herded into concentration camps under deplorable conditions.

We have legislation before Congress for an $8 billion five-year program to help Central American countries establish viable economies and social reforms. Less than a quarter of that amount is to provide help to their security forces so that the social and economic programs can be implemented.

Thank you for giving me a chance to reply.

Sincerely,

Ronald Reagan

Mr. Harry A. Ide
Ithaca, New York

May 31, 1984

Dear Miss Roberts:

In reply to your letter of April 27th I can understand how you have a mis-perception about my speech in China, there was a certain amount of dis-tortion in the press accounts. Actually there was no "incident" worthy of a press story. Relations with the Chinese leaders were and are on a sound friendship basis.

The theme of their remarks and mine was one of recognizing the differ-ences between us but emphasizing how many things we had in common. In my speech I made no criticism of their system or philosophy but in the context of getting to know each other better I sketched the basics of our system so they could understand where we were coming from. At the same time I contrasted them and ourselves with the country which has 56 divi-sions poised on their border. (We only have 17 divisions in our entire army.) I also mentioned that countries [*sic*] expansionist policies which have them promoting the conflict in Vietnam and Kampuchea on China's Southern border. All of these things had been discussed with my hosts and we were in agreement.

I believe some burocrat [*sic*] at a lower echelon took it upon himself to edit out those few lines possibly because of the impending visit of a Soviet diplomat who incidentally cancelled his visit probably because of China's movement of troops to the Vietnam border. By the way, my line about the "greatest threat to peace in the world today" was a report of what Premier Zhao had said to me.

Well you see your letter did get to me and I don't take daily zzzzz's. That's another distortion by the press. I'm enclosing your letter just in case you'd prefer to have it in someone else's possession.

Sincerely,

Ronald Reagan

Miss Joan Roberts
Portsmouth, New Hampshire

General Winn, a decorated command pilot, was shot down over North Viet-
nam in August 1968 and remained a prisoner of war until March 1973.

WASHINGTON

June 10, 1984

Dear General Winn:

Thank you very much for your insightful letter and wise words. I am writing this as I return from the Summit in London.

In spite of the usual slanting and inaccuracies of the media, who consider
such meetings failures unless there is friction or a feud to write about, the
meeting on the whole was good and worthwhile. There was consensus on
some of the issues you raised in your letter with regard to the anti-freedom
forces in the world and more realism than in some past Summits.

Indeed, it was easier to achieve consensus there than in Washington with
some of the factions in Congress. General Winn, I believe that again the
media has exaggerated supposed differences within our Administration. It
is true I encourage presentation of all facets but there is no compromise
with principle on my part, nor has such been urged upon me.

I'm most grateful for your letter and strengthened by the points you made
with such eloquence and logic. Thank you and God bless you.

Sincerely,

Ronald Reagan

Brigadier General David W. Winn, USAF, Ret.
Colorado Springs, Colorado

John Neil (Moon) Reagan, two years older than Ronald, also attended Eureka College and later became a vice president in the McCann-Erickson Advertising Agency in New York City.

June 21, 1984

Dear Moon:

Just a quick line to let you know I got your letter and have arranged for the V.I.P. White House tour. I can't do the book foreword for David Miller but I'll write and let him know. I'm sorry because I'm a fan of General George Armstrong Custer. The problem is it would be commercializing the office, etc.

I'm sorry to hear about your hand. You know I've been thinking about an operation after the election on that one bent finger of mine. It's not curled over as much as yours but you're giving me some second thoughts.

Ireland was great. You can add "Mary Queen of Scots" to the family tree. They brought in a young man who is actually of our family line and it was a shock to all of us, there actually was a physical resemblance. All in all, it was a great experience. I saw the book and the original handwritten record of our great-grandfather's baptism at age three days in 1829.

Nancy sends her love to you both as do I.

Sincerely,

Dutch

Mr. J. Neil Reagan
Rancho Santa Fe, California

Norman Lear served in the Army Air Corps in World War II, and later in Hollywood wrote and produced award-winning radio and television shows including "All in the Family." Cofounder of Tandem Productions in 1959, he also served as president of the Southern California Civil Liberties Union. He organized a liberal advocacy group, People for the American Way. Lear arranged to have excerpts from President Reagan's June letter printed in the New York Times *on September 9, 1984, and longer excerpts in the October 1984* Harper's *magazine.*

WASHINGTON

June 25, 1984

Dear Norman:

I won't attempt to respond to the quotes you listed in your letter not knowing the context in which they were uttered. It does seem to me, though, that people of any persuasion urging their associates to participate in political activity is pretty much what democracy is all about. And I say this even though I'm sure I would disagree with the course they might be suggesting we follow.

But in mentioning one form of such activity, you referred to me as lobbying for government-mandated prayer readings. That is how the school prayer amendment was defeated. Its opponents made the argument that we were advocating mandated prayer. We were doing nothing of the kind; to the contrary, we opposed mandated prayers. We wanted nothing more than recognition that the Constitution does not forbid children from praying in school if they so desire.

Norman, my father moved around a lot in search of better opportunities. As a result, I attended six different schools in the eight years of elementary school. There was never one in which there was prescribed prayers yet we knew we could pray if we wanted to. You asked about the case I mentioned of a child not being allowed to say grace in the school cafeteria. Without looking it up, I believe the locale was New York and it was children not child. The school authorities thought they were required to forbid the practice. Evidently some parents made a case of it and the courts upheld the school authorities.

I am not using this office as a pulpit for one religion over all others, but I do subscribe to George Washington's remark regarding high moral standards, decency, etc. and their importance to civilization and his conclusion that to think we could have these without religion as a base was to ask for the impossible.

Obviously, when I'm addressing an audience who share my own religious beliefs—indeed, a religious group—I see nothing wrong with talking of our mutual interests. I can recall no instance where I have ever tried to proselytize others or impose my beliefs on those of other faiths. Madelyn Murray O'Hare [American atheist and reformer] demanded and got denial of anyone's right to pray in a school. I simply ask that children be allowed to pray if they so desire—and that prayer can be to the God of Moses, the Man of Galilee, Allah, Buddha, or any others.

I said I would not take up the quotes of the clergy you brought to my attention, but isn't it possible those quotes were defensive rather than aggressive? Possibly they were in response to such statements as made in "The Humanist" by Paul Kurtz: "humanism cannot in any fair sense of the word apply to one who still believes in God as the source and creator of the universe. Christian Humanism would be possible only for those who are willing to admit that they are Atheistic Humanists. It surely does not apply to God-intoxicated believers."

Then there is the statement by John J. Dunphy (same magazine) that the battle for humankind's future will be waged and won in the public school classroom and the new faith of Humanism will replace the "rotting corpse of Christianity."

Believing that both of us are arguing for individual liberty, I have to call to your attention that it is Humanist doctrine that "we must relinquish some of our liberties and that religious values are overridden by what government determines is the general welfare or in the public interest."

Well, I've gone on too long. It was good to hear from you.

Sincerely,

Ron

Mr. Norman Lear
People for the American Way
Washington, D. C.

June 27, 1984

Dear Doug:

Congratulations to you both—but what's so great about a mountain [Everest]? Have you ever climbed the Capitol steps to get to the Congress? No—seriously, I'm very happy for you. Your account of the adventure was exciting reading.

Yes, I did get your other messages and have to say I've never had an Easter greeting from such a location. Thank you. I'm glad our people contributed along the way to your comfort and pleasure. Thanks for your generous words about them, especially the Ambassador. I'll be talking to George Shultz about him. As you know, the State Department rotates these career diplomats on a fairly regular basis. In this case, however, both Ambassador Coon and his wife have requested a return to the States to take up studies. He's going to one of our universities here in Washington, and she'll be at the American Enterprise Institute. I don't believe this means retirement for either of them.

Doug, you've just confirmed a long-held belief of mine. Well, no, you only reported the confirmation—Margot did the confirming. All of this talk on the part of some women about equality is foolish. The plain truth is they are superior, as she clearly demonstrated. I don't know about you, but I don't mind a d—n bit that they are. As a matter of fact, it's rather comforting.

During the recent Summit one of our members—leader of one of the seven nations—gave Margaret Thatcher a bad time. Later I said to her that he was certainly out of line and shouldn't have talked to her that way. She pleasantly and calmly said, "Oh—women know when men are being childish."

Well, welcome home and I echo Margot's question—"What do you do for an encore?"

Nancy sends her best as do I.

Sincerely,

Ron

Mr. Douglas Morrow
Glendale, California

President Reagan wrote these comments for publication in Runner's World *magazine for the July Olympic Games in Los Angeles.*

[July 1984]

I don't know whether everyone who participates in sports has daydreams of the Olympics but I did. I was a high school quarter miler and member of our 880 relay team. Then in college I came to the moment when a choice had to be made between running and swimming and the latter was my choice. My daydreams were first that and never taken so seriously that I felt any pain.

I would feel pain—great pain if ever the games were discontinued. They were born in a time and place where war was constant. They were designed to help bring peace. They are needed as much now as they ever were. They are an inspiration to millions of people in all the world.

July 3, 1984

Dear Mr. Collins:

Thank you very much for your letter of May 28. I don't know when I have been so moved, unless it was at the ceremony [at Arlington Cemetery] itself where I had trouble getting the words past the lump in my throat.

If I have done anything to help bring a proper focus on the noble purpose [Vietnam War] you all served so well, I'll be more than proud. You fought as bravely and as well as any American in our history, and literally with one arm tied behind you. Sometimes two.

The tragedy—indeed, the immorality—of those years was that for the first time in our history our country and its government failed to match your heroic sacrifice. This must never happen again.

Again, thank you for writing as you did.

God bless you.

Sincerely,

Ronald Reagan

Mr. B. T. Collins
Sacramento, California

July 9, 1984

Dear Mr. Muggeridge:

I'm sorry to be so late in answering your letter of March 14. Through some mix-up it made the trip across the ocean twice and has only just reached me.

Thank you for your generous words. I share your feelings about the slaughter of innocents by the practice of abortion. It seems to me the problem has a simple answer: no one has proved, nor can prove that the unborn child is not a living being. Unless they can—and until they can—we must by every moral standard opt for life.

Again, thank you, and please give my regards to Mrs. Muggeridge. Nancy joins me in this.

Sincerely,

Ronald Reagan

Mr. Malcom Muggeridge
Robertsbridge
Sussex, England

Norman Cousins, a former editor of the Saturday Review, *wrote to Reagan about the place of religion in American society and offered to send him a copy of his book,* In God We Trust, *which describes the religious views of the Founding Fathers.*

WASHINGTON

July 17, 1984

Dear Dr. Cousins:

Thank you very much for your letter of June 20 and for your offer of a copy of *In God We Trust*. I'd be very pleased to have it and to read it.

I know with our European heritage there were those in our early times who thought in terms of state religion and others who had a bias against particular religions. Indeed, I can recall as a boy when there was a very pronounced prejudice against Catholicism. My father was Catholic, my mother Protestant, and my brother and I were raised in our mother's church. We were raised to be intolerant of one thing—intolerance. It's hard to believe now, but some of our boyhood battles were in response to charges by other kids that the basement of the local Catholic Church was filled with guns for the day when the Pope gave the order to take over the country. Sounds silly, doesn't it? Yet ours was a typical Midwest small town.

I believe that today an ecumenical spirit is the nature of religion in America, and certainly there is no move by religionists to force their belief on anyone. My criticism of the Court decision on the right to pray in schools is that it in fact is contrary to the Constitution in that it forbids the individual's right to practice religion.

Again, my thanks to you and we'll look forward to seeing you at the wedding [of Patricia Ann Reagan, the Reagans' daughter].

Sincerely,

Ronald Reagan

Dr. Norman Cousins
Los Angeles, California

July 17, 1984

Dear Mrs. Taylor:

Thank you very much for your letter and for your generous words of support for me. I'm proud to have your approval and will do my best to be deserving of it. We are in agreement about the family and government's all-too-often intrusion and interference in family affairs.

On the other hand, government in my view has a sacred responsibility to protect the constitutional rights of every individual wherever and whenever those rights are being unjustly denied. We both know there was a long time when the U.S. government did not fulfill that duty when blacks were being denied virtually every constitutional right. We have finally, thank Heaven, wiped out that great sin against God and man, and for as long as I'm here I'll do everything I can to see it stays wiped out.

You asked about the Supreme Court decision regarding the seniority decision. This was a case brought to the court when a city faced with laying off policemen had to choose between affirmative action and their own rules about seniority rights. It was a tough situation. Admittedly, the black officers did not have the seniority of the others due to that period of bigotry when blacks weren't hired. At the same time, however, to ignore the seniority rights with regard to layoff would be discriminatory against individuals who had earned a lawful right. True, there were blacks among them whose seniority rights were recognized also, but they were few in number.

It was a hard decision to make because, either way, there was an element of unfairness: on the one hand was the situation due to past injustice; on the other, injustice to individuals who had earned a right through time in service. There is no easy or simple answer, but one thing I do know is that together we must do our utmost to see that everyone in this land has an opportunity to work and progress as far as their own ability will take them without regard to race, religion or sex.

Thank you again for writing as you did, and may I say I admire you very much for what you have done and for your courage and your outlook.

God bless you.

Sincerely,

Ronald Reagan

Mrs. Ernestine Taylor
Hamilton, Georgia

July 17, 1984

Dear Officer Bernstein:

Forgive me for being so late in answering your letter of May 29. Sometimes it takes awhile for mail to reach my desk.

I can't tell you how much your letter meant to me and how much I appreciate your writing as you did. You who served in Vietnam fought as well as any Americans ever fought and you did so in a worthwhile and noble cause. You were betrayed by indecision and strategic blunders in high levels of government. Yours was not so much a war as it was one long battle in an ongoing war—the war in defense of freedom which is still under assault. Forgive if you can those who let you down, but stand proud of what you and your comrades did in our country's behalf.

Thanks again and God bless you.

Sincerely,

Ronald Reagan

Officer John W. Bernstein
Houston, Texas

President Reagan wrote the following comment for a story in USA Today *on James Brady, his press secretary.*

[July 1984]

After the shooting in March of '81 my lowest moment came when they wheeled a stretcher by mine and I was told it was Jim Brady and that his chances were slim. Jim the unflappable, the generous, the witty, the one who had become such a trusted friend. It was the first I knew others had been shot and I really started praying.

I thought I knew and appreciated all Jim's good qualities before that day but new ones were revealed in the months that followed, the greatest of which was courage.

Ronald Reagan

WASHINGTON

July 17, 1984

Dear Mr. Bollinger:

Thank you very much for your letter of July 3rd. Thank you too for sending the draft of Steve's letter. It means a great deal to me. His loved ones have been in our thoughts and prayers.

The other day I read a verse—author unknown, which seemed to me a most comforting thought for those who have said goodbye to a loved one or friend.

The poet wrote of seeing a ship, all sails set put out to sea. As he watched, the ship grew smaller and smaller and finally was entirely out of sight. It was gone. But then he said somewhere else the ship was coming into view just as large and real as when he'd watched it sail away. It was not gone it had just gone to another place beyond our sight.

It was the poet's explanation of death. I'm sure Steve has gone to another place—the better place we've all been promised.

Thanks again.

Sincerely,

Ronald Reagan

Mr. Paul P. Bollinger, Jr.
Washington, D.C.

August 28, 1984

Dear Terri:

It was great to get your letter and learn that your dream came true.* Thanks, too, for sending the picture. Guess what? I, too, am riding a Hanoverian gelding, a boy like yours. He stands almost 18 hands and was a national champion hunter in Brazil. I keep him here in Washington and ride him at Camp David. He replaces "Little Man," the thoroughbred I had ridden until the end came several months ago. Before him I had ridden his sister, "Nancy D," and before her their mother "Tar Baby" who was in the movie "Stallion Road" that I made back in the '40's. Thirty-seven years those three had carried me.

I wish you and Hampton the very best and I'm very glad that ten-year-old girl wrote to me thirteen years ago.

Happy riding.

Sincerely,

Ronald Reagan

Miss Terri Menendez
Morgan Hill, California

* In 1971 Governor Reagan received a letter from a ten-year-old girl who wanted to own a horse. He urged her to save some of her allowance to buy one. She saved her money and now owned a three-year-old Hanoverian gelding.

August 28, 1984

Dear Mr. Hutton:

I'm sorry to be a month late in answering your letter of July 30th but it takes a while before letters reach my desk.

I can't tell you how much I appreciate your kind letter and generous words. I'm proud to have your support. Your letter was especially meaningful to me because nothing has frustrated me so much as the image created of me as a bigot and anti-Black. My parents would have turned me and my brother out of the house if either of us had shown a trace of racial or religious bigotry.

As a sports announcer broadcasting major league baseball in the 1930's, I campaigned for an end to the "whites only" rule in organized baseball. Our family was plugging for civil rights before the term had ever been used. I believe I have appointed more Black citizens to executive level positions in the Federal government than any other Administration and, as Governor, it was more than all California's Governors put together.

Forgive me for going on like this but you brought it on yourself because of your kind letter. Again, please know how truly grateful I am.

Sincerely,

Ronald Reagan

Mr. Anthony M. Hutton
Oakland, California

The Sisco sisters wrote about an injury to their horse, Dar-Si-Ah. The sisters made leather belts and also offered to make one for the Vice President George Bush.

September 14, 1984

Dear Miss Sam and Miss Bertha:

I was sorry to hear about Dar-Si-Ah's latest accident but happy to get the word that Dr. McCrystle [the veterinarian] did his usual magnificent work. I've just dropped him a line.

With regard to the Vice President and a belt, I have to tell you I'm not inclined to believe that's his style. He's a boater not a horse person like us. He's out on the ocean in a speed boat every chance he gets. Let me also say he's a great partner and Vice President.

Now about me and Christmas—remember last year's gift was to be for two years. So it is our coming gift just delivered a little early.

My secretary will send some campaign buttons as soon as she can locate them. I understand the ones with pictures are a little hard to come by so it may take a while, but she'll do her best to find some.

Best to Buzzy.

Sincerely,

Ronald Reagan

Misses Sam and Bertha Sisco
Healdsburg, California

October 30, 1984

Dear Mrs. Collins:

I have no words to tell you how very much your letter meant to me. My heart has ached for all of you who bear such a burden of sorrow and then to have the added pain of someone telling you the sacrifices your loved one made were for no reason.

Mrs. Collins, there was a reason and a cause. The cause was peace and your son and those other fine young men died [in the Beirut bombing October 23, 1983] because the enemies of peace knew they were succeeding. Now your letter comes and with all you have to bear you express concern for me. I have asked, with regard to men like your son, where do we find such men? Now I ask where do we find such women as you?

God bless you and from the bottom of my heart I thank you.

Sincerely,

Ronald Reagan

Mrs. Doris Collins
Gardendale, Alabama

November 1, 1984
Aboard Air Force One

Dear Drs. Shelton:

. . . I appreciate your suggestions about the "Star Wars" matter. That term was never mine—it was dreamed up by the press and now they saddle me with it. Actually I called for scientists to research to see if a defensive weapon against nuclear missiles could be found. But your suggestion of creating an umbrella-like image is very sound. I still believe if a defense can be found it is far more civilized than to continue relying on the threat of destroying millions of lives in retaliation for an enemy attack.

Nancy sends her best. Again, thanks.

Sincerely,

Ronald Reagan

Dr. Ivy Mooring Shelton and
Dr. John Shelton
Los Angeles, California

WASHINGTON

November 3, 1984
Aboard Air Force One

Dear Mr. and Mrs. Smith:

I'm terribly sorry to be so late in replying to your letter of August 22 but I have only just received it. It takes awhile for mail to reach my desk and, sometimes longer than other times, depending on the overall mail flow. Please forgive me.

I know there are no words that can lessen your pain—I wish there were.* But, believe me, those men aren't forgotten—by me or by the American people. And nothing has angered me more than those who, for political purposes, have charged they were not serving a worthwhile cause. Our Marines and all of you deserve better than that.

Their cause was peace, and for the better part of a year they were succeeding in that cause. It was for that very reason the forces who don't want a just peace in the Middle East turned to acts of terrorism. First, as you know, it was sniping, then mortar and artillery fire, and finally the suicide bombing. The commanders who approved making the headquarters building a barracks did so because the building offered the best protection against artillery and small-arms fire.

Even now, the possibility of a final peace in that tragic land exists only because of the presence of our Marines and their fellows in the multinational force during that year.

They had made possible the removal of 15,000 P.L.O. radicals and stopped the full-scale war that was going on in the city of Beirut with the thousands and thousands of innocent civilians maimed or killed. Only if we give up on trying to obtain peace will their sacrifice have been in vain. We will not do that.

I was present at Camp LeJeune for the memorial service last year and met the families of most of the men. There was another service this year at which General Kelly read a letter from me. I did not attend because I was sure the same people who have been using this tragedy for political purposes would accuse me of exploiting the event as part of the political campaign. Your son and his comrades deserve better.

Mr. and Mrs. Smith, I do understand your pain and sorrow. I am a parent myself but, more than that, I am so proud of the young men and women who serve in our military, and there is no greater burden in this office than having to make a decision that places them in danger.

I would be pleased to hear from you, but to avoid the delay, please send your reply in care of Kathy Osborne at the White House. In that way your letter will reach me immediately.

Sincerely,

Ronald Reagan

Mr. and Mrs. Joseph K. Smith, Jr.
Middletown, Connecticut

* Their Marine son died in the October 1983 Beirut bombing.

December 10, 1984

Dear Bill:

Of course you'll continue in Kabul, your sentence has four more years to run and no time off for bad behavior. I appreciate your kind words about my letter but I don't know Latin—that was just my poor writing and a certain weakness in spelling. Do you suppose that's how Latin got started in the first place?

I was glad to get your input on Van. Some of our gang thought he wanted a return to private life. Actually we haven't gotten into either of those posts yet. I'm scheduled to meet with Jeane [Kirkpatrick] in the coming week. So far we've been living and dreaming budget cuts and tax reform. In addition to that we've just been given a 10-week-old pup. It's an unbroken (house wise) sheep dog. May I say that while she's cute as a cabbage patch doll, she adds an unexpected complication to White House living. How do you teach a puppy to scratch an elevator when she wants out?

Nancy sends her love and love to Pat from both of us.

Sincerely,

Ron

The Honorable William F. Buckley, Jr.
New York, New York

December 18, 1984

Dear Ms. Guillory:

Thank you for your letter of November 13. It has just reached my desk, hence this delay in responding.

I hope you won't think I'm taking advantage of you but your letter was so forthright and fair, I'm compelled to do a little soulbaring in reply. Nothing has been so frustrating to me in public life as the image that has been created of me—a false image—may I say, with regard to my approach to racial differences.

I grew up in an America that had yet to hear the term "civil rights." We lived in a small town in northern Illinois but segregation as a matter of course was in place to almost the same extent it was in the deep south. The only exception was the public school. We were poor but I was blessed with a mother and father who raised me and my brother to believe there was no greater sin than racial or religious prejudice and bigotry. My father being Irish had known and experienced in his youth the bitterness of bigotry. You know, there was a time in this country when you could find signs on certain establishments: "No dogs or Irish allowed."

Well, anyway, in my college football days I played in the line besides a young Black man. We fought and bled together and became the closest of friends, a friendship that lasted until his death just a few years ago. I thank God I was able to have him here in the White House before that sad day.

My first career was as a radio sports announcer broadcasting major league baseball—the Cubs games out of Chicago. I had no Willie Mays or Don Newcombe to talk about. The Spalding Baseball guide said baseball was a "game for Caucasian gentlemen." I was one of a small group in the early '30's who editorialized and complained that the game should be open to Blacks as it finally was.

When I became Governor of California, I discovered the civil service tests were rigged to keep Black State employees pretty much at the bottom of the ladder. I changed that. As Governor, I appointed more Blacks to executive and policymaking positions than all the previous California Governors put together.

Now, in my present job, I've continued that practice. We have opened government contracts to minority-owned businesses, and launched a program to preserve the historic Black colleges and universities among other things.

Forgive me for belaboring you with my frustration but please be assured I am and will be a President of all the people. Like you, I don't feel "freebies" are the answer. Equal opportunity is. Wherever in this land someone's Constitutional rights are being denied, it is the duty of the Federal government to enforce those rights at the point of bayonet if necessary. And your friend was right; the first President to do that was Dwight D. Eisenhower.

Again, thank you for writing as you did and for giving me the opportunity to sound off.

Sincerely,

Ronald Reagan

Ms. Dorothy J. Guillory
Oakland, California

Sam Donaldson was the forthright ABC network reporter covering the White House.

WASHINGTON

December 20, 1984

Dear Sam:

I'm delighted that you are staying on the White House beat. I hope you won't be so self-effacing, quiet and shy as you have been in the past. Speak right up when you have a question.

Your compassionate master,

Ronald Reagan

P.S. I've worn a brand-new suit twice and you haven't noticed or asked me about it.

Mr. Sam Donaldson
Washington, D.C.

President Reagan visited with the students at the Congress Heights Elementary School in the District of Columbia on a March morning and answered their questions about the presidency and his life. A surprised Rudolph Hines was chosen to become the President's pen pal. Several months later Reagan visited Rudolph at his home and gave him a jar of jelly beans.

WASHINGTON

December 26, 1984

Dear Rudy:*

I'm on my way to California for New Year's but had to drop you a line to thank you for my Christmas gift. I can't tell you how happy I am to have that book on Western movies. I just happen to be a fan of Westerns. In fact when I was making movies I always wanted to be in more Western movies than I ended up doing.

Thank you again. Please give my regards to your parents and I hope you had a very Merry Christmas.

Sincerely—Your Pen Pal,

Ronald Reagan

Rudolph Lee Hines
Washington, D.C.

* In a subsequent letter to the President, Rudolph Hines signed his own name as "Ruddy" and the President then adopted this spelling, or addressed him as "Rudolph."

1985

—

My father was an alcoholic; I loved him and love him
still, but he died at age 58 and had suffered from heart
disease for a number of years before his death. He was
the victim of a habit he couldn't break.

·Letter of January 28, 1985·

S UBZERO temperatures paralyzed Washington, D.C., on Sunday, January 20, as Reagan's friend, the Reverend Billy Graham,
asked God's blessings for the reelected President, his cabinet,
and the American people. Because of the weather, the tradi-
tional parade and numerous other celebrations were canceled.
The next day President Reagan reenacted the swearing-in ceremony as
millions watched on national TV. His second presidential term began with
fresh optimism among his supporters for new domestic programs that
would modify New Deal government legislation. This confident president
believed the ongoing American military buildup and diplomatic negotiations would lessen tensions with the Soviet Union and restore peace to
Central America. And he hoped Congress would recognize the threats to

Central America posed by Daniel Ortega. Staff changes included the appointment of Don Regan as chief of staff, James Baker III as secretary of the treasury, and Edwin Meese III as attorney general. Elected in a landslide and endorsed by almost 60 percent of the voters, President Reagan began another year of personal correspondence.

Fewer letters about the domestic economy arrived at the President's desk in the White House. As always, Reagan looked forward to reading the concerns and compliments of ordinary citizens as well as the friends who wrote. Topics in letters included Social Security and farm problems along with job creation and civil rights. Reagan read and answered letters from his young pen pal, Rudolph. In his replies, the President told of his admiration for President Calvin Coolidge, of his various hobbies and boyhood jobs in Illinois, and of his road to the presidency. And a clever correspondent brightened Reagan's day by suggesting that the President change his young dog's name from Lucky to "Deficit" so if the dog were lost, the President could say, "Deficit's gone."

Foreign relations with the Soviet Union entered an entirely new era when Mikhail Gorbachev came into power as General Secretary after the death of Konstantin Chernenko in March. Major reductions in nuclear weapons appeared possible. President Reagan, while calling for an early meeting to discuss arms limitations, remained cautious in his hopes for substantial success. At the two-day November summit in Geneva, the fourteenth U.S.-Soviet conference, Reagan and Gorbachev held private discussions (with only their translators present) for six hours; however, they reached no agreement on the Strategic Defense Initiative before adjourning.

Plans for Reagan's visit to the Bitburg military cemetery and the Bergen-Belsen concentration camp in Germany to recognize American-German friendship and reconciliation on the fortieth anniversary of Germany's surrender produced a cascade of vehement public opposition in the media and the Congress in April and May. Ordinary citizens writing to the White House also questioned this visit. Among the more than two thousand German soldiers buried at Bitburg were the remains of forty-nine German SS soldiers, infamous for their atrocities against Jewish prisoners of war. Historian Elie Wiesel, a survivor of Auschwitz and Buchenwald, who would receive the Nobel Peace Prize in 1986 for his writings on the Holocaust and his dedication to justice, made a personal and public plea to Reagan at the White House to visit a different site. Other public figures, such as Senator Robert Dole and Prime Minister Margaret Thatcher together with the American Legion, agreed with Wiesel's view. Reagan was supported by former president Richard Nixon and Nixon's secretary of state, Henry Kissinger, who endorsed the trip. General Matthew Ridgway, the last living four-star general who fought in Europe, hoped to lessen the tension and graciously offered to lay the wreath at Bitburg. Although grateful, the President declined the offer. Finally, having promised Chancellor Helmut Kohl, who opposed any changes, that he would make these visits, Reagan refused to remove Bitburg from the upcoming travel schedule. He would go there, and as he said in Germany, "old wounds have been reopened."

At Bergen-Belsen, where sixty thousand persons died, Reagan delivered a magnificent speech that included phrases he had dictated with great emotion days earlier: "Here they lie. Never to hope. Never to pray. Never to love. Never to heal. Never to laugh. Never to cry." He also read from the diary of Anne Frank, who died just three weeks before the British army liberated the concentration camp, and he added that all of God's children must make a better world, that "never again" should such nightmarish suffering and brutality occur. In the afternoon, the President and Mrs. Reagan visited Bitburg with General Ridgway. During the eight-minute visit, Reagan laid a wreath and fulfilled his obligation to Chancellor Kohl.

Many Americans believed Reagan's trip to Bitburg was a serious mistake. His relationship with many American veterans and the Jewish community in the United States suffered. As Reagan biographer Lou Cannon wrote, "the decision to hold the ceremony at all demonstrated a failure of historical understanding by Reagan and Kohl that was compounded by the political selfishness of the West German chancellor and the stubbornness of the American president." This bitter time weakened the public's admiration for a president who in fact was truly sensitive to the Holocaust. During these weeks, the President wrote to numerous correspondents who criticized the German visit, telling them that it was morally the right thing to do and that former enemies now are friends and allies.

From West Germany the Reagan entourage traveled to Madrid and then Strasbourg, France, where he addressed the European Parliament about Soviet arms. A day later he addressed the National Assembly in Lisbon, Portugal, before returning to the United States. His address to the graduating class at the Naval Academy would be followed by trips to Virginia, Wisconsin, Pennsylvania, Oklahoma, Georgia, Alabama, New Jersey, Indiana, Texas, and Illinois. Despite all the travel, he continued to write to his friends and other correspondents until July 13, when doctors at the Bethesda Naval Hospital removed a cancerous polyp from his colon. His rapid recovery from the painful colon resection surprised the medical staff as well as his friends. Within a few weeks he resumed writing to his friends and other Americans. Six weeks later the President went horseback riding at Rancho del Cielo near Santa Barbara. During this time in August the first secret shipment of arms to Iranian moderates began. President Reagan hoped these intermediaries would deal with the kidnappers to obtain the freedom of American hostages held in the Middle East.

January 7, 1985

Dear Nackey:

Nancy and I are sorry you won't be coming to the "party" but do you know we kind of envy you. Don't get me wrong, I'm glad I still have the job but I think one Inaugural should be enough for two terms.

Nackey, I can assure you I'll miss Bill Clark. He's done a fine job at Interior, and I'll follow him with someone of the same philosophy. Bill has stayed on about two years more than he wanted to and now feels he must get back to the ranch. You know I'm responsible for his being in public service eighteen years. His ranching is not vacationing as mine is. It's a working ranch and he feels a real need to get his hands on the reins.

As for Jeane [Kirkpatrick], I have someone in mind who will be as solid as she has been at the UN. In the meantime I'm trying to arrange something that will keep her in the Administration. She has just had all she can take of that puzzle palace on the East River.

Nancy sends her best and we hope your holidays were happy.

Sincerely,

Ron

Mrs. William Loeb
Manchester, New Hampshire

January 23, 1985

Dear Francis Albert:

I still feel that saying thank you as many times as I tried to say it isn't enough. As a matter of fact there probably aren't enough words to express how grateful Nancy and I are and that goes for everyone here who had anything to do with the Inaugural.

The Gala was a smash hit and we're hearing that from everyone. Of course, we don't have to hear it to know that, we saw for ourselves. It really was a great show, Frank, and I know it didn't just happen. You put it together and I think I have some understanding of how much work it took, to say nothing of the touches that were all yours, the little girl who sang the National Anthem is just one example.

Nancy and I will be forever grateful. Again, a heartfelt thanks and love from both of us.

Sincerely,

Ron

P.S. Just received your gift—the framed cartoon. Thank you very much, we're both delighted to have it and to hang it in the W.H.

Mr. Francis Albert Sinatra
Rancho Mirage, California

January 24, 1985

Dear Rudolph:

I just received your letter and I was glad to hear from you. You asked some questions about the Inaugural, but maybe now that it's over you already have the answers. Just in case you missed a few, I'll answer anyway.

The Inauguration is the swearing-in of the President. Once elected (or re-elected as I was) your term begins at noon on January 20th with you taking an oath to uphold the Constitution and fulfill the duties of the Presidency.

This year the 20th fell on Sunday, the first time since President Eisenhower's Inaugural. So I had to take the oath on Sunday, but repeated it on

Monday for the public. I told some of our Congressmen that maybe we should change the Constitution so that when the 20th was on a Sunday the President would still be President until Monday noon.

Over the years traditions have built up so that a big entertainment takes place the night before. Ours was at the Convention Center with Frank Sinatra in charge. Then on Inaugural Day there is a parade. Ours was cancelled because of the cold. On Inaugural night there is a big party. That custom started back in 1789 when George Washington became President. Now our country has become so big we had to have eleven of them. Nancy and I showed up and made an appearance at all eleven. This was the 50th Inauguration in our country's history.

I mentioned the cold and cancelling the parade; this was the coldest Inaugural Day we've ever had and the first time the outdoor events had to be cancelled. Let me tell you how cold it was. Upstairs in the White House there is a big potted plant in front of the window we open at night for fresh air when we go to bed. This time I only opened it about two inches. In the morning the plant was dead. It had frozen.

I'll look forward to hearing about the science fair and hope you succeed in the rocket launch. Please give our regards to your folks.

Best wishes from your pen-pal,

Ronald Reagan

Rudolph Hines
Washington, D.C.

WASHINGTON

January 28, 1985

Dear Scott:

I have your letter and was happy to hear from you. Your mother keeps me posted on your progress and your intention to study architecture. I think that's great, but don't be surprised if you undergo a change of mind or, for that matter, more than one in the years ahead. I majored in economics and then wound up a sports announcer and later an actor.

I don't say this to suggest in any way your choice isn't the right one, it's just that in these next few years you'll be exposed to a number of new viewpoints and you should follow your own instincts. Architecture is a fascinating profession and a happy marriage between art and practical construction.

Scott, I shouldn't do this, but I have to argue with you a bit on your postscript about age 18 and the right to drink. Forgive me, but voting and soldiering are different than starting in on what we have to recognize is actually a form of drug. Now don't think I'm a hypocrite—I enjoy a cocktail now and then before dinner and have a taste for a good dinner wine. I also recall feeling exactly as you do now and, looking back, I realize the Lord must have been watching over me. At that age (about 18) getting drunk seemed like the thing to do, the point of drinking. Then, before something too awful happened (although there were a few near scrapes) I realized that I was abusing the machinery, this body. We only get one you know. But more than that, I had an example to look at. My father was an alcoholic; I loved him and love him still, but he died at age 58 and had suffered from heart disease for a number of years before his death. He was the victim of a habit he couldn't break.

Forgive me for playing grandpa—but think about it a little. Become an architect or, if you change your mind—whatever, and we'll celebrate your graduation with a champagne toast, and I'll furnish the wine.

All the best to you.

Sincerely,

Ronald Reagan

Mr. Scott R. Osborne
Fair Oaks, California

January 28, 1985

Dear Mr. Wilson:

Thank you for your letter. You'll never know how much it meant to me. I've been frustrated by our inability to get our story through the wall of silence to the Black community. Right now we continue to try to persuade Congress to give us what we call "enterprise zones." It is a program to use tax incentives to bring business and industry into depressed inner city neighborhoods to provide jobs and opportunity for the people there. We're also battling to get a lower minimum wage for young people with no work experience so they can get that first job. The present minimum has priced them out of the job market. The Council of Black Mayors support this because Black teenagers have the highest rate of unemployment in the land. We'll keep trying.

You are right also about how government programs have kept Blacks in poverty, dependent on government handouts. I want to help them become independent.

Thank you again, and very best wishes to you.

Sincerely,

Ronald Reagan

Mr. Donald Wilson
Jersey City, New Jersey

January 28, 1985

Dear Ms. Sellers:

Thank you very much for your letter and good wishes and for sharing your views about South Africa. All of us find apartheid repugnant but so do many people in South Africa. We are working quietly to persuade and to help the South African government improve the situation there and we've had some real success.

You are right about the importance to us and the free world of South Africa as a trade partner. Indeed, our own national security is at stake. I'm sure we can be of greater help to the disadvantaged Blacks in South Africa by continuing our present policy than by taking to the streets in demonstrations. Again my thanks to you.

Sincerely,

Ronald Reagan

Ms. Joan Joyce Sellers
Camarillo, California

President Reagan's answers to questions for a USA Today *automobile supplement.*

[January 1985]

1. *What was your first car?*
   1934 Nash Lafayette Coupe

2. *What was your most memorable car, and why?*
   A jeep I was given for x-mas by Nancy in 1963—I'm still driving it.

3. *What car would you like to forget, and why?*
   I won't name the brand but it was a luxury lemon. Even the trunk lid would pop open while I was driving.

4. *What type of car do you own now?*
   Jeep, Pick-up truck.

5. *What is your ideal car?*
   The one I've had lately. I just get in the backseat and someone drives me to where I'm supposed to be.

January 29, 1985

Dear Mr. Huntley:

Thank you very much for sending me the copy of Calvin Coolidge's Christmas Greeting of 1927.* I'm delighted to have it. I happen to be an admirer of "Silent Cal" and believe he has been badly treated by history. I've done considerable reading and researching of his presidency. He served this country very well and accomplished much before speaking the words, "I do not choose to run."

Sincerely,

Ronald Reagan

Mr. James M. Huntley
White River Junction, Vermont

[December 25, 1927. To the American People:] * Christmas is not a time or season, but a state of mind. To cherish peace and goodwill, to be plenteous in mercy, is to have the real spirit of Christmas. If we think on these things, there will be born in us a Savior and over us will shine a star sending its gleam of hope to the world. —Calvin Coolidge.

February 21, 1985

Dear Mrs. Smith:

I was very happy to receive your letter and learn that you are out of the hospital and recovering from your surgery. Don't overdo or push too hard yet. You know, someone has said that a surgeon's scalpel is five months long.

Thank you for your generous words about my performance before the Congress, but I'm also grateful for your approval of "Storm Warning." That was my first picture after coming out of the hospital—I had broken my thigh. It looked for a while as if I might do the picture using a cane, but we settled for a limp instead.

Nancy sends her best and her thanks for your kind words. Again my thanks for your good wishes.

Sincerely,

Ronald Reagan

Mrs. Hilda W. Smith
Richmond, Virginia

WASHINGTON

February 22, 1985

Dear Alan:

. . . Regarding your question about Tip [O'Neill] and Ted [Kennedy] and their reaction to my address: Tip had to applaud, he was on camera right over my left shoulder. Ted was seen by someone to have softly patted his hands together once but that was the extent of it.

Nancy sends her love. Again thanks.

Sincerely,

Ron

Mr. Alan Brown
APO New York

March 4, 1985

Dear Stephan [age 11]:

Thanks very much for your letter and your suggestion about a name change [to "Deficit"] for our dog, Lucky. I've thought it over and have decided to keep calling her Lucky. You see, I'm doing my best to make the deficit go away, but I don't want her (our dog) to go away. If I'm lucky we'll eliminate the deficit, but we'll still have Lucky. You'd like her, she's only 6 months old and a lot of fun.

Best regards,

Ronald Reagan

Stephan Lieske
La Canada, California

March 4, 1985

Dear Mr. Moulton:

Thank you for your letter of February 22nd and may I say, "right on." Since you wrote, I've made a couple of speeches and done one of my Saturday radio broadcasts touching on the theme you so eloquently expressed in your letter.

Yes, we have compassion for those who've tried and failed or who, through no fault of their own, must seek our help. But we can't impose unfairly on those who carry the load and make this country go and whose taxes pay the freight. For too long the forgotten American has been the citizen who sends the kid to school, goes to work, supports church and charity and pays taxes to keep the wheels turning. We'll keep on thinking of and caring for these Americans. Again, thanks.

Sincerely,

Ronald Reagan

Mr. Irving R. Moulton
Perrysburg, Ohio

March 5, 1985

Dear Mr. Puleo:

Your letter has only just arrived at my desk, so forgive the delay in answering. Thank your for your kind and generous words. I'm most grateful. I'm sorry about the schedule changes in the Inaugural and hope they didn't spoil anything for you.

You asked at what time in my life did I even entertain the thought of the presidency. Well, I can honestly say that throughout my years in pictures and TV, the thought of public office never occurred to me. I always believed in paying my way, life had been good to me so I campaigned for people and causes I believed in. Then, in '64, I went all out for Barry Goldwater. Late in the campaign, I made a speech in his behalf on NBC TV. The speech rang a bell I guess and raised a lot of money, etc. In '65 with the California Governor's race coming up in '66, a group of Republicans called on me asking that I run against the incumbent Governor Pat Brown. The party was terribly split as a result of the '64 primary between Goldwater and Rockefeller; they cited my speech and said I could unite the party. I dismissed them out of hand. I was very happy in show business. They kept coming back until Nancy and I were worn down and thought maybe we did have a duty.

As Governor, I was asked to be a favorite son candidate for President to hold our California party together. I agreed on the condition that that was as far as I would go. I would not be a real candidate.

Well, to shorten this down, the first time I ever thought of seeking the presidency was in 1976 because I felt Jerry Ford could not beat Jimmy Carter whom I'd known as a Governor. In 1980, after 4 years of the Carter Administration, I decided to make a race again because I believed it would do some good. I can honestly tell you that until that 1965–66 period, I had never thought of public office at all.

Sorry to be so long about it, but that's the story. Please give my best to your wife.

Sincerely,

Ronald Reagan

Mr. Dennis Puleo
Center Ossipee, New Hampshire

WASHINGTON

March 7, 1985

Dear Ms. Cox:

Your letter of January 31 has just reached my desk, so pardon my late reply.

Since your letter was written, we have done some things to help the farm situation. We have some four and a half billion dollars in credit available for farmers this year, including a special 650 million dollar program to help with refinancing. Of course, our regular crop loans and deficiency payments are continuing and will, by April 1st, amount to 12 billion dollars since last December.

There are 2.4 million farms in America and the overwhelming majority are not experiencing financial difficulties. About half have no debt at all. The present situation involves the middle-range family farmers. And of those, numbering in total 679,000, only 229,000 have problems in any degree. The problem group breaks down into 136,000 who can get through this year, but might face a problem in the next two to five years, and just under 100,000 who have an immediate problem. Of that last group, about half do their borrowing at the Farmers Home Administration and will in almost all cases be able to get through the year.

There will be some who can't be helped, but we believe our program will lend a hand to most of those in greatest need. Incidentally, we have tried to call attention to the good that communities and neighbors can do by rallying around and pitching in.

Thanks again for your letter.

Sincerely,

Ronald Reagan

Ms. Linda R. Cox
Kerman, California

March 7, 1985

Dear Dick:

Thank you very much for sending me the poem "The Hermit of Shark Tooth Shores."* If I sound a little vague on issues for the next few weeks it will be because I'm trying to memorize the poem. I'll add that to my repertoire of Dan McGrew and The Cremation of Sam McGee. Maybe it will take more than a few weeks, "The Hermit" looks pretty long.

Again, thanks, Dick.

Best regards,

Ronald Reagan

The Honorable Dick Cheney
House of Representatives
Washington, D.C.

* An unpublished poem by Robert Service.

Walter Annenberg established a magazine, radio, television, and newspaper empire. Ambassador to Great Britain from 1969 to 1974, he would be knighted by Queen Elizabeth II and awarded the Medal of Freedom by President Reagan in 1986.

WASHINGTON

March 26, 1985

Dear Walter:

You shouldn't be thanking me for something I was so happy to do. Walter, some people see a need, shake their heads and go off clucking, "my, my, someone should do something about this." Well, someone does, and more times than not, the someone turns out to be Walter Annenberg. We all owe you thanks for so many good deeds.

Nancy sends her love, and from both of us to Lee. How long is it to New Year's?

God bless you.

Sincerely,

Ron

The Honorable Walter Annenberg
"Sunnylands"
Rancho Mirage, California

Jeane Kirkpatrick was U.S. Ambassador to the United Nations from 1981 to 1985, and later, professor at Georgetown University and senior fellow at the American Enterprise Institute.

March 29, 1985

Dear Jeane:

I'm sorry I can't be with you in person but believe me my heart is there. Being a convert myself let me say a heartfelt welcome and assure you the water is just fine on this side of the dam and I'm sure you'll be very happy among us elephants. I can tell you we're more than happy to have you.

You are being hosted by the GOP Women's Political Action League at their first major function. Carla Hills, Nancy Reynolds and my daughter Maureen came together on a very wonderful idea and all the others there tonight also thought it was a great idea. They have come together to raise money and provide support for women candidates for State and Federal offices.

In 1984 our party had a net gain of 95 women legislators at State and Federal levels—a record. The goal is record numbers in '85 and '86. So you see, here is a new world to conquer which is just what you did as a truly great Ambassador to the United Nations.

Thank you and God bless you.

Sincerely,

Ronald Reagan

The Honorable Jeane Kirkpatrick
The Waldorf-Astoria
New York, New York

April 4, 1985

Dear Earl:

Believe me, I agree with "the former Ambassador to Cuba" [Smith] that Nicaragua is Cuba all over again. But try to convince a majority of the Congress of that—including a goodly number of Republicans.

The pro-Sandinista lobby on the Hill is about as sophisticated an operation as I've ever seen. I have to say though that this time the Secretary of State is on the side of the good guys. Our problem is the Congress. Tip O'Neill is influenced by someone in one of the religious orders and gets vehement about our hostility to the Sandinistas.

We're announcing a proposal this afternoon appealing for negotiations between the Contras and the government with the Church on hand as a participant. This is the result of our efforts to get funding for the Contras. We've been told by our own people there is no way we can get a straight up or down vote on money for the Contras so we're making the money part of this whole proposal.

Believe me, Earl, we're as solid on this as we can be and you are right that Nicaragua is nothing but a Soviet-Cuban base on our mainland.

Nancy left for California this a.m. and Thank Heaven I follow her tomorrow. Love to Lesly.

Sincerely,

Ron

The Honorable Earl E. T. Smith
Palm Beach, Florida

The announcement of the President's forthcoming visit to the Bitburg Military Cemetery for a wreath-laying ceremony came on April 11. Within two days, reporters discovered that forty-nine SS soldiers were among the two thousand buried there. Angry and vehement protests by American leaders, including Elie Wiesel, filled newspaper columns and TV programs. M. Z. Rosensaft was a biographer of Moshe Sharett, an Israeli statesman and colleague of David Ben-Gurion, a principal founder of Israel and its Premier and Defense Minister, 1949–1953, and 1955–1963. Rather than cancel the Bitburg visit, Reagan added a ceremony at the Bergen-Belsen Concentration Camp, where over 59,000 persons died, half of them Jews.

April 23, 1985

Dear Mr. Zeeman:

I'm sorry to be so late in answering your letter of March 30. I've been away, as you know, so it wasn't brought to my attention until a few days ago.

Believe me, I can understand your feeling of outrage [because the President would not visit Dachau Concentration Camp] and, yes, that of Mr. Rosensaft, but I would like to point out that the presentation of this episode in the media has been grossly distorted. Let me put the matter in proper perspective.

I will be in West Germany at the end of this month, as a guest of the German government, as we commemorate the 40th Anniversary of the end of World War II. Chancellor Helmut Kohl approached me some time ago as to what might be a proper observance of that event. I expressed the opinion that it was time for the world to view the day as one of gratitude that we have achieved friendship between former enemies, and forty years of peace. Of the seven nations represented at the Economic Summit, three were enemies of the other four in World War II. Now we meet annually as Allies.

Some time later, Chancellor Kohl asked me to be a guest of his government for a state visit following the Summit. He outlined a schedule which included our joint visit to the Bitburg Cemetery on our way to a visit with our American troops. Although the idea of a visit to Dachau had been raised, I had the impression that the German government preferred that I not visit that camp. I felt that for me to ok this on my own while a guest of the German government would be taken as an affront to the people of Germany, and would be at odds with the spirit of reconciliation the Chancellor was trying to achieve. I am afraid I did not explain this very well when the question was asked in the press conference.

Only a short time ago did I learn that there had been some confusion, and that a visit to a concentration camp was being suggested by the German government as part of the official itinerary. I, of course, immediately accepted.

Mr. Zeeman, my feelings about the Holocaust can be summed up in the words I have used a hundred times, "we must never forget and it must never happen again." Since I have been President, we have regularly hosted gatherings in the East Room of survivors of the Holocaust. I am more pleased than I can say that the visit to a concentration camp will be a part of the official program.

Thank you for giving me a chance to explain and to respond to Mr. Rosensaft's article.

Sincerely,

Ronald Reagan

Mr. Jesse A. Zeeman
Washington, D.C.

April 26, 1985

Dear Judge Zingales:

I have just received your letter of April 16 and will probably be in Europe by the time you receive this. I want you to know how very much I appreciate your kind thoughtfulness in writing as you did.

These have been trying days for one who feels as deeply as I do about the inhumanity of the Nazi period. The Holocaust must never be forgotten and must never happen again. My purpose in accepting the chancellor's invitation was to emphasize that fact.

I hope the words I'll utter on that occasion will make plain that I'm not asking forgiveness for those who perpetrated the monstrous crime only remembrance so as to ensure it will never happen again.

Thanks again for an act of kindness I shall always remember.

Sincerely,

Ronald Reagan

Judge Joseph A. Zingales
Redford, Ohio

April 29, 1985

Dear Mr. Carowitz:

I hope you won't mind my answering your letter to Nancy. She is most grateful for your generous words about her activities. She passed your letter on to me because of the concerns you'd expressed about my coming visit to the cemetery in West Germany.

I, too, am an admirer of the late Scoop Jackson and endorse everything he said to you in his [1978] letter.* While I will be making my first visit to a camp, Bergen-Belsen, I had early exposure to the horror of those places. In World War II I was adjutant of an Air Corps post directly under Air Corps Intelligence. One of our tasks was putting a film report together for the General Staff in the Pentagon. We received the first film taken by combat crews when our forces overran a number of the camps, Auschwitz, etc. None of us who worked on that report will ever forget the horrors we saw—the living and the dead.

I say with all my heart—this must never be forgotten and it must never happen again. Chancellor Kohl of Germany asked me to join him on this 40th observance of the war's end not to honor the dead in the cemetery but to point up that we erstwhile enemies—now close allies, who have lived in peace for 40 years, are united in our determination that the Holocaust will never be repeated. It seems to me this is a worthwhile and morally right thing to do.

Thank you for giving me a chance to explain.

Sincerely,

Ronald Reagan

Mr. Michael Carowitz
Ann Arbor, Michigan

* Regarding German brutality against the prisoners in Buchenwald.

Elsa Sandstrom, a delegate to the Republican National Convention in 1964 and 1972, was also a presidential elector from California. She was president of the California Federation of Republican Women from 1970 to 1976.

May 17, 1985

Dear Elsa:

Just a quick line to say a heartfelt thank you for your kind letter. I regret very much the media effort to raise a firestorm over the Bergen-Belsen, Bitburg trip. It actually turned out alright and certainly wasn't a big blunder in planning. From the first moment Chancellor Kohl asked me to do it, I felt it was the morally right thing to do.

Your letter was a very warm and kind reassurance and I'm most grateful.

Sincerely,

Ron

Mrs. Elsa Sandstrom
La Jolla, California

May 23, 1985

Dear Mr. Atkins:

Thank you very much for your letter of May 11. Anne Higgins saw that I got it.

You and I are tracking together on what should be said to Mr. Gorbachev. I've had the opportunity to say something of the kind to Foreign Minister Gromyko and Mr. Shcherbitsky when they were here. I look forward to saying it to the headman.

My dream is to take them to see some of our residential areas and farm country, and ask them why they think people who live as we do would ever want to go to war with them. I'd also like to ask when, if ever, they think their system can produce anything like what we have here.

Thank you again for your kindness in writing.

Best regards,

Ronald Reagan

Mr. Warner L. Atkins
Pinehurst, North Carolina

May 23, 1985

Dear Mr. Muntean:

I'm sorry to be so late in replying to your letter, but it didn't reach me until I returned from our European trip. Thank you for writing as you did. It is true there are too many who take freedom for granted and don't realize that every generation must fight for it and pass it on to the next.

We have not given up on the Nicaraguan situation. We'll try again, and I'm still optimistic. A number of those who voted against us in the Congress have had a change of heart since Nicaragua's President Ortega took his trip to Moscow.

Again, my thanks for your letter. You were kind to write as you did and I'm most grateful.

Sincerely,

Ronald Reagan

Mr. Livius Muntean
Morgan City, Louisiana

May 28, 1985

Dear Bill:

Following our phone conversation, I received your Bitburg column which appeared in the New York *Daily News* May 9th. So now another thank-you is in order.

Thank you very much, my friend, for your kind and, as always, eloquent and well-chosen words. I especially loved your "tag line," the final paragraph about being owed an apology I'll never get.

Sincerely,

Ron

P.S. Keep this up and I may transfer you from Kabul to Bermuda.

Mr. William F. Buckley, Jr.
New York, New York

May 31, 1985

Dear Jan and Mickey:

Sorry you can't make it June 12th [for dinner at the White House], but you have an ongoing rain check. While we'll miss you, we're happy you are working, 'cause that means pleasure for a lot of people.

Mickey, I'll bet you don't remember the first time we met. The year was 1937 or thereabouts. I was new in Hollywood, living in the Montecito Apartments. Someone had run over a dog in the street outside. You came in to look for a phone book so you could find the nearest veterinarian and take the dog to him. I figured this had to be a nice guy, and I was right.

Nancy sends her best and so do I.

Sincerely,

Ron

Mr. and Mrs. Mickey Rooney
Hollywood, California

Paul Harvey began his radio career in Tulsa in 1933 and became a famous
coast-to-coast newscaster.

WASHINGTON

June 21, 1985
Aboard Air Force One

Dear Paul:

Thank you very much for "Mr. President, Spare My But." You made my
day, and that goes for our top staff people—I gave them copies. You certainly helped our tax reform campaign also.

Paul, I understand you have just had or are slated to have a meeting with
our leader of the Red Cross. He told me of your concern about the Red
Cross seemingly refusing to help in the hostage situation [Americans held
in Lebanon]. This was another press error. We never asked the Red Cross
to intervene, nor will we. They have been most helpful in the ways they
are set up to help—contact with the hostages to see they are being properly cared for, etc.

Well, again, my heartfelt thanks to you, and

Warm regards,

Ronald Reagan

Mr. Paul Harvey
Paul Harvey News
Chicago, Illinois

June 28, 1985

Dear Mr. Garrison:

Thank you very much for your warm letter and welcome support. You have brightened my day considerably. I'll go into the battle for tax reform greatly heartened.

I share your feelings about the situation today faced by your generation, and promise I'll stay in the fight to eliminate the inflation that has contributed so much to the conditions you described so eloquently. Of course, there is much more than that yet to do. But with the support of people like yourself, I'm convinced we'll get the job done.

Your comparison of your lifestyle and your father's brought back many memories. When I graduated from college and got my first job, I splurged and treated myself to my first tailor-made suit. It cost $18.50. When I got my first Hollywood contract, I jumped to a magnificent $8,000 a year and immediately bought a Cadillac. I know we'll never see those figures again, but we can bring about a better ratio between income and prices.

Thanks again for your generous words and your support.

Sincerely,

Ronald Reagan

Mr. Gary L. Garrison
San Antonio, Texas

June 28, 1985

Dear Glenn [high school junior]:

I'm glad you have given me an opportunity to correct what is obviously some misinformation you have received. I'm curious as to who might have misinformed you. Whoever it was, either was ignorant of the facts or was guilty of an outright lie. I think the figures I've enclosed will prove that I have not been lying.

Glenn, before you check out the figures let me give you some additional facts. Our missiles, the landbased ICBMs, are not more sophisticated and superior. Our latest, the Minute Man III, is over 15 years old and doesn't have the accuracy or power needed to handle the hardened silos of the Soviets. That's why we want the MX. It is equal to the Soviet's SS-18s and 19s but we're only asking for 100 of these and they won't all be operational for several more years.

By 1981, the Soviets had achieved an advantage in nearly every measure of strategic capability such as strategic missiles, warheads, bombers and throw-weight. At the same time, they continued to tilt the conventional and nuclear balance in Europe further in their favor; they increased and modernized their already considerable forces in Asia, and they increased their ability to project their forces and those of their allies throughout the 3rd World.

We are trying to modernize at the same time we seek effective arms reductions to reduce the risks of war and to increase global stability.

If you need any additional information, please let me know. If you write, address the letter to me—the White House, but mark it "Attention Kathy Osborne." That way, it will come directly to me.

Sincerely,

Ronald Reagan

Glenn Ball
Wisconsin Rapids, Wisconsin

July 2, 1985

Dear Bill:

Have your letter in hand and hasten to reply before you get lost somewhere in the Pacific. Robert Bork has been on the Circuit Court since February of 1982 which, as you know, is as high as you can go except for the Supreme Court. I know of no change with regard to him, but the top court is not on the front burner because no one seems inclined to retire as yet.

I think whatever rumor you heard has to do with general conversation quite awhile back regarding the fact that, to our knowledge, no Italian-American has ever been on the Court. But all of that was in the context of possibly having a number of appointments open up before I ride off into the sunset.

Now the important thing is a sailing trip to New Guinea! I know you've been holed up in Kabul for a long time—don't you know we have ships that don't need sails anymore? It all started with a fellow named Fulton. You can get to New Guinea several times as fast lolling in a deck chair—without pulling and hauling on a lot of ropes. Just a thought for you to conjure with.

Love to Pat.

Sincerely,

Ron

Mr. William F. Buckley, Jr.
New York, New York

Governor Cuomo commended President Reagan for his continuing restraint with firmness regarding the release of thirty-nine Americans aboard hijacked TWA flight 847 in the Middle East. All these TWA hostages were freed on June 30. Covert operations to secure freedom for the seven kidnap victims noted by Reagan would turn into the Iran-Contra affair.

July 5, 1985

Dear Governor Cuomo:

Thank you very much for your kind letter of June 27. It was good of you to write as you did and I'm most grateful. I'm grateful, too, for so many who prayed, and to God for answering those prayers. Now we must go on until we have secured the freedom of the seven kidnap victims. They, too, must be brought home.

Again, my thanks to you.

Sincerely,

Ronald Reagan

The Honorable Mario Cuomo
Executive Chamber
Albany, New York

July 31, 1985

Dear Mrs. Hardie:

Our friends . . . made sure I received your message and the word of your own experience thirty years ago. Thank you so very much. You were more than kind to think of me.

I'm already feeling fine and, while I won't be chopping wood for a while, I expect to be on a horse in a few more weeks.* Do you know the most encouraging part of your message was to learn you've managed without popcorn for thirty years. I received the same orders you did—no popcorn, nuts, etc. from now on. I happen to be a popcorn freak and will eat any given amount. I've been wondering what life will be like without it. You've reassured me that I'll be able to adjust.

Well, again, my thanks. Nancy sends her regards as do I.

Sincerely,

Ronald Reagan

Mrs. Teresa A. Hardie
San Diego, California

* The President had intestinal surgery on July 13.

Brooke Astor, a New York City philanthropist, wrote several books and numerous magazine and newspaper articles. She also was awarded six honorary university degrees. The President was surrounded, as he noted, by Marines.

WASHINGTON

August 6, 1985

Dear Brooke:

Thank you for your kind letter. I'm happy to say I feel just fine and expect to be on a horse in about a week or so when we get to the ranch.

I'm also happy to tell you that Monday I had a short question and answer session with the press and one of the questions had to do with the attacks on George Shultz. It was my pleasure to tell them how much confidence I had in him and how utterly false were the charges some crackpots were making about him. Incidentally, did you know George was a Marine and served in the Pacific in World War II? Of course he doesn't use the past tense—he says, "Once a Marine, always a Marine." I'm surrounded—Don Regan, Bud McFarlane and Jim Baker.

Nancy sends her love and again, my heartfelt thanks.

Sincerely,

Ron

Mrs. Vincent Astor
Northeast Harbor, Maine

Eddie Albert, Reagan's friend from Hollywood days, continued his movie and TV career into the 1990s. His wife, Margo, had died shortly before he wrote to the President.

August 11, 1985
Aboard Air Force One

Dear Eddie:

Nancy and I were deeply moved by your letter and we both send you our love and, as you already know, our deepest sympathy. You and I have been richly blessed. We can only be grateful to God and now have faith in his infinite wisdom and mercy. We're all still on location, Margo has just finished her scenes and gone home. Her performance was magnificent and one day you'll be able to tell her so. We have His promise on that.

Eddie, in reference to your words about preventive medicine, I believe I'm correct in saying that our National Health effort is devoting a major portion of its resources to that cause.

Thank you for sending the clipping, and please give our best to the younger Alberts. You are in our prayers.

Sincerely,

Ron

Mr. Eddie Albert
Pacific Palisades, California

August 14, 1985

Dear Ms. . . .*:

I'm sorry to be so late in answering your letter of May 20 but I've only just received it.

It is not my intention or right to pass judgment on the decision you made, but I do believe that an unborn child is a living human being and is entitled to life as we all are. Having an adopted child of my own, I'm also convinced there are alternatives to abortion that solve the problems of an unwanted pregnancy without going to the extreme of an abortion.

Sincerely,

Ronald Reagan

* Name and address withheld.

August 14, 1985

Dear Sgt. . . .*:

Thank you for your letter of June 25th, and pardon my late reply. It takes a while for mail to reach my desk. I welcome this chance to express my appreciation for your service in Beirut. You are correct about accomplishing your mission; it was because you did that the terrorists launched their all out effort against you. You were not withdrawn because of failure, but only because required defensive measures made continuation of your mission impossible.

Sgt., the sense of guilt you say you felt is typical of combat. I first learned of it in WWII, even though my service never included combat. It isn't given to us to understand the fortunes of war—why some are called upon to die and others spared. We must have faith in God's infinite wisdom and mercy. He alone decides, and when we are spared it is because He has things for us yet to do.

Thank you for writing but, more important, thank you for what you are doing.

God bless you,

Ronald Reagan

* Name and address withheld.

September 9, 1985

Dear Ruddy:

It was good to hear from you and to hear about your vacation trip. Thank you very much for our gift. Nancy joins me in this—we both think the glasses are lovely with those beautiful ring-necked pheasants on them. I assure you, we'll use them with great pleasure.

Don't worry about asking questions. Feel free to ask them anytime. About the one on riding, when I was in high school and college I spent my summers as a lifeguard at a river beach in my hometown. The man who took care of the park had a horse for pulling some of the equipment he used in keeping the park clean. Sometimes at the end of the day he would ride the horse bareback (no saddle) down to the beach. One day he teased me into riding the horse and, before I knew it, I liked riding. Later, when I was a sports announcer near an Army cavalry post, I became a reserve officer in the cavalry.

Riding is a wonderful sport and a very healthy sport. An old cavalry saying is, "nothing is so good for the inside of a man as the outside of a horse." It's only natural to be afraid of a horse at first, but that goes away as you begin to ride.

You asked me about learning Karate and how to breach the subject to your parents. Ruddy, being a parent myself, I can tell you your parents are the best friends you'll ever have. The best way is to simply talk it over with them. The decision they make will be based on what they think is best for you right now. Listen to them and accept their decision knowing they have your best interest at heart. I can recall some turn-downs by my parents when I was young. At the time I was pretty upset and thought my parents were wrong but, as time went by, I usually looked back and decided they had been right.

By the way, Ruddy, parents worry and are sorry they can't spend more time with their children. It's just that life gets a little complicated, what with making a living and all.

Thanks again for our beautiful gift, and happy school days. The enclosed is a little going-to-school gift.

Sincerely,

Ronald Reagan

Rudolph Hines
Washington, D.C.

WASHINGTON

September 18, 1985

Dear Teddy and Otis:

What a surprise! Your letter and promotion for "Asia Pacific Magazine" has just reached us. I know your letter was dated August 1 but sometimes it takes a while before mail makes its way to my desk. First of all, thank you for your good wishes and your prayers. They weren't in vain. I finished the last 8 days at the ranch riding every morning and pruning trees in the afternoons. I feel great.

I wish you well with the new magazine and now we'll be praying for you. I'm more than ever convinced of the future of the Pacific rim. Not too long ago I received a letter from a young man from Vietnam. Ten years ago (remember only 10 years) he was in a boat off Vietnam. They were out of food and almost out of water. He was 13 years old.

They were rescued by a passing ship and he was dropped off at an island refugee camp. Sometime after, he was shipped to the U.S. He learned our language, graduated from high school and was given a scholarship to Harvard. He (now 23 years old) is in Dartmouth Medical School studying to be a doctor. Could any of us have done something like that?

Nancy sends her love and again best wishes from both of us.

Sincerely,

Ron

Mr. John Otis Corney
Cora, Wyoming

WASHINGTON

September 26, 1985

Dear Paul:

I know I'm kind of late in answering your letter, but it takes a while before mail gets to my desk. I'm glad you wrote. I've heard the same things that Irish teacher said from some here in our country who always seem to blame America first and for any and every thing. Well, don't you believe him.

First, on the economic side, we've had the greatest and fastest recovery from recession over the past three years that we've ever had. In the last 33 months we've created more than 8 million new jobs. We have more people employed than ever before. It's true that since 1979 we've lost 1,600,000 manufacturing jobs. But we've added more than 9,000,000 new jobs in service industries and transportation alone. Just since 1982 some 2,000,000 new businesses have been started in our country.

As for government spending, yes, that's been out of line for 50 years and we must reduce our deficit, but we're on the way to doing that. Our European friends haven't added one new job in more than 10 years. We're trying to help them out of the recession they are still having with an unemployment rate that is two or three times the size of ours. In my last meeting with the leaders of those nations they called what we are doing "the American miracle," and they asked me to tell them how we did it.

As for the military situation, he was as far wrong as he was on the economy. It's true that when our Administration started in 1981 our military had been allowed to slide downhill very badly. Today we are in better shape than we've been since World War II. Our new weapons systems are superior to just about anything in the world. Our Navy is being restored with new aircraft carriers and the Trident submarine; airplanes, tanks, weapons of every kind are coming on line and our readiness has never been better. It's true the Soviets have more tanks and artillery and more men in uniform, but remember they have to face not only the U.S. but all our allies—West Germany, England, France, Italy and so on.

You are right that ours is the greatest nation in the world. You young people are going to have things we never dreamed of just as we had it better than our parents before us. So stick to your dream. I wish you well in your plan to sign on for military aviation.

Best regards,

Ronald Reagan

Mr. Paul E. Bulman, Jr.
Scituate, Massachusetts

September 26, 1985

Dear Marjorie:

Thanks to Katherine I have your reproduction of the 1926 *Dixonian*. Please thank her for me and bless you for making it all possible. I've had a few days of warm nostalgia and happy memories. There will be more for I still have it on my desk so I can sneak another look every once in a while.

Speaking of memories, I have one that has to do with Franklin Grove. When I was drum major of the YMCA boys band we were asked to lead the Decoration Day parade in Franklin Grove. The parade marshall on a big white horse rode back down the parade at one point which left me out in front. No one had told me the parade route so I kept on marching. He rode back up the line just in time to have the band turn a corner. I was left marching up the street all by myself. I didn't look around until the music began to sound faint and far away. Then I cut across backyards and got back in front again.

Well, thanks again and best regards.

Sincerely,

Dutch

(Ronald Reagan)

Mrs. Marjorie Cushing Bidwell
Franklin Grove, Illinois

September 26, 1985

Dear Virginia:

Thank you for your letter of August 8 and forgive me for being so late in answering but your letter has only just reached me.

Believe me, I understand your frustration; in fact, I was pretty upset with all those "anniversary" programs about Hiroshima. You are right about horrors perpetrated by our enemies in World War II. In fact, the Japanese killed more people—innocent civilians—in the occupation of Nanking, China, than the atom bombs killed in Hiroshima and Nagasaki together.

I know there are some films that have been shown about Pearl Harbor, but I have some concerns about documentaries that might build up a hatred in our young people toward the Japanese people. For virtually the first time in history, we have buried our hatred and now find Japan and West Germany our firmest friends and allies. We must remember that most of the people in those countries weren't born or were mere babies when that war took place. Would it be right to impose the sins of their fathers and grandfathers on them?

Would it not be better if our own media refrained from bashing us for what we did in the war and spent more time telling how we helped rebuild the countries that were once our enemies?

Again, let me say I know how you feel and have wrestled with my own anger.

Thanks again and best regards.

Sincerely,

Ronald Reagan

Miss Virginia Sica
Akron, Ohio

September 26, 1985

Dear Mike and Maureen:

Say—writing the above struck a familiar note. I addressed letters to my first two children that way many years ago—Mike and Maureen.

Thanks for your good wishes and your prayers. I feel great. The doctors have just given me a rating of a "100% complete recovery." And thanks for your generous words about our relations with Japan and the Pacific Basin countries. I truly believe they are the wave of the future. I value highly my friendship with Yasu [Yasuhiro Nakasone, Japanese Prime Minister] and will do all in my power to see it continues. Of course, I'm most happy to have help in that from a fine Ambassador.

Nancy sends her best to you both as do I.

Sincerely,

Ron

Ambassador Mike Mansfield
APO San Francisco, California

September 27, 1985

Dear Mrs. Schoper:

Thank you for writing as you did. Perhaps I'm more understanding of your kind of farmer than you know. I started life in a small village in Illinois. It was a farm community existing to serve the needs of farmers. On Saturday the streets would be full of teams and wagons as the farmers from the surrounding countryside came to town to buy and sell. We in town were visitors, especially at threshing time, to our farmer friends. In my family's case, our farm friends would pick us up in town because we couldn't afford any kind of transportation—horse-and-buggy or Model T.

Please, Mrs. Schoper, don't say your America is dying. Most Americans are still ready to lend a hand to a neighbor who needs help. Some 65 million Americans give time to volunteer causes just as you do.

Yes, we give away surplus cheese, just as the government has welfare programs. But I've been trying to get government to help hard-working Americans like you and your family. We've brought inflation down from 13% to 2.5% for the last four months. Interest rates are less than half what they were five years ago, and now I'm asking for a tax reform that will reduce your income tax sizeably. Most importantly of all, we are trying to restore the economy so there will be a market for the things farmers produce. We have created 8 million new jobs in the last 33 months.

Bless you, I know you aren't out for a free ride. We just want you to have more opportunity and a fair return for your work. Our goal, too, is to continue reducing interest rates.

Sincerely,

Ronald Reagan

Mrs. JoAnn Schoper
Jeffers, Minnesota

WASHINGTON

September 27, 1985

Dear Ms. Roe:

I'm sorry to be so late in answering your letter but it has only just now made its way to my desk. . . .

Like you, I was disturbed by the one-sided editorializing that was carried on during the 40th anniversary of Hiroshima. I've become more and more conscious of an element in our land, of people I call the "blame America first" crowd.

We have every right to stand tall. Our country is unique in all the world. A former Prime Minister of Australia said some years back, "I wonder if anybody has thought what the situation of the comparatively small nations would be if there were not in existence the United States—if there were not this giant country prepared to make so many sacrifices."

In the days following World War II, Pope Pius XII said, "The American people have a great genius for splendid and unselfish acts. Into the hands of America God has placed the destinies of an afflicted mankind."

We have kept our rendezvous with destiny. Thank you again.

Sincerely,

Ronald Reagan

Ms. L. Dianne Roe
Gales Ferry, Connecticut

October 28, 1985

Dear Ruddy:

Well, it was good to hear from you and I'm glad school is going so well and that you like your teacher. Good luck with the Karate lessons.

I ride on weekends up at Camp David. I tried Rock Creek Park once but so many Secret Service Agents had to go along and the concern about security was so great it didn't seem worth it. I'll just keep on doing it at Camp David and, of course, I'll be there this Thanksgiving for a few days and riding every day.

You asked about the Presidential Seal. It remains the same for each President but can only be used as the seal for whoever is President and while he is holding that office.

I've met the photographer Ansel Adams. He does specialize in scenic photos and has covered many if not all of our National Parks.

It was good to see you in the Rose Garden. I hope the pamphlet on the Royal coat-of-arms gave you the information you wanted. I had it on my desk to be sent with this letter, but when I saw you out there, I hadn't finished this letter, so I figured I'd hand it to you.

My best wishes to your folks.

Your Pen Pal,

Ronald Reagan

Ruddy Hines
Washington, D.C.

George Montgomery arrived in Hollywood several years ahead of Reagan and achieved fame in western films before joining the Army Air Corps in World War II. A talented artist, he made bronze sculptures of Reagan and several other movie stars.

WASHINGTON

November 12, 1985

Dear George:

Thank you for your letter and for the photos. Sculpturing has always been an unknown art to me, and now I have some inkling of how it's done and I find it fascinating.

You are right about the Russian people and how little they will be allowed to know. I have just received the Izvestia interview I did with four reporters. The parts of my answers they omitted did, in many instances, actually change the meaning of what I had said.

Nevertheless, I'm looking forward to the meeting [at the Geneva Summit with Mikhail Gorbachev] and continue to hope that maybe we can reduce some of the distrust between us.

Nancy sends her best and, again, thank you.

Sincerely,

Ron

Mr. George Montgomery
Los Angeles, California

November 25, 1985

Dear Elsa:

Thank you very much for your Thanksgiving greeting and your warm letter. You were more than kind and I'm deeply grateful for your generous words.

I think I was aware of all the prayers in my behalf, particularly when I was alone with Mr. Gorbachev.* Strangely enough, in those meetings he twice invoked God's name. I think in our next meeting I may question him on that subject. My only reservation is the need to talk through an interpreter. It's not exactly like being alone.

Congratulations on your new assignment with the California Federation. They made a wise choice.

Nancy sends her love as do I.

Sincerely,

Ronald Reagan

Mrs. Elsa Sandstrom
La Jolla, California

* Geneva Summit with Mikhail Gorbachev, November 19–21.

November 25, 1985

Dear Murph:

Well we're home at last and I must tell you that sitting at the table in Geneva was a lot like those old days across the table from the Studio heads in Hollywood. Turns out that was pretty good training.

We didn't go there concession minded and we stayed that way. Murph, I have to say George Shultz has quietly done some housecleaning without conducting a purge. Our team was solid as a rock and no one was trying to budge me out of my stubborn tracks. As a matter of fact they were urging me on. I'm sure some of those other elements are still in the woodwork waiting for us to go away but all in all the level I'm dealing with seems pretty solid. Incidentally, that press stuff about a feud is just their same old witchhunting. Cap's man, [Richard] Perle, was one of our team in Geneva. Now don't worry that I've lost my bearings, I can still spot those other types and I'm always watching for them. . . .

I've been keeping in touch with our old friend Roy Brewer, and he comes up with some darn good information. Some of the old names like Gus Hall are still mounting the rostrum in California.

Please give Bette our best, Nancy sends her love.

Sincerely,

Ron

The Honorable George Murphy
Palm Beach, Florida

This top-secret letter to Mikhail Gorbachev was declassified in October 1991.

November 28, 1985

Dear Secretary General Gorbachev:

Now that we are both home and facing the task of leading our countries into a more constructive relationship with each other, I wanted to waste no time in giving you some of my initial thoughts on our meetings. Though I will be sending shortly, in a more formal and official manner, a more detailed commentary on our discussions, there are some things I would like to convey very personally and privately.

First, I want you to know that I found our meetings of great value. We had agreed to speak frankly, and we did. As a result, I came away from the meeting with a better understanding of your attitudes. I hope you also understand mine a little better. Obviously there are many things on which we disagree, and disagree very fundamentally. But if I understand you correctly, you too are determined to take steps to see that our nations manage their relations in a peaceful fashion. If this is the case, then this is one point on which we are in total agreement—and it is after all the most fundamental one of all.

As for our substantive differences, let me offer some thoughts on two of the key ones.

Regarding strategic defense and it's [*sic*] relation to the reduction of offensive nuclear weapons, I was struck by your conviction that the American program is somehow designed to secure a strategic advantage—even to permit a first-strike capability. I also noted your concern that research and testing in this area could be a cover for developing and placing offensive weapons in space.

As I told you, neither of these concerns is warranted. But I can understand, as you explained so eloquently, that these are matters which cannot be taken on faith. Both of us must cope with what the other side is doing, and judge the implications for the security of his own country. I do not ask you to take my assurances on faith.

However, the truth is that the United States has no intention of using it's [*sic*] strategic defense program to gain any advantage and there is no development underway to create space-based offensive weapons. Our goal is to eliminate any possibility of a first strike from either side. This being the case, we should be able to find a way, in practical terms, to relieve the concerns you have expressed.

For example, could our negotiators, when they resume work in January, discuss frankly and specifically what sort of future developments each of us would find threatening? Neither of us, it seems, wants to see offensive weapons, particularly weapons of mass destruction, deployed in space. Should we not attempt to define what sort of systems have that potential and then try to find verifiable ways to prevent their development?

And can't our negotiators deal more frankly and openly with the question of how to eliminate a first-strike potential on both sides? Your military now has an advantage in this area—a three to one advantage in warheads that can destroy hardened targets with little warning. That is obviously alarming to us, and explains many of the efforts we are making in our modernization program. You may feel perhaps that the U.S. has some advantages in other categories. If so, let's insist that our negotiators face up to these issues and find a way to improve the security of both countries by agreeing on appropriately balanced reductions. If you are as sincere as I am in not seeking to secure or preserve one-sided advantages, we will find a solution to these problems.

Regarding another key issue we discussed, that of regional conflicts, I can assure you that the United States does not believe that the Soviet Union is the cause of all the world's ills. We do believe, however, that your country has exploited and worsened local tensions and conflict by militarizing them and, indeed, intervening directly and indirectly in struggles arising out of local causes. While we both will doubtless continue to support our friends, we must find a way to do so without use of armed force. This is the crux of the point I tried to make.

One of the most significant steps in lowering tension in the world—and tension in U.S.–Soviet relations—would be a decision on your part to withdraw your forces from Afghanistan. I gave careful attention to your comments on this issue at Geneva, and am encouraged by your statement that you feel political reconciliation is possible. I want you to know that I am prepared to cooperate in any reasonable way to facilitate such a withdrawal, and that I understand that it must be done in a manner which does not damage Soviet security interests. During our meetings I mentioned one idea which I thought might be helpful and I will welcome any further suggestions you may have.

These are only two of the key issues on our current agenda. I will soon send some thoughts on others. I believe that we should act promptly to build the momentum our meetings initiated.

In Geneva I found our private sessions particularly useful. Both of us have advisors and assistants, but, you know, in the final analysis, the responsibility to preserve peace and increase cooperation is ours. Our people look to us for leadership, and nobody can provide it if we don't. But we wont [*sic*] be very effective leaders unless we can rise above the specific but secondary concerns that preoccupy our respective bureaucracies and give our governments a strong push in the right direction.

So, what I want to say finally is that we should make the most of the time before we meet again to find some specific and significant steps that would give meaning to our commitment to peace and arms reduction. Why not set a goal—privately, first between the two of us—to find a practical way to solve critical issues—the two I have mentioned—by the time we meet in Washington?

Please convey regards from Nancy and me to Mrs. Gorbachev. We genuinely enjoyed meeting you in Geneva and are already looking forward to showing you something of our country next year.

Sincerely yours,

Ronald Reagan

Jo Regan's husband, Phil, began his movie and radio career in Hollywood in 1934 with Warner Brothers and starred in musicals for two decades. As a public relations counselor, he campaigned for Reagan in the California governor's race.

December 10, 1985

Dear Jo:

Thank you very much for your very nice letter and generous words. I'm most grateful.

I know what you mean about the press, although our gang here insists that on State of the Union addresses and that sort of thing they only hand out in advance a few hints to help build audience for the speech. One thing though, for sure, is the press insists after my speech on telling the people their version of what I said, which often doesn't match with my remarks. The TV fellows are the worst. I finish a speech, then turn on the set and hear them telling the people who just listened to me what I said. I don't think they'll ever change.

Tell Phil I have a multiple vitamin called Multicebrin every morning with breakfast and a vitamin C capsule. Nancy's father, who was a surgeon, started us on this habit some years ago.

Nancy sends her love to you both and so do I.

Sincerely,

Ron

Mrs. Phil Regan
Pasadena, California

December 19, 1985

Dear Barney and Vada:

Thank you for your letter and "wreath" of holiday greetings. Nancy and I hope the holiday season is all you want it to be.

Russia again! I can't keep up with your travels. Let me tell you how the movie bit came up at the Summit. I had suggested to the General Secretary that we leave one of the plenary sessions and walk down to the lakeshore where there was a pool house complete with roaring fire. We were there for about an hour and a half for a one-on-one discussion. On the way down I told him to tell [Georgiy] Arbatov all my pictures weren't B's. Arbatov had made a statement to the press and TV that I was just a B movie actor. The General Secretary told me he had seen one of my pictures. He didn't remember the name but said I'd had my legs cut off. I told him it was "King's Row" and he said "yes, that was it."

Shortly thereafter I invited him to come to the United States next year and he accepted. Then he invited me to Moscow in 1987 and I accepted. Our people couldn't believe it had been that easy. They thought future visits would take long, hard negotiations.

Well, knowing the post office, I'll say I hope you *had* a Merry Christmas and Nancy does, too.

Sincerely,

Ron

Col. and Mrs. Barney Oldfield
Beverly Hills, California

December 19, 1985

Dear Murph:

Thanks for your good letter and that most generous review of my performance in Geneva. I must say I enjoyed playing the part and the show
did have something of a happy ending. Maybe I should say—"tune in next
year for the second installment."

Seriously, it was worthwhile but it would be foolish to believe the leopard
will change its spots. He is a firm believer in their system (so is she), and
he believes the propaganda they peddle about us. At the same time, he is
practical and knows his economy is a basket case. I think our job is to
show him he and they will be better off if we make some practical agreements, without attempting to convert him to our way of thinking.

I've turned the information on . . . over to Jim Baker at Treasury. I'm sure
he'll look into it. One thing I know about myself, having this job hasn't
weakened my prejudice about the I.R.S.

You and your roommate have a Merry Christmas and a Happy New Year.
Me and my roommate send you both our love.

Sincerely,

Ron

The Honorable George Murphy
Palm Beach, Florida

December 24, 1985

Dear Miss Sam and Miss Bertha:

Thank you for our gift—the splendid (as always) leather engraving and most important, those wonderful quotes. They will be a valuable source for me in future speeches but also just to refer to for my own good feeling.

I've enclosed the Charlton Heston remarks, autographed by me as you requested. As for the baseball story there was no script on that, I ad-libbed. So enclosed is a handwritten account to Buzzy.

Again, my thanks.

Sincerely,

Ronald Reagan

Misses Sam and Bertha Sisco
Healdsburg, California

[December 24, 1985]

Dear Buzzy:

Many years ago I was a radio sports announcer and used to broadcast by telegraphic report big league baseball games.

I would sit at a microphone in the studio and on the other side of a glass window a telegraph operator would receive from the ball park in Morse code each play of the game. He would type the message as it came in and slip it under the window to me. For example his note to me would say— s one c. That meant the pitcher had thrown a called strike to the batter and I would describe it as if I were at the game seeing it happen.

Well I was doing a game between the Chicago Cubs and the St. Louis Cardinals. The score was tied, nothing to nothing in the 9th inning. A Cub player Billy Jurges was at bat. I saw my operator begin to type so I had the pitcher wind up and start his throw to the plate. Just then I was handed the slip of paper and it said: "the wire has gone dead." I had a ball on the way to the plate. The only thing I could think of that wouldn't get in the records was a foul ball so I had Jurges foul one down back of 3rd base.

My operator first shrugged and indicated he was getting no message from the ball park. There were several other stations broadcasting that game and I knew I'd lose my audience if I told them we'd lost our telegraph connection so I took a chance. I had Jurges hit another foul. Then I had him foul one that only missed being a home run by a foot. I had him foul one back in the stand and took up some time describing the two lads who got in a fight over the ball.

I kept on having him hit foul balls until I was setting a record for a ball player hitting successive foul balls and I was getting more than a little scared. Just then my operator started typing. When he passed me the paper I started to giggle—it said "Jurges popped out on the 1st ball pitched."

I've waited a long time to tell that story. And didn't tell it until after I was no longer a sports announcer.

All the very best to you, Buzzy. Give Miss Sam and Miss Bertha my very best regards.

Sincerely,

Ronald Reagan

Buzzy Sisco
Healdsburg, California

1986

—

D—n it, yes, we sold them a few spare parts and
weapons but the stake was a contact that could give us
a chance at a relationship with Iran, and we were
succeeding. A plus on the side was returning three
hostages & [it] could have been five if the media hadn't
blown our cover.

·*Letter of November 24, 1986*·

THE space shuttle *Challenger* explosion on January 28 stunned the nation, especially millions of television viewers. The seven-crew members included Christa McAuliffe, a high school teacher chosen from thousands of applicants for the space voyage. President Reagan joined other citizens in calling the crew members "heroes" in a Houston ceremony three days later.

International terrorism supported by Colonel Muammar Qaddafi triggered American trade and other commercial sanctions against Libya during the first month of the new year. On April 15 Air Force bombers flying from England struck military bases near Tripoli and Navy aircraft from the *Coral Sea* and *America* bombed other bases near Benghazi. In a national television address, Reagan explained that Libyan agents were responsible for the disco bombing in West Berlin several weeks earlier. Bipartisan supporters applauded the President's determination to destroy terrorist sanctuaries wherever they may be located.

U.S. relations with the Soviet Union continued to be prominent in the President's answers to those who wrote him at the White House. The missile shield known as the Strategic Defense Initiative (by its supporters) or Star Wars (by others), grain sales, Soviet labor camps, and spy exchanges were 1986 topics. Reagan's brief summit meeting with Mikhail Gorbachev, who suggested they meet in Iceland in mid-October, collapsed as the Soviet leader insisted that the United States place a ten-year moratorium on testing the Strategic Defense Initiative. Reagan went to Reykjavik, Iceland, having learned enough Russian to say to Gorbachev in Russian "Trust but verify." To Gorbachev's irritation, he would repeat this phrase in many of their subsequent meetings in the Soviet Union and America on arms control.

The President's ongoing crusade to eliminate Soviet and Cuban power in Central America continued as Reagan sought $100 million in assistance from Congress for the Contras in Nicaragua. Before March ended, the House rejected this military aid package. However, in late June it voted $70 million in military aid and $30 million in civilian assistance. Congressional members read Reagan's high popularity rating and finally supported his appeals for assistance despite the opposition of Massachusetts congressman House Speaker Tip O'Neill.

Violence in the Middle East continued to be a major presidential frustration, verging on despair. The freeing of seven American hostages, including William Buckley, a CIA officer in Beirut who had been seized by Iranian-sponsored Hezbollah terrorists, became one of Reagan's secret objectives in the months after his recovery from colon surgery in July 1985. Hopeful that moderate Iranian agents, known by the Israelis, would negotiate with the kidnappers if the agents received antitank arms and other missiles, Reagan gave approval for the weapons transfer plan designed by National Security Advisor Robert McFarlane. Iran, engaged in a brutal war with Iraq, needed weapons desperately. In August 1985 the first transfer of missiles from Israeli supplies (which would be replenished by the United States) was made; in September there was a second shipment, and one hostage, the Reverend Benjamin Weir, was freed. A third sale followed in November. The Americans had not known at the time they requested the September freeing of William Buckley that he had died in captivity three months earlier; and the terrorists substituted Weir for Buckley.

In early December a fourth arms transfer was discussed in the White House by Reagan and National Security Advisor John Poindexter, Chief of Staff Don Regan, cabinet officers Casper Weinberger and George Shultz, and CIA Deputy Director John McMahon. Weinberger, Shultz, McMahon, and Regan questioned and finally opposed another sale. However, anxious to secure the release of the hostages, and not seeing the arms sales as trading arms for hostages but rather having a sympathetic intermediary deal with the kidnappers, Reagan, with support from Central Intelligence Agency Director William Casey, gave formal approval in January for another transfer of defensive arms. Once again the President hoped it would bring about the release of the five remaining hostages.

In February, May, and October 1986 several thousand TOW [tube-launched, optically tracked, wire-guided] antitank missiles and some spare parts for HAWK [Homing All-the-Way Killer] antiaircraft missiles would be sold via the CIA to Iran. Apparently in a scheme devised by Colonel Oliver North, some of the money from inflating the price of the arms shipment would be diverted to the Contras in Nicaragua. In July Father Lawrence Jenco was taken from Beirut, Lebanon, to Damascus, Syria, and freed by the Hezbollah terrorists; however, in August two more and in October one more American were kidnapped. As Shultz and Weinberger had feared, the Hezbollah continued to kidnap more Americans, and the tradeoff failed. Amazingly, in the last days of October, another missile shipment to Iran from Israeli suppliers took place. On November 3 David Jacobsen was freed. Although three hostages were liberated, only two were freed as a result of the arms transfer to Iran. No more would be freed during Reagan's presidency.

On November 3 *Al-Shiraa,* a Lebanese magazine, broke a story on the secret American missions to Iran, and three days later the American media began publishing details. In the weeks and months that followed, independent counsel Lawrence Walsh, a board headed by John Tower, and select committees of the House and Senate investigated the Iran-Contra affair. Their exhaustive research and reporting revealed the complex, at times bizarre, negotiations and results. The President, convinced he had done the right thing, was angry with the media and dismayed at the congressional and public condemnation of the various schemes to free the hostages. The affair was a personally and politically painful episode in Reagan's presidential career, second only to the Bitburg furor.

Shortly before his 75th birthday, President Reagan wrote out these answers to questions sent to him by syndicated White House and State Department correspondent Trude B. Feldman regarding his childhood and adult life.

[January 28, 1986]

1. *Does your brother still treat you like a BABY brother?*
    No, and any tendency towards that disappeared a long time ago. As we both grew older, the two-year difference in age seemed to shrink. Another thing that helped was my going to college first. After my first year, when he saw it could be done and enrolled as a freshman, our roles were sort of reversed.

2. *Did you grow closer over the years, and how so?*
    As the juvenile sibling rivalry disappeared, we did become closer.

3. *What are you named for? How did you happen to be named Ronald Wilson?*
    My first name would have been Donald but my aunt had my cousin first, so my mother settled for Ronald. Wilson was my mother's maiden name.

4. *Is that the name you were born with?*
    Yes. When I got in pictures the studio (Warner Bros.) routinely started to find a name for me. I reminded them I already had a pretty widely recognized name from my sports announcing. They said "Dutch Reagan!" with some sense of shock. I had used my nickname. I said—tentatively—my given name "Ronald" and they agreed to it.

5. *Would you recall the day of the week and the time and the name of the hospital you were born in? (your brother said he forgot . . .)*
    What a thing for him to forget. There wasn't a hospital in Tampico, Illinois. I was born at home—home was a flat above the local bank.

6. *What do you want for THIS birthday? Why?*
    I'd be happy if those who want to give me something would send the money to Eureka College—the small school that gave me my start.

7. *What are some of the myths of aging?*
   I don't know that I have an answer to that. Maybe it is the idea that at certain specific ages you are supposed to think of yourself as middle-aged or old. I've never done that or even thought about it.

8. *Something like: It's not how long you live . . . but HOW you live your life . . . and Ronald Reagan shows us HOW to live . . . it's not the quantity, but quality . . .*
   Quite sometime ago I attended an old school reunion. I was struck by the fact that I instantly recognized some old friends, yet others equally well known and remembered by me had to be named before I knew who they were. Later, I recalled that almost without exception the ones who still looked pretty much the same as when they were young were enthusiastic about what they were doing. The others hardly mentioned their work.

9. *Your brother recalled the gift that touched you the most—when, in your name, he bought clothing and food for a poor family in Hollywood . . . for Christmas BUT that doesn't fit in with the birthday theme . . . so do you have a SIMILAR anecdote . . . of a gift that most touched you, perhaps from your mother or father? or one birthday that was more outstanding than the other? Five years ago, after you moved here, there was a party in the East Room for you. Were you surprised at it, and/or WHAT do you most remember from your first birthday party in the White House? Why do you think people like you, trust you, have confidence in you?*
   That first birthday party in the White House was very enjoyable with virtually every friend present. But what I remember best is that Nancy kept it a complete secret. Even when a columnist said it was going to take place, I joked about the inaccuracy of the press. It was a total surprise.

10. *Did you ever celebrate a birthday in a foreign country? (If so, when and which country . . . ?)*
    Not that I can recall.

11. *Do you drink from a special fountain of youth? To what do you attribute your long and healthful life—and your vigor?*
    I don't know. Maybe the fact that I was totally wrapped up in athlet-

ics in my younger days. Going through school, I lifeguarded for seven summers, played football, ran the quarter mile in track and then, when school days ended, I discovered horses. There is an old saying that: "nothing is so good for the inside of a man as the outside of a horse."

12. *How old do you FEEL TODAY? How does age affect you? How have you aged on the job?*
I have a philosophy—getting old is always fifteen years from where you are now.

13. *IF you could live your life again what would you do differently? (personally, professionally)*
On the whole, I've enjoyed my life as it is. Even when there were setbacks, I recalled my mother saying—"everything happens for a reason and for the best. If you accept what seems a disappointment at the time, there will come a day when you'll look back and see that if it hadn't happened, some of the good things that followed wouldn't have happened."

14. *As you reach 75, how has your thinking and attitudes changed?*
Well, I have to believe I've matured some. As the Bible says—"When I was a child, I spoke as a child, and did childish things. When I became a man I put aside childish ways."

15. *Did you ever go through a mid-life crisis? Have you changed over the years in a significant way?*
How could I? I haven't reached mid-life yet.

16. *Have your values changed? How?*
I have a greater appreciation of things I might have taken for granted.

What have your close friends added to your life?
I treasure friends. As the poem says: "Age is measured by the number of friends not the number of years."

Have you always had good health habits? Ever smoke?
I've already spoken of health habits. I did smoke a pipe for a time but only occasionally, never inhaled, never smoked when I was in training

for football, track or swimming. Then, a long time ago, I gave it up entirely.

Have you always been realistic about using your time wisely?
I don't know whether I've always used my time wisely. Sometimes I think time I wasted was, in retrospect, the best times of all.

WASHINGTON

February 10, 1986

Dear Joe:

It was good to get your letter. Yes, I have written and have personally met the families of our lost heroes.*

I've looked into the matter you suggested about future appointments to the military academies and find that only in the case of the children of either active duty or retired military personnel does the President have the power to nominate. Since I won't be President when the children of the CHALLENGER astronauts come of age, all I can do is request that a future President consider appointing them if they desire to attend one of the academies. I am prohibited by law from requesting appointments for the children of McNair, McAuliffe or Jarvis because they were not military. Rest assured yours was a fine suggestion, and I'll do all I can for all the families.

You were right about this tragedy and its impact on the nation. I'm very much aware of a close, family kind of feeling among all Americans.

Nancy sends her best and give our regards to Dorothea.

Sincerely,

Dutch

Mr. S. Joseph Penberthy, Jr.
Farmington, Michigan

* *Challenger* crew members.

February 10, 1986

Dear Mrs. Massie:

Thank you very much for your warm letter, your good wishes and your generous words. I was pleased to hear your views on the summit and the "man in the [Russian] street" reaction.

I'm not going to let myself get euphoric but, still, I have a feeling we might be at a point of beginning. There did seem to be something of a chemistry between the General Secretary and myself. Certainly it was different from talking to Gromyko. Incidentally, twice in our private conversation he invoked the name of God and once cited a Bible verse. This has stuck in my mind and stays a nagging question that won't go away. I hope nothing comes up to interfere with our next meeting, which I hope will be in June.

Again, my thanks and very best wishes.

Sincerely,

Ronald Reagan

Mrs. Suzanne Massie
New York, New York

February 25, 1986

Dear Mrs. Morgan:

It takes a while for mail to finally reach my desk, hence the lateness of my response to your letter of January 8.

I share your feeling about the need for our schools to instill patriotism in our children, but, regretfully, I must say a mandate by me or the Congress is not the answer. In our Federal system of government, where much authority is left to the States and local governments, education is one of the responsibilities left primarily to the community. This was done so that parents could have more of a say with regard to their children's schooling. We've had some instances in recent years where the Federal government has invaded the public school system with programs and excessive regulations, and I have opposed this and sought to preserve autonomy at the local level.

Mrs. Morgan, as I said before, I share your feeling about the Pledge of Allegiance and the National Anthem having a place in our schools. May I suggest you talk to some of the other parents to see if they won't join you in going to either the school officials or, probably better yet, the local school board. That really is where this matter should be resolved. I hope you'll try this, and I wish you well.

Nancy thanks you for your kind words and sends her regards to Joey, as do I.

Sincerely,

Ronald Reagan

Mrs. Mary Morgan
Lexington, Kentucky

February 25, 1986

Dear Charlie:

Thanks for your letter and the enclosed correspondence re the IRA. Your reply to Mr. Hawksley-Cooke* was right on. We know there are some of Irish heritage who contribute to the terrorists in Northern Ireland, but they are more than matched by those who preach the opposite. The Irish Ambassador, as well as quite a few of our citizens, including many from Boston—such as speaker Tip O'Neill—take to the speaking circuit to plead for no contributions.

Love to Carole.

Sincerely,

Ron

The Honorable Charles H. Price II
American Ambassador
London

* Hawksley-Cooke had written to Charles Price criticizing the support U.S. citizens were giving to the Irish Republican Army.

March 10, 1986

Dear Mr. Robinson:

I'm sorry to be so late in responding to your letter of January 3rd, but I have only just received it. It does take a while before letters can make it through the bureaucratic process and to my desk.

With regard to your concern over a possible four billion dollar handout to Mexico at the same time 80,000 of our farmers were being notified of foreclosure, I'm afraid the press was a little less than accurate. The matter of credits to help some of the debtor nations has to do with our participation, along with our trading partners, in international programs such as the World Bank and the International Monetary Fund. It is not a handout by our country.

As for the 80,000 foreclosure notices—so called—that, too, is a little more complicated than the oversimplification in the media. During my terms here in Washington, financial aid to farmers is and has been at a higher level than anytime in our history. The Department of Agriculture did send 65,000 letters—not 80,000—to farmers who were delinquent in their payments to creditors. With those letters went information as to where and how they could seek further help to renegotiate their debt. Foreclosure will be contemplated only in those cases where a farmer has not made a payment in three or more years. Even in these extreme cases, we will find a way to help most of these farmers continue farming.

Thank you for writing and expressing your concern and for giving me an opportunity to explain.

Sincerely,

Ronald Reagan

Mr. Robert M. Robinson
Elma, Washington

Henry Salvatori chaired Barry Goldwater's presidential campaign in California and Reagan's campaigns for governor and president.

March 17, 1986

Dear Henry:

Thanks for sending the editorial. I hadn't seen it and it sure brightened my weekend. Thanks, too, for your generous words.

I've been meeting with Congressmen and Senators both Republican and Democratic trying to get them to see why we have to send help to the Contras. I really don't know where we stand as of now but I'm saying a prayer. I can't understand the reluctant ones, the issue is so clear-cut.

Nancy sends her love and from both of us to Gracie.

Sincerely,

Ron

Mr. Henry Salvatori
Los Angeles, California

March 17, 1986

Dear Bess and Moon:

. . . I wonder if your Navy friend knows of a little social incident involving San Diego Naval Forces some years ago? It seems the fly-boys invited the submariners to come over and see how things were done in the air. They got them off the ground and, then, indulged in a lot of acrobatics that brought them down a little airsick and more than a little scared.

Sometime later the submariners returned the courtesy and invited the fly-boys over to see what things were like under water. They went into a dive and, then, red lights started flashing, bells were ringing and men were running around turning valves, etc. The subcommander told the fly-boys they couldn't get the sub out of the dive, and they were fast approaching the depth limit beyond which the sub would be crushed by the pressure.

About the time the dial registered them as having gone too far, a sailor climbed the ladder into the conning tower and opened the hatch. They had never untied from the dock.

Nancy sends her love—so do I.

Sincerely,

Dutch

Mr. J. Neil Reagan
Rancho Santa Fe, California

President Reagan wrote out these comments for Time *magazine regarding his opening-day appearance at the Orioles baseball game.*

[April 1986]

1. *How did the President feel being at the ballgame? What did he enjoy most about it?*
   Well, as someone who used to make a living broadcasting (on radio) major league baseball, going to a game and being sort of backstage; in the dugout instead of the grandstand, it's a happy experience. It's hard to pin down one single thing as more enjoyable than another. I was glad to find out I could still throw a strike even if it took two tries. (I still claim my first throw was high because I was afraid I'd hit some of the photographers who had ganged up around the catcher.)

2. *Does he feel he was bad luck for the Orioles?*
   You can't be around the sports world without sharing some of the superstitions that go with the game. For example, never talking about a no-hitter if the Pitcher seems to be on the way to one. Yes, I'm bothered by the fact that I've been to 4 opening games and all four times the Orioles have lost. I promised them that if I'm ever at another opening day I'll sit in the visitors dugout.

April 21, 1986

Dear Brute:

Bless you and thank you. Your column really tells the story, and I hope it does get to the people on the Hill. A number of them have bought the Sandinista disinformation line hook, line and sinker, and I'll bet only a few have ever looked at *The Grenada Papers* since the State Department published the book. Brute, if we had secretly come upon documents signed by people like Gromyko and Ogarkov—among others—and someone had leaked them they'd be on most of the front pages in America. But here are hundreds of documents we've willingly offered to the public and, as far as I know, only one journalist, a fellow named Krulak, has seen their importance and their worth.

God bless you.

Sincerely,

Ron

Lt. Gen. Victor H. Krulak, USMC (Ret.)
San Diego, California

April 22, 1986

Dear Rudolph:

I'm glad to hear about your Easter Break. Out in California we read and heard about the wonderful weather you were having. Ours was nice, but not quite as summery as what you were having back here.

We went to church on Easter at a little country church down in the valley. Then every day for the rest of the week we had a horseback ride, usually in the morning. In the afternoons we cleared some of the riding trails that had gotten overgrown. All in all, it was a good time and a nice change from the Oval Office.

The end of this week will see us on our way to the Island of Bali and Japan. On Bali, we'll have meetings with some of the leaders of Indonesia, Malaysia, Singapore, the Philippines and some other Asian governments. They are joined in an organization called ASEAN [Association of Southeast Asian Nations].

From there we'll go to Tokyo for the annual Economic Summit with the leaders of England, France, Italy, West Germany, Canada and Japan. It will be a busy time. We have a lot to talk about, including terrorism and what we can do about it. We'll be back in Washington May 7th. Since the time difference is 12 hours, I think we'll have a little trouble with jet lag.

Best regards,

Your Pen Pal,

Ronald Reagan

Rudolph Hines
Washington, D.C.

WASHINGTON

May 12, 1986

Dear Ruddy:

It was good to see you at the White House when we returned from Japan. That was quite a trip. We were in the plane, actually flying, a total of 38 hours and gone a total of 13 days. Two of the flights were over 14 hours each.

On the way out we stopped overnight in Los Angeles and two nights in Honolulu. This was to help us adjust to the time change which totaled 13 hours. While we were in Bali and Japan, it was daytime there when it was night in Washington. It does get you a little mixed up as to sleeping. You can change your clock, but you can't change that inner clock in each of us that tells us when to get sleepy.

You know there is a line known as the international date line out in the Pacific Ocean. It is where yesterday or tomorrow and today meet. For example, going to Bali we left Hawaii about 10:00 a.m. Monday morning and that afternoon as we crossed the date line it became Tuesday. Coming home from Tokyo, we left there at noon Wednesday, crossed the date line and arrived in Washington at two o'clock that same afternoon, although we'd been flying 14 hours with a one-hour stop in Alaska to refuel. We'd flown through the night and seen the sunrise, but it was still Wednesday. You can get a little confused.

The trip was worthwhile. On Bali we met with the President of Indonesia, a country of 165 million people on 13,600 islands spread over 3,000 miles of ocean. We also met with the foreign ministers of five other Asian countries.

All those countries are important trading partners of ours, and we had a lot to talk about. In Tokyo we met with heads of state of Japan, England, Germany, Italy, Canada and France. We are all allies and meet each year to discuss our mutual problems. I think it is wonderful that three of those countries now our good friends were our enemies in World War II.

Now all I have to do is get readjusted to sleeping on Washington time, which isn't easy.

Give my regards to your folks and all the best to you.

Sincerely,

Ronald Reagan

Rudolph Lee Hines
Washington, D.C.

May 22, 1986

Dear Mr. and Mrs. Van Cutsem:

Our mutual friend, Ambassador [Charles H.] Price, has forwarded your letter to me, and I want you to know how very much I appreciate your writing. You are more than kind.

I know there are people in both our countries [England and United States] who disapproved of the action we took in Tripoli, but I'm sure they lack understanding of what is at stake.*

I shall be forever grateful to your Prime Minister for her courage and for the bond of friendship between us and between our two countries. You have just eloquently expressed that friendship.

Thank you very much and God bless you.

Sincerely,

Ronald Reagan

Mr. and Mrs. Hugh van Cutsem
Suffolk, England

* On April 14 U.S. Navy and Air Force bombers struck Benghazi and Tripoli in Libya to retaliate for a West Berlin disco bombing where an American serviceman was killed.

Decades earlier, Reagan had welcomed numerous Western Station Wagon Tours to California. Composed of Michigan teenagers, these groups were directed by Chet Sampson. Nelle Reagan, at her son's request, served as go-between for Sampson and actor Reagan.

May 22, 1986

Dear Chet:

It was good to hear from you. Thanks for the jam and for all the Gipp mementos and for those letters of my mother's. You are very kind.

You wondered about Gipp and whether this might be a forgotten part of my past. Quite the contrary. He has remained very much a part of my life, indeed, playing him was the role that moved me into the star category. Curiously enough, at political rallies during my last campaign, there would always be signs out in the crowd referring to me as "The Gipper." And, believe me, I like that very much.

When you make that trip to Washington, let the girls know your schedule in advance and a meeting will be arranged. It will be good to see you.

Thanks again.

Sincerely,

Ron

Mr. Chet Sampson
Hollywood, California

May 28, 1986

Dear Ms. Mertens:

Thank you very much for your kind letter and the snapshots. I'm truly grateful. I had no idea there was such a marker or that those graves were there.*

My father was orphaned at six years of age so we know very little of his family except for an old photo of his mother and father. Now, since coming to this office, the Irish government has kindly provided a family tree. William and Thomas Reagan are great uncles and Michael is my great grandfather.

Could I impose upon you for another kindness? Could you give me the names of someone connected with the cemetery who could give me an estimate of what needs to be done? Your photos seem to show that the problem has to do with the rock base underneath the monument. If you write again, address your letter to me here at the White House and on the front of the envelope write "Attention Kathy Osborne." This will speed up delivery to me and avoid some bureaucratic processes.

Again, my heartfelt thanks.

Sincerely,

Ronald Reagan

Ms. Maxine Mertens
Keystone, Iowa

* William, Thomas, and Michael Reagan graves at the Fulton, Illinois, cemetery.

WASHINGTON

May 30, 1986

Dear Mr. Post:

Your letter of April 17 has finally reached me. It sometimes takes a while for mail to get to my desk and this was particularly true in light of my recent trip to Asia.

I appreciate your sending me the article on our expenditures in behalf of foreign countries [*New Haven Register*, October 31, 1971]. In the past, long before I ever thought I'd be doing what I'm doing now, I did a lot of public speaking. Frequently my subject was the waste and extravagance connected with foreign aid. I'm pleased to tell you we've taken steps in these last five years to eliminate waste and fraud with some success.

But I've studied very carefully the article you sent me and let me point out something having to do with the time period, 1946–1971. Back in 1946 [1948], you may recall, we created the Marshall Plan to help rebuild the war-ravaged nations, both friend and enemy. Just picking out the nations listed in the article helped by this plan accounts for more than half the total spending.

I don't think we can or should ignore the great benefit provided by that plan. Today three of our staunchest allies, West Germany, Italy and Japan were our enemies in World War II, and we've known 40 years of peace.

We continue to have a foreign aid program today. Its purpose is to help developing countries build an economic structure so as to reduce poverty and misery and resist the overtures of the Soviet Union which is bent on an expansionist policy in an effort to make the whole world into a single Communist state. Also much of that aid is to help those countries have a defense capability of their own which is less costly than if we had to provide that defense with our own forces.

But please be assured we continue to search for ways to eliminate unnecessary spending both at home and abroad.

Thanks again for your letter.

Sincerely,

Ronald Reagan

Mr. Edwin E. Post
East Haven, Connecticut

WASHINGTON

[June 1986]

Dear Peggy:

There are so many things I want to say. First is my heartfelt thanks to you for all you have done. It just won't seem the same to look for that "Noonan" on the top right-hand corner of the script and not find it there. It always meant I was going to like what I read.

I wish you well in your new undertaking, but you are going to be missed. Whenever I hear references to the "great communicator," I will think of all the fine work you did for me.

I appreciate your offer of help and will take some comfort from it. Again my thanks, very best wishes, and warmest regard.

Sincerely,

Ronald Reagan

The Honorable Margaret Noonan
Special Assistant to the President for Speechwriting
The White House
Washington, D.C.

Sammy Davis, Jr., an old friend of Reagan's, was deeply concerned about the plight of South African blacks.

June 24, 1986

Dear Sammy:

My friend, I have your wire and want you to know we are doing all we can about the tragic situation in South Africa but are as frustrated as you are with our lack of progress.

Sammy, it is a much more complex problem than it appears on the surface. The Botha regime is trying and has made a number of changes for the better. However, there is an opposition party in that government which opposes the things he has done and makes it difficult for him to attack the ultimate problem of apartheid. It's a little like our own situation where in the opposition party, a majority, in one house of Congress can throw roadblocks in our way.

Some of the things proposed here such as all-out sanctions and disinvestments by American firms in South Africa would hurt the very people we are trying to help and would leave us no contact with South Africa to try and bring influence to bear on their government.

The American-owned industries there employ more than 80,000 Blacks. And their employment practices are like they are here with no discrimination. An American Minister named Leon Sullivan, a Black himself, created an employment policy which the American employers adopted and which is very different from the normal South African customs. Sanctions such as the House of Representatives has passed would wind up eliminating thousands and thousands of jobs in the South African–owned mines and industries, and in addition would find us shooting ourselves in the foot. For example, chrome which is essential in our steel-making comes from South Africa. The only other source is the Soviet Union. I'm sure you can see what that would do to us. Not only would we be at the mercy of the Soviets, we would be helping a nation that violates human rights as much or more than any other. Incidentally, one of the products we buy from South Africa and which isn't available anywhere else is essential in the manufacture of the catalytic converters in our automobiles.

Now Sammy, I don't want you to read this as putting such things before the great moral issue involved in apartheid. Believe me, I see apartheid as an evil that must be eliminated. We must continue our efforts to bring this about. But we have a better chance of doing so if we maintain contact than if we pick up our marbles and walk away. You have my promise we won't let up.

Best regards.

Sincerely,

Ron

Mr. Sammy Davis, Jr.
Beverly Hills, California

July 2, 1986

Dear Nackey:

. . . What we are seeing in this Manion case is another lynching in which some Senators are trying to bring down a better man than themselves.* And, of course, as always, there are some deluded souls who believe the falsehoods of the lynchers and go along with the mob.

Nackey, our dog situation is one of youthful exuberance, on the part of the dogs—not us. We were well along in training Lucky before she took residence at the ranch, but, even so, she forgot her lessons when the helicopter (which meant Camp David) was on the lawn.

Now we're doing a repeat—in spades. Rex is still only a pup and, when the chopper comes in, he just tunes us out. I think he believes "MARINE I" is his personal dog basket.

You know there is always a crowd on the South Lawn, not just the press, both when we leave and when we return, and Rex does get excited with the clapping and waving, etc. I have a sneaking feeling he'll still be doing this when we take our final lift-off in January 1989. From then on he better quiet down, because there will be horses in his life.

Again, thanks for the clippings.

Sincerely,

Ron

Mrs. William Loeb
Manchester, New Hampshire

* On June 26 the Senate voted 48 to 46 to confirm the nomination of Daniel A. Manion as the United States Circuit Judge for the Seventh Circuit. Opposition to this vote by Democrats, led by Robert Byrd of Virginia, resulted in a motion to reconsider on July 23. This motion to reconsider was rejected by a vote of 49 to 49.

July 7, 1986

Dear François:

Just a line to say how good it was to see you here for Miss Liberty's birthday celebration and to hear that you, too, enjoyed the celebration. It was very kind and generous of you to make the trip, and I thank you on behalf of all Americans.

Now, may I impose on you further? One of our most prestigious religious figures, the world-renowned Reverend Billy Graham, is holding a crusade this September in Paris in the new Bercy Sports Stadium. We have been close friends for many years. Our Ambassador [Joseph M.] Rodgers will be speaking to you about a possible appointment with Reverend Graham while he is there. I would be most grateful if you could find time to see him. The Ambassador has all the information about dates, etc.

Now, and having nothing to do with the above request, I must share with you an item I just read on my way home in one of our prestigious magazines, the *Reader's Digest,* July issue, page 148. It says that British genealogists in 1984 traced my family back to a connection with Riagain, kin to the Irish king Brian Boru and this made me a cousin to, among others, President Francois Mitterrand. So our recent get-together was something of a family reunion.

All the best and I look forward to hearing from you following your trip to Moscow.

Sincerely,

Ron

His Excellency
François Mitterrand
President of France
Paris

July 14, 1986

Dear David:

There are no words to properly thank you for that magnificent birthday party.* You took a great city, a vast harbor, several islands and made them into a stage on which you produced a show for an entire nation. And an entire nation's heart was touched.

Even with my past experience in show business, I can't begin to comprehend the enormity of your effort. I only know it was beyond anything ever done before and will be remembered forever.

Nancy and I are humbly grateful for being allowed to participate. Thank you and God bless you.

Sincerely,

Ronald Reagan

Mr. David L. Wolper
Burbank, California

* The 100th birthday of the Statute of Liberty, an extravaganza produced by Wolper in New York City, July 3 to 6.

July 14, 1986

Dear Mr. Capen:

Thank you for sending me your column on drugs [July 6, 1986], and thank you for writing it. You and I are in agreement on the need for a concerted national effort. At the Federal level we've stepped up, as you know, our effort to limit the supply, and vastly increased our seizure of drugs. At the same time, we're aware the drug supply has increased at an even greater pace.

It's apparent that Nancy has been on the right track. We must concentrate on taking the customer away from the drugs. The other way won't solve the problem. We are studying now how a nationwide effort can be mobilized. Whatever we come up with, I know the news media will play an important role, and I'm happy to know of your own interest and concern.

Again, thanks.

Sincerely,

Ronald Reagan

Mr. Richard G. Capen, Jr.
The Miami Herald Publishing Company
Miami, Florida

July 17, 1986

Dear Judge McDevitt:

Thank you very much for writing as you did and telling me of the moment with your mother.* I'm happy that I played a part, even though it was by accident.

I understand your situation because in my mother's latter years in a nursing home she no longer recognized me or my brother. Sometimes she would tell me incidents about her son Ronald as if I were some new acquaintance. But, as I look back at those days, I wonder if this wasn't something of a God-given mercy. She was apparently content in that little world into which she had retired. She would have been miserable if she had retained all her faculties and awareness and yet been physically helpless and restrained, no longer able to do the things she so much enjoyed.

Again, my thanks to you for your kindness in writing.

Sincerely,

Ronald Reagan

The Honorable Leonard M. McDevitt
Folcroft, Pennsylvania

* The judge's elderly and forgetful mother, a nursing home resident, suddenly recognized the judge during Reagan's TV commencement address at Glassboro High School.

July 23, 1986

Dear Mrs. Asheraft:

I'm sorry you feel as you do, because I believe with all my heart that the unborn child is a living human being and abortion is murder. Yes, these years have gone by, and we haven't been able to get the necessary action to change the Constitution, which is the only way to reverse the Court opinion. There could be another way, of course, if a case were brought before the Court and the Court reversed its decision. As you know, in the last term of the Court, we filed a brief in a case involving this issue, but lost 5–4. But that's progress. The original Court vote was 7–2.

I assure you I'll keep trying, and I "Wave" to the pro-lifers because their effort to mobilize public opinion is most important to the cause.*

Sincerely,

Ronald Reagan

Mrs. Teresa Asheraft
Columbus, Texas

* The President waved to pro-life marchers who went to Washington, D.C., every January 22, the date of *Roe v. Wade* abortion ruling.

August 1, 1986

Dear Larry:

It was good to hear from you and, as always, you are right on target. This place—this Capital, leaks like a sieve. I don't know which is worse—the leak of a truth or the leak like the one you forwarded that is not based on fact. We will not allow SDI to become a bargaining chip. My own view is that we may be able to develop a defensive shield so effective that we can use it to rid the world once and for all of nuclear missiles. Then—since we all know how to make them, we preserve SDI, as we did our gas masks, in the event a madman comes along someday and secretly puts some together.

Larry, we haven't agreed to any artificial time restraints. We have a good idea of about how long research will take and are basing our proposals on that, since research is within the restraints of the ABM treaty. We'll make no unrealistic longtime agreements reaffirming or pledging to observe the treaty.

You know, those people who thought being an actor was no proper training for this job were way off base. Every day, I find myself thankful for those long days at the negotiating table with Harry Cohen, Freeman, the brothers Warner, et al.

Well, thanks again. Nancy sends her love and so do I.

Sincerely,

Ron

Mr. Laurence W. Beilenson
Los Angeles, California

Reagan's friend, John Howard, served with valor in World War II and was awarded two Silver Stars and two Purple Hearts. Later he became president of Rockford College before heading the Institute.

August 11, 1986

Dear John:

Bless you and thank you for your kind letter and generous words. I'm most grateful.

It behooves us all to counter the wave of feeling and lack of understanding about the South African situation. Of course, we are all opposed to apartheid and injustice, but causing economic hardship and unemployment for millions of Black workers is not the answer. I've just had a remarkable, statesman-like letter from [Mongosuthu Gatsha] Buthelezi, the leader of all the Zulus, the largest group among the Blacks of South Africa. He details what punitive sanctions would do to his people and the other tribes as well, and it's a very ugly picture.

Again, you were kind to write—thank you.

Sincerely,

Ronald Reagan

Dr. John A. Howard
President
The Rockford Institute

Alonzo Smith, Reagan's classmate at Eureka College, urged the President to meet with the presidents of Black colleges and universities in the United States during their Washington, D.C., conference and reception.

October 1, 1986

Dear Alonzo:

What a nice surprise to hear from you after all these years we've been away from "The Elms upon the Campus." We just had a fund-raising dinner for Eureka last week. Did you know that Coach Mac [Ralph McKinzie], now in his 90's, is still assisting the football coach at Eureka? He may outlast all of us.

I was pleased to be invited to meet with the Black College and University Presidents when they were here. Alonzo, I've been able to lend a hand to the Black College fund-raising group and share your feeling about those schools. When I first took office, I learned of a debt problem involving the government and Meharry Medical School that threatened to close the school down. We were able to take care of that situation. As you know, the Black medical college has graduated half or more of all the Black doctors in the country. Believe me, I share your feelings about those schools and will do all I can to see that they continue doing what they have been doing so well for all these years.

Thank you for writing. It was good to hear from you. If you are talking to Tubby Muller [Reagan's fraternity brother] again give him my best regards.

Sincerely,

(I'm supposed to sign letters Ronald Reagan)

I'll sign this one—Dutch

Mr. Alonzo L. Smith
Jefferson, Texas

October 3, 1986

Dear Mr. DiMarco:

Thank you for sending me your article on the Gipper. Some of the things you told were familiar to me and many of them I hadn't known. One question you asked and couldn't answer had to do with Gipp's dying request of Rockne to ask a Notre Dame team to win a game for him. I believe I have the answer. Rock's widow, Bonny Rockne, spent some time on the set while we were making the picture. She was asked that question and her answer was, "Yes, it was true and, word for word, was in Rock's diary." Incidentally, I didn't have to learn those particular lines. As a sports announcer for WHO radio station in Des Moines, Iowa, in the 1930's, I told that part of the Gipp story on one of my broadcasts. When I was put under contract at Warner Brothers in 1937 I almost immediately started talking to everyone who would listen about doing the life story of Rockne. Of course, I had one thought in mind—I would play George Gipp.

Well, thanks again, and all the best to you.

Sincerely,

Ronald Reagan

Mr. Tony DiMarco
Los Angeles, California

October 6, 1986

Dear Barney:

I haven't been there yet, but just having finished *Red Storm Rising* by the author [Tom Clancy] of *Red October*, I think I know every square foot of Iceland. If you haven't read it, it's worth the effort.

Here's my latest from the Soviet Union to reward you for the stories. It's night time, a soldier calls to a citizen walking by and orders him to halt. The citizen starts running, the soldier shoots him. Another citizen asks the soldier why he did that. The soldier replies, "curfew." "But it isn't curfew time yet," the citizen says. "I know," said the soldier, "but he's a friend of mine. I know where he lives. He couldn't have made it." I'm assured this is a story the Russians are telling each other.

Thanks again, and best to your lady.

Sincerely,

Ron

Colonel Barney Oldfield, USAF (Ret.)
Beverly Hills, California

October 16, 1986

Dear Larry:

It was good to get your letter and your confirmation regarding SDI. I wasn't aware that Sam Donaldson had said what he did about McFarlane, and I question whether Bud said such a thing.* Certainly he knew better.

Yes, I've quoted from your books on a number of occasions and will continue to do so because they make such good sense. When I finally decided to move on what has become SDI, I called a meeting of the Joint Chiefs of Staff. I said that, until nuclear weapons, there had never been an offensive weapon that hadn't inspired a defense—all the way back to the spear and the shield. Then I asked them if in their thinking it was possible to devise a weapon that could destroy missiles as they came out of their silos. They were unanimous in their belief that such a defensive system could be developed. I gave the go-ahead that very day. The scientists working on this have achieved several breakthroughs and are quite optimistic, although they say we have several years to go. I have never entertained a thought that SDI could be a bargaining chip. I did tell Gorbachev that if and when we had such a system they would join us in eliminating nuclear missiles; we'd share such a defense with them. I don't think he believes me.

Well, it was good to hear from you and thank you for the confirmation. Nancy sends her love.

Sincerely,

Ron

Mr. Laurence W. Beilenson
Los Angeles, California

* According to Reagan's correspondent, Sam Donaldson said on the air on October 12 that Bud McFarlane told Donaldson that he, McFarlane, gave the President the idea of using SDI as a "bargaining chip."

October 21, 1986

Dear Suzanne:

It was good to get your letter and your kind words. Your estimate of the Iceland affair is very reassuring.* You mentioned their ability to wait. I'm wondering if things won't be on hold until after our election and, possibly, even after the West German elections in January.

They created another little haggling point with their ousting of five of our people from the Embassy in Moscow and the Consulate in Leningrad. Well, we are going to respond in kind. They greatly outnumber us in their Embassy here and their San Francisco Consulate. We are going to reduce their majority shortly.

I've had quite an experience meeting with the Orlovs.† I had a phone conversation also with Dr. Goldfarb, but it wasn't very satisfactory. His voice was so weak I had trouble hearing him. I can only say I was aware he was thanking us and was happy to be here.

Nancy sends her best and, again, my thanks.

Sincerely,

Ronald Reagan

Mrs. Suzanne Massie
Cambridge, Massachusetts

* Reagan's meeting with Gorbachev in Reykjavik, Iceland, October 11 and 12.
† Yuri and his wife, Irina, both dissidents, emigrated to the United States as part of the exchange of Gennady Zakharov, a Soviet spy, for Nicholas Daniloff, Moscow correspondent for *U.S. News & World Report.* Geneticist Dr. David Goldfarb and his wife also emigrated; they had been trying to leave the Soviet Union for eight years.

October 21, 1986

Dear Nackey:

I'm glad your two letters and editorials arrived on my desk at the same time. I enjoyed the one dated October 14 more than the October 7 mailing. I do agree however that your suggestion in the earlier letter about the news media creating a false message is true and I'm grateful for your prayers.

The column by Jim Finnegan was appropriately titled—"Lies, Lies, Lies"—because that's what it was.*

Nackey, of course we wanted [Nicholas] Daniloff back.† But we told the Soviet Union, everything—their spy, their invitation to a meeting, etc.—was on hold until Daniloff was freed. When they did that we then told them we'd do what Presidents before me had done 3 times before in similar cases, exchange their guilty spy [Gennady Zakharov] for Soviet dissidents. Our choice was [Yuri] Orlov and his wife [Irina Valitova]. By pleading no contest their spy acknowledged his guilt and we were saved months of trial while the Orlovs remained victims of Soviet cruelty.

Mr. Finnegan was off base again when he declared we were reneging on the Soviet intelligence agents we were sending home from the U.N. All 25 are now back in Moscow. There was never a question but that we were kicking them out.

Thanks again for your prayers and good wishes.

Sincerely,

Ron

Mrs. William Loeb
Union Leader Corporation
Manchester, New Hampshire

* The Finnegan column stated that Reagan lied when he pledged early on that there would be no prisoner exchange for Daniloff.
† Daniloff, Moscow correspondent for the *U.S. News & World Report*, was accused of spying.

William Buckley's column, "Saved from the Brink," praised Reagan for his de-termined stand at Reykjavik and his leadership for the Strategic Defense Ini-tiative.

October 22, 1986

Dear Mr. Ambassador:

All the way from Kabul you brightened my day. Thank you for your gen-erous words and that includes the column also.

I'll wait till we can have a talk to relay all the details but it was quite a ten or eleven hour set-to—no plenary meetings, just the two of us plus [Ed-uard] Shevardnadze, [George] Shultz and interpreters. I even spoke Rus-sian to him: "Doveryai no proveryai." It translates, "Trust but verify."

Thanks again and love to Pat. Nancy sends love to you both.

Sincerely,

Ron

The Honorable William F. Buckley, Jr.
New York, New York

November 6, 1986

Dear Ruddy:

Just got back to Washington and found your letter awaiting me. I've been out campaigning for our candidates through 22 states and wound up in California.

Ruddy, I think we made great progress in Iceland, and now our arms negotiating teams are continuing to meet in Geneva, Switzerland. We'll have a better idea of our chances in a few days after Secretary of State Shultz' meeting with the Soviet Foreign Minister in Vienna.

Iceland was something of a different world, but the people are very nice and very friendly. They are also proud of their country and their way of life.

It's true that the only trees are in and around the city. They have been brought into the country and planted by the people. There are no trees natural to Iceland. There is plenty of green grass for the raising of sheep, cattle, etc. It is studded with black volcanic boulders and ridges on the low hillsides. This time of year daylight is only five hours long and, yes, it does seem strange to be in darkness at about 3:30 in the afternoon. Our flight there was about six hours long.

Your trip [to Luray Caverns in Virginia] sounds interesting and fun. Thanks for my "worry stone." Now that the election is over, I think I'll make use of it.

I'm sorry to hear about your mother's operation and hope everything went well and that she's recovering nicely and without much pain. Please tell her for Nancy and me that she's in our thoughts and prayers. She's right about the stones—they would be quite a project. How many in the class could match that?

All the best to you.

Sincerely,

Ronald Reagan

Rudolph Hines
Washington, D.C.

November 12, 1986

Dear Dr. Rodgers:

Thank you for sending me the book *No, I'm Not Afraid* by Irina Ratushinskaya. You were very kind and I'm most grateful.

Quite some time ago I received, by way of our United States Information Agency, a letter from a Soviet labor camp. It was handwritten and so tiny (only four inches in width and three quarters of an inch from top to bottom) that it must have been interpreted by using a powerful glass. It was in Russian, but an English version was provided by those who saw that the smuggled letter reached me. It was a letter congratulating me on my election. It contained 47 words, plus the salutation, and the signatures of 10 women prisoners. Accompanying it was a four-inch by four-inch, handmade chart—in the same tiny writing—the record of the hunger strikes by the ten women between August 1983 through December 1984.

As I read Irina's book, something prompted me to get out this letter. The ten signatures are the women Irina writes about in her book, including herself of course. I'm sure you can understand what meaning the book has for me now. Thank you for your kindness.

Sincerely,

Ronald Reagan

The Reverend Dr. Richard Rodgers
Birmingham, England

The Reagan administration sold antitank and antiaircraft weapons to Iran from the late summer 1985 to mid-fall 1986. These sales violated both its policy of refusing weapons transfers to terrorist nations and also an embargo on arms sales to Iran. Some of the money from the sales was diverted to rebel forces in Nicaragua, also defying congressional restrictions.

WASHINGTON

November 21, 1986

Dear Jim:

It was good to hear from you and to learn how well you are doing. Prayers are answered. Thank you for including me in your article. You gave me a better press than I've been getting the last several days here inside the "beltway." I don't think I'll plan a vacation to Iran.

Nancy sends her best, as do I, and give our love to Mary.

Sincerely,

Ron

Mr. Jim Curtis
Johnstown, Colorado

WASHINGTON

November 24, 1986

Dear Bill:

I'm sorry I didn't get to see you at the dinner, but they kind of rushed me in and rushed me out so there was no time for this rusher to look for another Rusher.

Anyway, thank you for your column. It did buck the tide and for that I thank you. I'm really upset by what so many of your contemporaries have done.

D—n it, yes, we sold them a few spare parts and weapons but the stake was a contact that could give us a chance at a relationship with Iran, and we were succeeding. A plus on the side was the return of three hostages and [it] could have been five if the media hadn't blown our cover. I don't know if we can put it back together. If we can't it's a great loss of all the Western World.

Nancy sends her love. Again, thanks.

Sincerely,

Ron

Mr. William A. Rusher
Publisher
National Review
New York, New York

November 24, 1986

Dear Paul:

Thank you very much for your more than kind letter. You brightened my day considerably. I've felt like I've been swimming in a pool of sharks and there's blood in the water. But I console myself with thinking this too will end because what we did was the right and sensible thing to do. My real regret is that the irresponsible press may have made it impossible to continue doing it. We won't know the answer to that for a while.

You are right about "Star Wars." I'm not about to give up on that.

Again, thanks. Nancy sends her best.

Sincerely,

Ron

Mr. Paul Trousdale
Santa Barbara, California

December 2, 1986

Dear Dolores:

It was good to hear from you to know how much you have come to love the West. I'm a midwesterner (Illinois) but I became a westerner after a short time and know how you feel. I guess the poet Robert W. Service said it when he wrote the line, "The land of gold held him as if in a spell."

I'm sorry campaigning doesn't provide time for visits but it was great to see you. If I didn't look like I recognized you, put it down to self-consciousness. I'm always aware that I'm facing the crowd and they'll wonder what I'm doing if I appear to be communicating with someone they can't see.

Thank you and Paul for all you did in the effort to get us a Senator [in Nevada]. You have every right to be proud because I'm convinced you made the difference in your precinct.

You are right about the media in this Iran thing. I've told them the absolute truth and they just won't accept it. I think, however, we are moving on a couple of fronts that will put out the fire and break up the lynch mob.

Please thank Sabrina for me for her letter and tell her she is still in our prayers.

Sincerely,

Ron

Mrs. Dolores M. Ballachino
Boulder City, Nevada

Jaquelin Hume, a stalwart supporter of the San Francisco area Republican Party, backed Reagan for governor in 1966 and served in Reagan's "Kitchen Cabinet," special advisors to the Governor. He established Citizens for America in 1983 to counter revolutionary terrorists in the Middle East and Nicaragua.

WASHINGTON

December 3, 1986

Dear Jack:

Thanks for your kind letter and warm words. I'm truly grateful. Thanks, too, for sending the copy of your letter to Jerry [Ambassador Gerald P. Carmen, Chairman, Citizens for America]. I know it will be helpful to him.

I keep telling myself the lynch mob will move on to other fields. They better, because I'm not about to let them tighten the rope around my neck. I think I've taken some steps that should speed the process—asking for an independent counsel etc. Actually, there is no case and no laws were broken or even bent. They just don't want to believe I've told them the "whole truth and nothing but the truth."

Thanks again for your letter and your faith. Love to Betty.

Sincerely,

Ron

Mr. Jaquelin Hume
San Francisco, California

December 4, 1986

Dear Nackey:

It was good to hear from you. This is just a line to bring you up to date. Evidently, my announcement on TV Tuesday, December 2, had something of an impact. Some have said it put a ring around the whole affair. Our own polls had begun to show a turnaround on the previous Sunday and by Tuesday afternoon were up several points, after a tremendous nose dive. I think most telling was my request for an "Independent Counsel"— we used to call them a "Special Prosecutor." They are the same thing—just the title is different.

So far we have only the two individuals who knew about the money transfer and didn't tell me. If the investigation reveals there were others, they, too, will go. Nackey, we had something good going that could have established a relationship with some responsible people in Iran. It is a distortion to suggest we were dealing with the Khomeini—we could never do that. In fact, the people we were talking to were risking their lives. Now all the publicity has destroyed what we were trying to do and may have destroyed those people as well. The business of the money transfer was none of our doing and a complete surprise to us.

Again, thanks for writing. Nancy sends her best.

Sincerely,

Ron

Mrs. William Loeb
Manchester, New Hampshire

Author of thirteen books on American quality management, Philip Crosby was an executive with ITT before establishing his own company and Quality College in Florida.

December 8, 1986

Dear Mr. Crosby:

Thank you very much for your letter and words of support. I'm most grateful.

I appreciate also your suggestion about getting a list of questions from Congress and supplying answers. Right now, however, we have a problem with that. I have given the Congress and the press all the information we have. That's why we are bringing in a Special Counsel. These are things about which we don't have the answers. I approved the plan of entering into dialogue with those Iranian individuals. When the leak led to the press exposure, I told them all I knew. The money problem was not known by me and was discovered by the Attorney General in his investigation. He told me what he had found out at 4:30 on a Monday afternoon. On Tuesday morning I told the leaders of Congress and the press what I had learned. Now there will be a House committee and a Senate committee, as well as the Special Counsel searching for whatever additional facts there might be.

Again, my thanks, and thanks for your prayers.

Sincerely,

Ronald Reagan

Mr. Philip B. Crosby, Sr.
Winter Park, Florida

December 9, 1986

Dear Murph:

It was good to get your letter and your reminders of other sharpies in days long ago. In our Hollywood adventure with infiltration and subversion, you and I picked up a lot of knowledge the pundits and the politicos don't have.

This whole fuss today is mind boggling. For two weeks or more the media is [*sic*] acting like they dug up the whole thing. I have to remind myself they got the whole story from me. When our own investigation turned up the alleged money transfer by way of a Swiss bank account, I went to the press room instantly with Ed Meese in tow. I broke the story, and Ed took their questions for an hour. Now they are acting like it was their story, and when am I going to come clean.

Well, there seems to be a weakening of their ardor. In fact, I understand a few have indicated they don't know how to get off the subject gracefully.

Again, thanks, and love to Bette. Nancy sends her love.

Sincerely,

Ron

The Honorable George Murphy
Palm Beach, Florida

December 16, 1986

Dear Larry:

This is to say thank you for two letters—the handwritten one and the letter of December 2. As always, you make good sense, and I'm grateful to you.

You know, Larry, this whole thing is hard to understand. I didn't try to do business with the Khomeini. I know he thinks I'm Satan. But it was others in his government who got word to us they would like to see if we couldn't establish a relationship leading to the future. With the strategic importance of Iran, I couldn't pass up this opportunity. They asked for a token arms sale to prove our sincerity. Our reply was $12 million worth of spare parts and anti-tank missiles. We told them we'd like concrete evidence of their anti-terrorism and that could be their effort to persuade the kidnapers in Beirut to free our hostages. By the way, countries in Western Europe have sold about $3.5 billion worth of weapons to Iran and $9 billion worth to Iraq. Our Communist friends (?) have sold about $5.4 billion worth to Iran and $24.0 billion worth to Iraq.* I don't think our sale tipped the military balance.

A leak by a radical weekly in Lebanon blew the cover. Because of the threat to the people we were dealing with, I begged the press to lay off. They didn't of course. But then our Attorney General looked into the whole thing to make sure there were no "smoking guns," and he turned up the supposed transfer of funds. I immediately went to the press and told them everything we had discovered about that. Now, for going on three weeks, the press, with the facts I gave them, are building a case that I'm covering up.

But you are right about the Contras. I'm convinced the case has become a battle between those who oppose helping the Contras and us who want to help. As this goes on, I think I'll point out that you can't be against the Contras without being for the Communist government of Nicaragua.

Well, I'm running on and better close. Again, thanks. Nancy sends her love.

Sincerely,

Ron

P.S. Merry Christmas!

Mr. Laurence W. Beilenson
Los Angeles, California

* Using unclassified CIA figures, staff members provided the numbers in this typed letter in place of Reagan's handwritten figures of $3 billion, $7 billion, $5.5 billion, and $24.5 billion.

WASHINGTON

December 22, 1986

Dear Mr. Murray:

Thank you very much for your wire and for giving me a chance to explain what our purpose was in this Iranian situation. I share your feeling about the present ruler of Iran and the treatment of our citizens several years ago and doubt I'll ever be able to forgive those responsible. At the same time, I can't find it in my heart to blanket-indict all the people of Iran. Nancy and I were guests of the Shah in Iran shortly before his overthrow. We had an extensive tour of the country and met many fine people, some of whom were later executed by the present regime.

Iran is of great strategic importance in the Middle East. We had been contacted by some individuals who wanted to establish a base for renewed relations between our two countries. I'm sure they are anticipating a new regime to succeed the present ruler, whose health in rapidly declining. At any rate, they were taking a great risk in contacting us and in proving their opposition to terrorism by getting the release of some of our hostages.

The news leak in Beirut, which precipitated the press furor here in America, has of course halted the progress we were making and may have caused the death or imprisonment of some of those who had contacted us.

Only time will tell whether we can re-establish relations and continue our effort to bring about peace between Iran and Iraq.

Again, my thanks to you for your understanding and support.

Sincerely,

Ronald Reagan

Mr. Warren Murray
Medford, New Jersey

1987

—

In all these years [1931–1981], no Congress ever
investigated a Democratic President. But every
Republican President was investigated, Ike for the
Sherman Adams affair, Dick for Watergate, Jerry for
CIA and now my own lynching. Well, so far they
haven't gotten the noose around my neck, and
they won't because I've been telling the truth for these
last eight months.

·Letter of July 21, 1987·

THE media frenzy that began in November 1986 over secret arms sales to Iran expanded in the early months of the new year. A harried president and his nervous staff, who feared impeachment and another Watergate-type upheaval, answered barrages of questions. The President's popularity rating sagged. In the midst of these probing questions on what did the President know, and when he knew it, Reagan was hospitalized again, for noncancerous prostate surgery on January 5.

Reports on the Iran-Contra secret maneuvers filled newspaper pages daily as the Tower board, a bipartisan committee appointed by President Reagan, began its inquiry in early December 1986. The board's target: the highly classified diplomatic negotiations, begun in late summer 1985 and concealed from Congress, for arms sales to Iran in order to open relations with Iranian moderates and, it was hoped, free American hostages. Testimony from sixty interviews would reveal the sale of thousands of antitank missiles and hundreds of spare parts for HAWK antiaircraft missiles to Iran. As noted in the introduction to the letters for 1986, although several hostages were freed, additional hostages were kidnapped. Almost $4 million from the arms sales went to support the Contras. Extensive investigations by independent counsel Lawrence Walsh and the Tower board never found evidence that President Reagan approved the diversion of funds to the Contras.

On Wednesday, March 4, Reagan admitted full responsibility for the Iran-Contra affair during a national TV address from the Oval Office. He said that several months earlier, he had told the American people he did not trade arms for hostages; however, the evidence and facts say this was not true. He then added, "What began as a strategic opening to Iran deteriorated in its implementation into trading arms for hostages." With emotion, he then stated: "As angry as I may be about activities undertaken without my knowledge, I am still accountable for those activities. As disappointed as I may be in some who served me, I am still the one who must answer to the American people for this behavior. And as personally distasteful as I find secret bank accounts and diverted funds, as the Navy would say, this happened on my watch." Staff changes included appointing Howard Baker in place of Don Regan as chief of staff, Frank Carlucci as National Security Advisor in place of John Poindexter, and William Webster as director of the CIA in place of William Casey.

Because of this speech, Reagan regained a good amount of support and understanding from the American public and from influential newspaper and TV commentators. The *New York Times* called the speech a laudable step. However, the continuing congressional and media investigations caused the President's correspondence to be colored by his frustration. Other critics accused the President, and especially certain influential administrative aides, including Oliver North, Robert McFarlane, and John Poindexter, with being naive, especially regarding the Middle East. Reagan, in his 1990 autobiography, *An American Life,* stubbornly maintained: "To this day I still believe that the Iran initiative was *not* an effort to swap arms for hostages. But I know it may not look that way to some people."

And he added that when he earlier called North a national hero, he was thinking about the colonel's Vietnam service. Despite North's alleged claims, there had been no frequent meetings between North and Reagan in the Oval Office and Camp David, nor did they speak frequently on the phone; none of this is true, the President wrote, he hardly knew North.

The President's foreign travel included a brief visit to Canada in early April followed by a carefully prepared ten-day trip to Europe: first to Italy for the Group of Seven Summit in Venice, and then to the Vatican to meet with Pope John Paul II before going on to Germany. In West Berlin, at the Berlin Wall, President Reagan gave one of his most famous speeches, urging Soviet leader Mikhail Gorbachev to give some sign that would signify that the Soviets wanted freedom and peace, that they would make substantial policy changes. Reagan then asked Gorbachev in the cause of freedom and peace to come here to this [Brandenburg] gate: "Mr. Gorbachev, open this gate! Mr. Gorbachev, tear down this wall!" The President hoped for significant Soviet changes because two months earlier, Secretary George Shultz had met with Gorbachev and Soviet Foreign Minister Eduard Shevardnadze and the two foreign ministers found agreement for an Intermediate Nuclear Forces (INF) arms control treaty.

At Washington, D.C., on December 8, Gorbachev and Reagan signed this treaty that called for their nations' elimination of intermediate-range and shorter-range nuclear missiles. For the first time, a Soviet–U.S. treaty mandated the destruction of nuclear weapons, with that destruction verified. Pleased, President Reagan repeated the old Russian maxim "Trust but verify" again to Gorbachev, who smiled. Conservatives were fearful and anxious about the import of this INF treaty. Democrats and Republicans in Congress were encouraged by the President's ongoing negotiations with the Soviets. Gorbachev's December visit gave new evidence of improved relationships between the two superpowers. Never before had a Soviet leader attracted such favorable reviews in the daily press and on television, as he courted American public opinion in press conferences as well as along the streets of Washington, where he stopped his car to greet well-wishers.

Other domestic efforts in 1987, such as President Reagan's attempts to obtain a line item veto and a constitutional amendment that required the federal government to balance its budget, made no progress in the powerful Democratic Congress whose members were preparing for next year's presidential election. The stock market's plunge on October 20, much worse than that of October 1929, sobered the financial community, private investors, and the White House. Despite this anxiety, a confident Reagan proudly reported on the economic recovery that had begun almost six years earlier and accounted for over 14 million new jobs.

Reagan's nominations for Supreme Court justices met prompt and positive receptions in a Republican Senate before 1987. His nomination of Sandra Day O'Connor in 1981 had been confirmed; his appointments in 1986 of William Rehnquist and Antonin Scalia also met with approval. Justice Lewis Powell's June 1987 resignation lead to Robert Bork's nomination. In the Senate, now Democratic, Bork became the target in a campaign led by Senator Edward Kennedy and waged daily on TV during the hearings on his nomination late in October; the Senate voted down the nomination, 58 to 42. Douglas Ginsburg, the next nominee, withdrew; and Anthony Kennedy won Senate confirmation in February 1988.

January 13, 1987

Dear Madeline:

It was good to hear from you, and we are both grateful for your kind, good wishes.

I found your letter here when I returned from the hospital. I'm happy to say the doctors are amazed at my swift recovery from the surgery.* I intend to keep them that way. You are right about someone helping me. Besides the wonderful people at the hospital and Nancy, I called on my deep belief in prayer, and my prayers were answered.

You surprised me with your reference to a song "Footprints In the Sand." I have a short essay or story by author unknown. It is titled, I believe, "I had a dream." It has to do with the author walking along a beach, accompanied by the Lord, while scenes from his life are pictured in the sky. Coming to the end of his walk, he looks back and sees the double set of footprints in the sand, except that each time his story in the sky shows him in trouble there is only one set of footprints. He cries out, asking the Lord why he deserted him when he was most in need. The Lord replied, "where you see only one set of footprints, it was then I carried you." Does that sound like the song you mentioned?

Well, thank you for your letter and birthday wishes. Just think, it will be the 37th anniversary of my 39th birthday. Nancy sends her best.

Sincerely,

Dutch

Mrs. Madeline K. Frazer
Dixon, Illinois

* Prostatectomy on January 5.

As sports director of Des Moines, Iowa, radio station WHO in 1934, Reagan began announcing baseball games of the Chicago Cubs, then managed by Marion Grimm's husband, Charlie, who had played major league baseball for twenty years.

WASHINGTON

January 15, 1987

Dear Marion:

From both Nancy and myself a heartfelt thanks for your cards, letters and prayers—and, might I add, your generous words of support.

Our holidays were happy. We spent New Year's in California. I even got in a couple of rounds of golf. Then it was back to Washington and the hospital. I'm happy to say there wasn't a hitch; all the exams came out A-plus and the surgery was a success. I'm back at the office now and feeling fine.

The only sour note is—as you yourself pointed out—the media. They are like a lynch mob looking for a victim. I know they've chosen me, but I don't think they can get the rope around my neck.

Nancy sends her best—as do I.

Sincerely,

Ron

Mrs. Charles Grimm
Scottsdale, Arizona

Ward Quaal suggested consideration of a national lottery as a means of reducing the national debt.

February 2, 1987

Dear Ward:

Your letter and the clipping are in hand. I've put the idea on the table, but the strongest argument against it was one this ex-Governor couldn't rebut. It would be the Federal government moving in again to usurp a revenue source the states are counting on.

I have to confess, I still have that little "blue nose" feeling that our Nation should be a little above that method of raising revenue. Incidentally, I haven't checked this out, but one history buff said Jefferson used a lottery to pay for the Louisiana Purchase.

Nancy sends her love, and to Dorothy from us both.

Sincerely,

Ron

Mr. Ward L. Quaal
Chicago, Illinois

Paul Newman served in the U.S. Navy in World War II. After studies at Kenyon College, Yale University, and the Actors Studio in New York City, he began his movie career in Hollywood, and received the Best Actor's Award in 1987. Also notable have been his charitable enterprises including foundations for terminally ill children; alcohol and drug abuse education; and famine relief for Africa.

WASHINGTON

[February 1987]

Dear Paul:

Having read your letter to Nancy, I am compelled to write: first, to reply to your suggestion that Nancy is less than dedicated to the anti-drug campaign and, second, to inform you that my own commitment is not "campaign rhetoric." There has been "rhetoric" over our proposed budget, and it is pure political demagoguery.

Nancy has traveled tens of thousands of miles to virtually every part of this country and to Europe and Asia motivated by her deeply felt devotion to the anti-drug crusade. I believe she has done more and continues doing more than any other single individual, particularly with regard to young people to whom she is totally dedicated.

Yes, we have proposed a smaller appropriation for the drug program than we had last year, but it is bigger than the appropiation for 1986, which was bigger than the one for 1985. Indeed, we have increased the appropriation every year since we've been in Washington. But the appropriation we've proposed for '88, it is true, is smaller than the '87 budget and for a very good reason. Several hundred million dollars were added to the '87 appropriation for one-time, program start-up costs and purchase of equipment and facilities such as radar balloons, helicopters, and planes. Some of that money is still being spent. These were, as I say, one-time expenditures. May I also say, those who have been loudest in their demagoguery have access to this information. It is they who are guilty of "campaign rhetoric."

302

I'm sorry you removed yourself from the proposed anti-drug film. It was a very worthwhile effort and should not be sacrificed on the altar of partisan politics. I assure you, our Administration and my wife are dedicated to the nationwide crusade against drug and alcohol use.

Sincerely,

Ronald Reagan

Mr. Paul Newman
New York, New York

John Cooper served in the U.S. Senate from 1946 to 1949 and later from 1952 to 1955 and from 1956 to 1973; and as delegate to the United Nations General Assembly from 1949 to 1951. He served as ambassador to India and Nepal from 1955 to 1956 and to the German Democratic Republic from 1974 to 1976.

WASHINGTON

February 9, 1987

Dear John:

I have just been given a copy of your letter in *The Washington Post,* January 21, and want you to know how grateful I am for your well-reasoned, commonsense response to the unfounded speculation which has characterized so much of the press reporting of the Iran situation.

When the press got wind of our effort to open a dialogue with certain Iranian individuals, both in and out of government, I immediately told them and the public what we had been trying to accomplish. When I subsequently learned there might have been some manipulation of funds, which was not part of our plan, I made what information I had available. I am still waiting to learn if this was indeed true and what the particulars might be. In short, I am not engaged in any cover-up; indeed, I'm anxious to have the truth known and will help in any way I can to learn what the facts are and to make them known.

Again, my thanks to you for bringing a touch of sanity to what has become a diatribe of unfounded charges and name-calling.

Sincerely,

Ronald Reagan

The Honorable John Sherman Cooper
Washington, D.C.

Stanford graduate, World War II Army captain, and oil tool company executive, William A. Wilson became a member of Governor Reagan's "Kitchen Cabinet" in California. He became the President's personal representative to the Vatican and, later, ambassador to the Vatican until 1986.

WASHINGTON

March 5, 1987

Dear Bill:

Just a few lines about your letter of February 20. You realize, of course, that you'll be reading the words of a Protestant, even though the son of a Catholic father. But I assure you, that latter point means I haven't even a tinge of religious prejudice.

Bill, I'm worried about two things having to do with the spiritual or moral fatigue [in Europe that] the Cardinal [William Baum] mentioned. One is general and, in my view, has to do with a secularism that is so prevalent today. An example—sex education in our schools. Well-intentioned though it might have been, it is taught in a framework of only being a physical act—like eating a ham sandwich. The educators are fearful that any references to sin or morality will be viewed as violating the church and state separation.

This has been carried into other things so that, outside the home or church, no values are being taught or emphasized.

With regard to the Catholic Church itself, I believe there is a faction within the clergy that is out of step with basic moral tenants [*sic*]. When I spoke a few years ago at the Notre Dame commencement, a group of Maryknoll nuns came down from Chicago and picketed the campus in protest against my being there. A sizeable number of that Order are today supportive of the Communist government of Nicaragua.

On the Protestant side, that division is also present in several denominations, as well as the National Council of Churches. By contrast the very fundamentalist denominations who stick closely to the Bible are showing an increase in followers. Maybe there is a clue there for all of us. "Let's get back to the Ten Commandments."

Well, that's enough of a lecture from me. Nancy sends her love to you both.

Sincerely,

Ron

The Honorable William A. Wilson
Los Angeles, California

President Reagan's visits with Prime Minister Yasuhiro Nakasone in Washington, D.C., and in Japan in 1983 brought about a personal friendship and an improved relationship between the two countries.

WASHINGTON

March 12, 1987

Dear Yasu:

Secretary Shultz has just delivered your letter to me, and I thank you very much. Of course, your comparing my [March 4] speech to some good golf shots reminded me of how much I miss those California golf courses while

I'm sitting here in the cold weather of Washington. But you and I will continue to work closely together, I assure you. I look forward with great pleasure to seeing you at the Summit.

Nancy sends her very best, and give our warm regards to Tsutako.

Sincerely,

Ron

His Excellency
Yasuhiro Nakasone
Prime Minister of Japan
Tokyo

WASHINGTON

March 23, 1987

Dear Paul:

Thanks very much for your letter and your kind words about me and your proper words about our friends (?) in the media.

Someone sent me a clipping from an Illinois paper. It carries quotes going back to 1858 in the press of that time about Lincoln. One paper called him everything from a thief to a gorilla. But when he was shot the same paper went into a mix of crocodile tears and a eulogy about this "great and good" man.

I hope I can avoid such a change of heart by today's press, considering the price.

Nancy sends her best.

Sincerely,

Ron

Mr. Paul Trousdale
Los Angeles, California

March 30, 1987

Dear Marion:

Thank you for your kind letter and generous words. I am most grateful. You are so right about the media; they seem to be in business not to report the news but to make it by attacking whoever is in charge. Just between us, I handle it by pretending I'm on the mound pitching and they are out in the right field bleachers.

Next time you see Tom [Chauncey], give him our best regards. Nancy and I have known him for a long time. And when and if you make that trip to Washington, let us know. In case they have me out of the country on May 7, let me say Happy Birthday now.

Again, my thanks for your kindness and your prayers.

Sincerely,

Ron

Mrs. Charles Grimm
Scottsdale, Arizona

March 30, 1987

Dear Barney:

Thank you for your good review of my go-around with the Fourth Estate. I must confess I really enjoyed it. I think we've really got this thing behind us, although I'm still waiting to find out where that extra money came from and where did it go. We didn't ask for it. Our price was $12 million and we got that. It appears that some of the "go-betweens" on the Iran side maybe upped our price and skimmed some profit off the top. We must not forget everything was taking place in the Middle East.

Again, thanks, and best regards.

Sincerely,

Ron

Col. Barney Oldfield, USAF (Ret.)
Beverly Hills, California

[March 30, 1987]

Dear Bill:

Knowing how busy you are with your ambassadorial duties, I won't (as Henry the 8th said to each of his 6 wives) "keep you long." But I just have to thank you for that wonderful, magical book you sent us. Clichés are statements repeated so often because they are truths. So the cliché I'm about to write is the only suitable thing to say—"I couldn't put it down." What warm, wonderful memories you all must have. And now you share them with the rest of us. Again my heartfelt thanks.

Nancy sends her love and love to Pat.

Sincerely,

Ron

The Honorable William F. Buckley, Jr.
New York, New York

April 6, 1987

Dear Heather [elementary school pupil]:

Being your seatmate the other day in Columbia, Missouri, and having the opportunity to observe firsthand the commitment to our basic educational skills was a real pleasure.

I thought you asked me about whether our Iran initiative was worthwhile, but apparently your question was much broader—whether being President is worth it. Well, the answer to both questions is yes.

To begin with, I enjoyed being an actor and never thought for a moment I'd ever seek public office. However, I've always believed that you should pay for the blessings you've enjoyed. My fellow actors elected me President of our union, the Screen Actors Guild, six times, and I was proud to serve them. I used to campaign for causes and political candidates I believed in. There came a day when, as a result of this campaigning for others, a group of people asked me to run for public office. I said no. But they kept after me until, finally, I gave in, without really understanding that I was giving up acting once and for all. That was more than 20 years ago, and I became Governor of California, a job I held for eight years.

Heather, a very wise man once said, "life begins when you begin to serve." He was right. I have discovered that serving my fellow man is more fulfilling than anything I had ever done before. Being able to deal with matters affecting the welfare of our people, instead of just making speeches about such things, is more than worth the loss of privacy and the other drawbacks you mentioned in your question.

I hope this answers your question and I hope sometime we might meet again and talk about this. It was a great pleasure meeting you, your classmates and your gracious teacher. Give them all my regards and, again, my apology for misinterpreting your question.

Sincerely,

Ronald Reagan

Heather Watson
Columbia, Missouri

James Schmidt, a San Diego savings and loan officer, served in three state transportation agencies during Governor Reagan's administration.

April 27, 1987

Dear Jim:

It was good to get your letter, and I appreciate your interest in our problem. Sometimes I wonder how they might look to me if I hadn't been a little conditioned by that mess we inherited in California.

Jim, I'm going to keep on fighting for that line-item veto, but I'm afraid a trade as you suggested for a tax increase isn't the answer. With the Democrats back in charge in both Houses of Congress, there are too many of them just waiting for a crack in the dam to flood us with tax changes to pay for a pack of new spending ideas, not deficit reduction.

I'll keep on trying for the veto, even if it's only for the next President, because you are right—it is the most essential tool to fiscal sanity. We are pushing for a whole new budget plan. You'd be amazed how Mickey Mouse the Federal budget policy is. I doubt if any State would put up with it for five minutes.

Thanks, again, and best regards.

Sincerely,

Ron

Mr. James C. Schmidt
San Diego, California

April 28, 1987

TO THE EDITOR:

I have only just received the April 9 issue of the *Purdue Exponent*. I found the questions on page 7 of the six students who responded to your query as to what one question they would ask me if given the chance. I'm sorry there was no opportunity for them to ask or me to answer.

I was so warmly received on your campus and so greatly impressed by all that I saw and heard, I thought the least I could do was answer those questions.

Sharon Cania asked if I thought the relationship between the United States and the Soviet Union would ever get better. I have to say, Sharon, I believe there is reason to believe it will. In my talk with Gorbachev in Geneva I told him our two countries didn't mistrust each other because we had weapons. We had weapons because we mistrusted each other, and reduction of arms would follow if we worked to eliminate the causes of our mistrust. Today we are both talking reduction of arms, and this is the first Soviet leader who has ever volunteered to destroy deployed weapons. I think there is reason to hope.

Shawn Baskett asked if I was squeamish about having my "innards" displayed on national television. Yes, Shawn, I was. I realize a great deal of privacy is sacrificed when you take this job but there should be some limits. I guess what I resented most was the attempt to make the whole thing look more serious than it really was.

Mark Peters asked what could be done to stop the spread of Communism in the Philippines. Well, the government of the Philippines is doing a lot now. First, there is no hesitation in using force to disarm and subdue the Communist bands who are using violence to impose their way on the people of the Philippines. At the same time, there is an education program to make the people realize that Communism is anti-freedom and rules always by a totalitarian dictatorship. At the same time, the government of the

Philippines is showing the people it is trying to bring about democratic reforms and equal opportunity for all.

Tammy Gatlin asked if I thought my loss of popularity over the Iran affair will hurt the Republicans in the upcoming elections. Well, Tammy, not if the truth—all the truth—finally comes out and is given fair treatment in the press. Very simply, we were dealing with Iranian representatives who claimed they wanted to establish a better relationship, looking toward the day when there will be a new government in Iran. Iran is a nation of 40 million people in a most strategic position in the Middle East. Apparently the Iranians' intentions were not as honorable as our own. So the plan went awry and we made mistakes, but it was no scandal. I hope the voters will keep in mind that by '88 the Republicans will have only [have had] a majority in both houses of Congress for 4 of the last 58 years and one house, the Senate, for 6 [8] years.* The Democrats will have dominated both houses of Congress for 48 [46] years and one house for an additional 6 [8].

Carol Gloyd wanted to know if I would run for a third term if the Constitution allowed it. Carol, I can't really answer because I've always believed the people let you know whether you should run or not, and since I've been 39 years old 38 times now, they might have some hang-ups about me serving another term. I will tell you this, though: I will support doing away with the 22nd Amendment for future Presidents. Why should the people be denied the right to vote for anyone they want and for as many terms? The President and the Vice President are the only Federal officers who are elected by all the people, and the President is the only one with a limit on how many terms he can serve. I think the 22nd Amendment limits the people's democratic rights.

Jerry Ryzowski wanted to know why I continue to make financial cutbacks which result in less fortunate students being unable to "go for further ed." Jerry, I'm afraid there has been some misunderstanding about our Student Aid programs. It is true we have proposed some changes because it was discovered that grants were going to students whose families were in income brackets above a level that would fairly qualify them for aid. We would shift some grants to loans and, in some instances, would eliminate the interest subsidy. Actually, the total financial support for education—Federal, State and local—is higher than it has ever been and 42 percent of all college students in the country are receiving some form of Federal help. The changes we've made are intended to direct more aid to the neediest students and away from those less needy.

Again, my thanks for a wonderful day on your campus.

Sincerely,

Ronald Reagan

Editor
Purdue Exponent
Room B-50
Purdue Memorial Union
West Lafayette, Indiana

* Republican majority in the Senate: from 1931 to 1933 and from 1981 to 1987.

WASHINGTON

April 29, 1987

Dear Courtney:

It was very nice of your to write as you did, and both Mrs. Reagan and I are most grateful for your letter. And please thank your sister for coloring that picture of us.

I hope I'm not too late with regard to your report on the White House. According to the Constitution, the President is the Chief Executive Officer of the government (that's like being the head of a big business concern) and is the Commander in Chief of the Armed Forces. The President is responsible for all national security.

As President, it was my job to select the people who would make up what is called my Cabinet. They each have a title of Secretary, except the head of the Department of Justice whose title is Attorney General. The Vice President is also a member of the Cabinet. Some of the others are Secretary of State, Secretary of Defense, Secretary of Agriculture, Secretary of Health and Human Services, etc. There are more, but that will give you the idea.

You asked what I do. Well, the days can be pretty full. At 9:00 a.m. every morning, Monday through Friday, I meet with my Chief of Staff, his assistant, and the Vice President. We go over things that are scheduled for the day, problems we may be having with regard to actions by the Congress, requests for me to appear and make speeches, and on and on.

Then, at 9:30 on a normal day, my National Security Advisor and his top assistant come in with the latest information regarding foreign affairs. He leaves me with a leather folder containing about a half-hour's reading on worldwide matters.

Throughout the day memorandums come to my desk, papers and laws that have to be signed or refused by me and, of course, mail. The President has a few thousand people in government who are appointed by him; and there are always some who are retiring and have to be replaced, so there are meetings with staff to do that.

I've enclosed a page for the month of May from what is known as an advance schedule. That means it isn't complete. There will be changes and additions for each day. Every evening I get a corrected and final schedule for the next day, plus information on the various appointments and meetings for that day. All of that is my bedtime reading.

Of course, there are occasional trips. For example, in June, I will go to Italy for a meeting with the leaders of six other countries and then a one-day stop in Germany.

I hope this gives you an idea of what the President does. Of course, there are happy times, too, such as getting a nice letter from a little girl named Courtney.

Best regards,

Ronald Reagan

Courtney Justice
Sierra Madre, California

Trude B. Feldman, a syndicated correspondent covering the White House and the State Department, submitted these questions in May 1987 to President Reagan, and he answered them on four handwritten pages. The President's answers, abbreviations, and punctuation are published as he penned them.

1. *Why are you so insistent against tax increases?*

   Early in this country classic ec. theory held that recurrent hard times were the result of govt. taking too big a share of gross national product in taxes. Since then general tax cuts such as those under Pres. Kennedy & our own in our "ec. Recovery package" resulted in govt. getting more revenue from lower tax rates because of the stimulant to the economy. I think a tax increase would risk bringing on a recession.

2. *Do you believe you can achieve a balanced budget in the near future without a tax increase?*

   Yes I do if the Congress will approve cuts we have recommended in domestic spending. If our budget for 1982 had been adopted, the cumulative deficit through 1986 would have been $207 bil. less.

3. *If defense expenditures should not be reduced (as you stated), and if Social Security benefits should not be curtailed, how much expenditures are left that could possibly be reduced by the $200-billion-dollar cut needed to balance the budget?*

   Only a few years before we came to Wash. & during Democratic administrations, defense spending as a share of the Nat. budget was nearly half. Today our defense spending is something less than 30% of the total budget. Social Security is not a part of the deficit. It is funded out of a trust fund that can't be used for any other purpose. Maybe if I use some figures for a 15 year period this question can best be answered. In the middle 1960's the "war on poverty," Pres. Johnson's great social experiment was passed and implemented. In the 15 years from 1965 to 1980 the fed. Budget increased to almost 5 times what it had been in 1965. The annual deficit increased to 38 times what it had been.

4. *Since large budget deficits are inflationary, does not the Federal Reserve have to exercise credit constraints, which means high interest rates?*

I did not understand the Fed. Reserve policy in the few years before we came here. The prime interest rate went to more than 20% and inflation reached double digits. Both of those figures have changed drastically & we've had more than 50 months of economic expansion with an increase of 13.6 mil. new jobs.

5. *Since issues of rising inflation, higher interest rates, and the decreasing value of the dollar are so critical, isn't it necessary to move quickly to reappoint Paul Volcker or to name his successor?*

   True—we haven't done any studying of the Federal Reserve situation & no decision has been made as yet. I'd rather not answer this Q.

6. *Don Regan, who is now focusing on current economic and financial problems, said Western nations better resolve their economic differences at the Venice Summit or face a cataclysm in the financial markets. Do you agree? Why or why not?*

   We have some serious ec. Problems to resolve at the Ec. Summit. Many of them have to do with unfair trade practices, closing of markets to certain products etc. We'll be dealing with those matters. Last year agreement was reached to re-open the "GATT" round of tariffs etc. for further studying. We'd been trying to persuade our partners to do this for a couple of years. Now we'll be doing that.

   a. *What was Regan's contribution to your Administration in the Economic arena?*

      One of his major contributions was laying the foundation for tax reform.

   b. *To you, personally?*

      He was a fine Sec. Of Treasury and he was fully supportive of our policies and worked to carry them out as chief of staff.

7. *When Regan and Berl [sic] Sprinkel were at The Treasury, they were against increasing the capital of the International Monetary Fund. Shouldn't we now be more supportive of strengthening the Fund in view of the debt crisis of many developing countries?*

   True we are supportive of the I.M.F. but haven't gotten into the specific thing you asked about. I'm still getting input.

8. *Are you disturbed by the shift of our country from being the world's largest creditor nation to the world's largest debtor nation?*

   We became the world's largest debtor nation because of the high value of our dollar in comparison to the currency of our trading partners. That has now been somewhat corrected and the change in the trade imbalance shows some improvement. I'd like to point out that the trade balance ignores some figures. For example a portion of our exports are services not goods. The trade balance figures do not include pay for services. Yes I'd like to see a better balance but at the same time I recognize we are the world's biggest customer of the less developed nations. We are helping them become more prosperous which means they will one day be able to buy more from us.

9. *It now appears that the national debt will triple during your terms in office, and much of our government bonds are owned abroad. Is this a source of concern to you? If so, what should we do to reduce that debt?*

   Yes the national debt & the continuing deficits are of concern to me & have been for half a century or more. For 46 of the last 56 yrs. The Dem. Party has had a majority in both houses of the Congress. The President can't spend a dime. Congress determines the amount of spending. Since W.W. II with only an exception here & there we have had deficits every year. When many of us complained (I used to make speeches opposing deficits) we were told, "it didn't matter we owed it to ourselves." Well now it's caught up with us and we see interest on the debt as one of our major spending items. What should we do? Make the Congress give the President the power of Line Item Veto which 43 of our State Governors have. Then amend the Constitution to provide for a balanced budget. Thomas Jefferson asked for that when the Constitution was adopted.

10. *Are you confident that the Japanese markets will be substantially opened to American goods and services?*

    I can only say we have made quite some progress and have had the cooperation of Prime Minister Nakasone. We are going to continue working on this.

11. *Dick Darman criticized American business management for our competitive weakness. What do you plan to do to improve business performance?*

We have prepared an entire set of legislation to the Congress aimed at making us more competitive world wide. We are making progress. Recently I visited the Harley Davidson Motor Cycle Plant in York Pa. [May 6]. A few years ago they were almost on the rocks due to foreign competition. They asked for help under the "201" program. We put this into effect for 5 years. More than a year early they told us to cancel the program, they didn't need it anymore. Management & labor got together in a team effort. Now that company is producing 24 different models, previously they only produced 3. They have reduced the number of hours it takes to make a motorcycle, they have cut prices on many models and—well the list goes on. I'll bet on American working men & women as being able to compete with anyone in the world.

WASHINGTON

May 27, 1987

Dear Todd:

I'm sorry to be so late in answering your letter of March 10. It sometimes takes a while for mail to reach my desk, and your letter has only just made it.

Thank you for writing as you did. I'm most grateful and I'm happy to share your viewpoint—yours and Karen's. Please give her my regards and tell her how right she is to feel the way she does.

When, after almost a decade of fighting in Vietnam, we signed the Paris Peace Accords to end the war between South Vietnam and the communist government of North Vietnam, we withdrew our forces. We had helped the South Vietnamese put together an army of half a million men. We believed this army, with the tanks, helicopters and artillery we left them, could defend their country if North Vietnam violated the peace treaty and attacked. We promised that if this happened we'd provide the fuel and ammunition for the things we left behind.

Well, the North Vietnamese did violate the treaty and attacked as soon as our forces left South Vietnam. When our President asked Congress for money to keep our pledge, the Congress flatly refused. Just as they are refusing to help the Contras now. The South Vietnamese army retreated, abandoning the things we'd left for them, and today the communist forces of North Vietnam have taken not only South Vietnam but Cambodia and Laos as well.

We must not allow this to happen in Nicaragua. The Sandinistas have a disinformation network that has many Americans confused about what's at stake, so just keep on preaching the gospel about Central America.

Again, thanks.

Sincerely,

Ronald Reagan

Mr. Todd L. Thornton
Columbus, Ohio

WASHINGTON

June 17, 1987

Dear Brute:

Thank you again! Your column on the Ayatollah is magnificent and puts the whole situation in focus, as a number of our Congressmen have been unable to do.

And you are right about another segment of the Congress—that endless hearing with its litany of hearsay that would never be allowed in a courtroom. I will say, however, the latest item—the memo supposedly written by [Oliver] North and intended for me—which has been termed a smoking gun, was never given to me. I've never seen it and, thus, was clearly telling the truth when I said I did not know of any Iranian money over and above the purchase price of the arms shipment. Today I had the pleasure of answering a shouted question from the press that "there ain't no smoking gun."

You know, even here in Washington the hearings are being ignored by more and more people, even though they are on TV, live, hour after hour.

Well, thanks again. You have a circle of fans here in the West Wing.

Sincerely,

Ronald Reagan

Lt. Gen. Victor H. Krulak, USMC (Ret.)
San Diego, California

Lorraine Makler, a thirteen-year-old movie fan in Philadelphia, wrote her first letter to Reagan in 1943, and he replied. In 1950, with her husband, Elwood Wagner, she went to Dixon to celebrate Reagan's career. Correspondence between the Wagners and Reagan continued until 1994.

WASHINGTON

June 25, 1987

Dear Lorraine and Wag:

Thank you for my Father's Day card and, even more, for your warm letter. It was good to hear from you. I was very interested in your adventure with Les Kinsolving [radio talk show host] and am most grateful for your setting him straight. I've heard there are a couple of books out that apparently were written out of complete imagination. Thank you for taking care of at least one of them.

You know Les was a White House correspondent for a while. Maybe he still is and is just doubling in brass. By the way, with regard to taking horses over fences, I regret to say—not anymore. We still ride, but since we only get to the ranch a few times a year and since my longtime favorite, "Little Man," has gone to horse heaven, I've decided it wouldn't be fair to the job I have. I used to feel that way when I was doing movies. While I was making one, I wouldn't jump. It is a sport where accidents can happen to the best of riders and, while I miss it, I have to feel it wouldn't be right to have to cancel a Summit meeting or such while some bones mended.

Thank you for your kind words about our present troubles. I think there is a kind of political lynching going on, but my conscience is completely clear, so I'm not losing any sleep. Nancy sends her best to you both, and so do I.

Sincerely,

Ron

Mr. & Mrs. Elwood Wagner
Philadelphia, Pennsylvania

WASHINGTON

June 25, 1987

Dear Phil:

Just a line to thank you and J. for your kind letter, good wishes and prayers. Our Summit was a complete success, but you'd never know it from the press accounts. Actually, we got everything we went for, and the relationship with our six allies has never been closer.

Let me assure you the Pope is still Catholic and, let me add, still a truly great human being. Our visit is something I'll long remember.

Nancy sends her love, and from both of us to Jo.

Sincerely,

Ron

Mr. Phil Regan
Pasadena, California

Actor Charlton Heston, an early supporter of Adlai Stevenson and John Kennedy, also campaigned for civil rights in the 1960s. He worked with Reagan during the Screen Actors Guild strike. In 1998 he became president of the National Rifle Association.

July 9, 1987

Dear Chuck:

Thank you very much for your kind letter and for writing to Ollie North as you did. These last few days I think he has captured the heart of America. In just two days—July 7 and 8 the White House has received almost 2,500 calls, 2,400 of them supportive and only 83 hostile.

Don't worry about me holding the "Bear" [Soviet Union] too close. I'm willing to dance but intend to lead. I'm sure you approve of our choice for the Supreme Court [Robert Bork]. We really touched a nerve in the ultra-liberal community, but he doesn't deserve the abuse he's taking. I've never thought the American Bar Association was overly conservative, but they've given him the highest recommendations they can make.

Nancy sends her love, and from both of us to Lydia. Again, thanks.

Sincerely,

Ron

Mr. Charlton Heston
Beverly Hills, California

July 16, 1987

Dear Mr. Stevenson:

Your letter of June 16 has only just now reached my desk—hence this tardy acknowledgement. I'm sure you know that, as of yesterday, July 15, Admiral Poindexter's testimony confirmed that I have been telling the truth for the last seven months. I did not know there was additional money from the arms sale or that it was being diverted to the Contras. Admiral Poindexter kept this information from me.

I look forward to making a statement when the investigation is closed. Then those "2/3 of the people" you mentioned will know I have not been lying.

Have a nice day.

Sincerely,

Ronald Reagan

Mr. John R. Stevenson
Elmira, New York

July 17, 1987

Dear Michel:

George Bush showed me your letter, and I hope you won't mind my responding.

First, let me say I have not reneged on my campaign promises to repeal the Windfall Profits Tax. I just haven't been able to get the Congress to move on it and now, with both Houses again in Democratic hands, they are even more dug in against repeal, as well as a whole package of measures. I've sought to help the energy industry. I have, for example, asked for repeal of the regulations on natural gas, with no success.

Possibly, some of their bullheadedness is brought on by their insistence on tax rate increases across the board. Michel, I assure you we have a package of measures leading off with repeal of the Windfall Profits Tax. That package has been introduced and reintroduced, and it's like my budget proposals, just ignored. Has the industry engaged in any activity on the Hill? I must say we've had affirmative votes on the Windfall Tax by itself a couple of times in the Senate, but it dies in the House. I was pleased, as I'm sure you were, to see a repeal provision included in the trade bill passed by the Senate earlier this week. But the House is where we need help now.

Believe me, I'll keep trying.

Sincerely,

Ronald Reagan

Mr. Michel T. Halbouty
Houston, Texas

WASHINGTON

July 21, 1987

Dear Murph:

Thanks very much for your good letter and call to arms. You are completely right about what's going on up on Capitol Hill. I'm waiting my turn. I won't comment publicly on this 'til the inquisition is all over, but when it is I'll go nationwide.

Murph, isn't it strange, the Democrats have had a majority in both Houses of the Congress for 46 [44] of the 50 years from 1931 to 1981. Republicans had the Congress for two years during Truman's Presidency and two years during Ike's two terms. I had one House Republican for six years and now am back to a Democratic majority in both Houses. In all these years, no Congress ever investigated a Democratic President. But every Republican President was investigated, Ike for the Sherman Adams affair, Dick for Watergate, Jerry for CIA and now my own lynching. Well, so far they haven't gotten the noose around my neck, and they won't because I've been telling the truth for these last eight months. It's fun now to see them and the press trying to get back off the limb they've all been out on.

I envy you the visits to the Grove, but, then, the day I can join you is coming closer.

Love to Betty.

Sincerely,

Ron

The Honorable George L. Murphy
Palm Beach, Florida

WASHINGTON

August 3, 1987

Dear Walter:

Just a line to thank you for sending that *Wall Street Journal* clipping.* I hadn't seen it, but it sure confirms a suspicion I've had for quite a while. You know, Walter, I've had some hints that some of today's faculty were the student demonstrators of the '60's. At any rate, there is no question but that our young people are getting a lot of indoctrination along with their teaching.

Nancy sends her love, and from both of us to L.

Again, thanks and best regards.

Sincerely,

Ron

The Honorable Walter Annenberg
Radnor, Pennsylvania

* "Endangered Species" in the July 10 *Wall Street Journal.*

Stuart Spencer, an astute strategist, worked on Reagan's campaigns for governor and president with the exception of 1976, when he supported President Gerald Ford.

August 3, 1987

Dear Stu:

Thanks very much for your helpful letter, and it is helpful. We're not too far apart on what should be said. I'll be able to say we have changed, and are changing, certain things. For example, I appointed the Tower Commission to study the entire workings of the NSC [National Security Council]. We have now reformed NSC according to their recommendations. We are also working with the Hill right now on intelligence and covert matters. That hasn't been easy because they really were out to have a lynching. Nevertheless, I think we have something going there that will smack very much of bipartisianship.

I do think, Stu, that a couple of real misconceptions must be wiped out. They have been firmly planted in the public mind by constant repetition. I was not doing business with the Ayatollah, for example, but with individuals who could have been executed if they were exposed. Another is that I was not trading arms for hostages; but, as it developed, Cap [Weinberger] and George [Shultz] were right when they argued that, if our arrangement ever became know, it would look like trading. That's what happened.

Nancy sends her love.

Sincerely,

Ron

Mr. Stuart K. Spencer
Irvine, California

October 20, 1987

Dear Donn:

I'm sorry to be so late in answering your letter of August 17, but I was away from Washington until early September, and then a cloudburst of activity hit me. Well, anyway, here I am at last. Donn, I want to comment on our meeting. I know the people you brought were sincere and believed they had seen and known the truth about Nicaragua. Once again I have to point out that we have sources of information that go deeper than what can be learned on a visit, no matter how dedicated the visitors are to learning the truth.

I'm enclosing Reverend Gary Demarest's account, which has only just now come to my attention. Donn, I can't be too detailed in relating things we know because it would reveal sources, etc. But, just as an example, those accounts of attending church, being in the homes of clergymen who attested to freedom of religion, etc.—I'm sure they spoke the truth as they saw it, but the truth is the Sandinistas have created a religious "Potemkin Village."* The Reverend Parajon is a supporter of the Sandinistas, and he has put together a group of churches where religious freedom is supposed to prevail, and does, so long as they support the government. It is all part of their very sophisticated disinformation campaign. There are more than 10,000 political prisoners held in captivity who have committed no crime.

I just had to call this to your attention and, as I say, there is more evidence, much of which I can't discuss.

Nancy sends her love.

Sincerely,

Ron

The Reverend Donn Moomaw
Los Angeles, California

* Russian field marshal Grigori Potemkin is alleged to have had sham villages built in the Crimea to impress Catherine II during her tour of the province in 1787.

October 20, 1987

Dear Mr. Avey:

Let me apologize for the tardiness of my reply, but I have only just now gotten your letter of July 25. Somewhere in the bureaucracy it must have become entangled or shelved for a time.

I appreciate your writing as you did and relating the story of your trip to the Soviet Union. I'll be sharing your account [about Soviet propaganda] with our people here in the West Wing. My own experience with the Soviet disinformation process took place in the late 1940's when they made an all-out effort to gain control of our motion picture industry. It was an era of communist front organizations and infiltration into a number of our unions. We eventually repelled them, but only after they had done considerable damage.

Again, my thanks to you.

Sincerely,

Ronald Reagan

Mr. C. K. Chuck Avey
Hilmar, California

October 21, 1987

Dear Ms. . . .*:

I'm sorry that I've only just received your letter of July 10, hence this tardy response. Since receiving your tragic story, our thoughts and prayers have been very much with you. I know that can be of very little comfort to you, in the face of such underserved horror inflicted on those you love.†

I assure you we have increased funding for research in our budget proposal, which Congress has not approved as yet. There is no question but that

"AIDS" is an emergency calling on all of us to do everything we can in the face of tragedies such as the one you are experiencing. Your letter has increased our determination to do everything we can to halt this dread disease.

Our deepest sympathy to you and your loved ones. God bless you and keep you.

Sincerely,

Ronald Reagan

* Name and address withheld.
† Her sister, brother-in-law, and their baby all had AIDS, caused by a transfusion of infected blood.

October 21, 1987

Dear Mrs. Siegel:

Thank you very much for your letter of September 21. I am in great agreement with you on your evaluation of Judge Bork and that his nonconfirmation will be a tremendous loss to our nation.

I want you to know that we've been working as hard as we can to change some of the negative votes, but the prospect is not promising. There is no doubt in our minds that the disgraceful distortion of fact in the hearing was politically motivated. There is no question but that the witnesses supporting Judge Bork were far and away of higher quality than those opposed, and it's also true they were not given equal exposure by the media.

Again, my thanks to you for writing as you did.

Sincerely,

Ronald Reagan

Mrs. Lynn Siegel
Palm City, Florida

October 21, 1987

Dear Morton:

Thanks for your letter of September 30 and for your help on the Bork matter. As you must know by now, we never had any intention of asking him to back away. In fact, I personally let him know we'd be with him whatever his decision might be. When he decided to stay in, I let him know we were happy with his decision.

Morton, I think there was a distortion of our position as to his philosophy. We never portrayed him as an Earl Warren type, nor did we ever use the word "moderate." It's possible some might have used that term in repudiating the charge that he was some kind of radical, but not any of us here in the Administration, to my knowledge.

Maybe we were overconfident, in view of the quality of our witnesses compared to those opposed: Chief Justice [Warren] Burger, seven former attorneys general for both Democratic and Republican Presidents, nine deans of prestigious law schools, the endorsement of the American Bar Association. By the way, I understand that one of the ABA board members who voted against him works for Senator [Joseph] Biden.

Well, perhaps by the time you receive this, it will be all over—I hope not—but, if so, I assure you I'll come back with a nominee as much like him as I can get.*

Again, thanks, and best regards.

Sincerely,

Ronald Reagan

The Honorable Morton C. Blackwell
Arlington, Virginia

* On October 23 the Senate blocked the confirmation by a vote of 58 to 42.

Singer Pearl Bailey was a special delegate to the United Nations in the Ford, Reagan, and Bush administrations. President Reagan's comment regarding the General Assembly refers to Nicaraguan president Daniel Ortega's address to the Assembly on October 8. When Ortega criticized President Reagan's call for re-newed aid to the Contras, the six-member American delegation walked out.

October 30, 1987

Dear Pearl:

Thank you for your kind letter and good wishes. I'm happy you agreed to serve at the U.N. and proud to have you representing us. I was very proud when I saw you on TV walking out of the General Assembly when that character was insulting our country. God bless you.

Nancy has had a fine recovery [from a mastectomy] and, according to the doctors, is way ahead of schedule. She sends her love, as do I.

Sincerely,

Ronald Reagan

The Honorable Pearl Bailey
United States Mission to the United Nations
New York, New York

Nick Ruwe had been on President Nixon's staff and served as chief of staff after Nixon resigned.

November 3, 1987

Dear Nick:

Howard Perlow delivered the translation of the article in *Timinn* regarding my (Icelandic?) parentage. I thought you might like to have my comments in case of future questions.

First of all, the story is without any foundation at all. My great-grandfather on my father's side hailed from Ballyporeen, Ireland. The pub there is named after me, and I've seen the church records and, no, I've never ordered them sealed.

But, to be specific, I was born in Tampico, Illinois. Beside the local records, I have an older brother who remembers my birth. He wasn't happy, he wanted a sister. There are a few people around who remember my birth. Of course, most have passed on, but I remember them and their relationship with our family.

Nick, I'm amazed at the detail in that story and it makes me wonder. I know there are at least two Ronald Reagans in addition to myself. One was a policeman in Sacramento when I was Governor. The second was an officer in the Army, World War II. I never met him, but other officers who had crossed paths with him at Fort Benning said he portrayed himself as Ronald Reagan the actor. He wouldn't sign autographs—said the Army had ordered him not to.

Well, enough of that. This Ronald Reagan is Irish, English and Scottish and made his first and, so far, only visit to Iceland at the invitation of General Secretary Gorbachev. As I said, that's quite a family history the *Timinn* printed; only it just ain't me.

Love to your lady, and warmest regards.

Sincerely,

Ron

The Honorable Nick Ruwe
America Ambassador
Reykjavik, Iceland

November 16, 1987

Dear Nackey:

Thank you for sending me the editorial. Needless to say, I share your high regard for Cap [Casper Weinberger] and, yes, I'll miss him. But Nackey, I must say the continued barrage from the media and the gossipers here "inside the beltway" is making for a distorted picture. Cap is leaving only because of his family situation, and his replacement [Frank Carlucci] is *his* first choice for the job. The supposed feud between Cap and George [Shultz] is greatly exaggerated. And, please, let me assure you that the picture which has been presented to you of my being steered, motivated and manipulated by people around me just isn't true. The thing that bothers me most is that some of this misrepresentation comes from a group who should be my allies, since they are self-declared conservatives.

But, again, to get back to your editorial—thanks for giving Cap the recognition he deserves. Cap has done a fantastic job of rebuilding our security forces, which were in a terrible state when we came here.

Best regards,

Ron

Mrs. William Loeb
Manchester, New Hampshire

November 20, 1987

Dear Alan:

Nancy and I thank you for your generous words and your condolences.

On the matter of Judge [Donald H.] Ginsburg, however, I think you've been victimized by press accounts that have distorted the situation in the interest of sensationalism.

The Judge is really a fine man and would have made an excellent Justice of the Supreme Court. He was overwhelmingly approved by the Senate committee little more than a year ago for the Court of Appeals and has actually been approved by the Senate for government positions two times.

Alan, the F.B.I., in their examinations, ask questions that would require answers as to whether an individual has ever been arrested for such things as drug possession, drunk driving, etc. I don't think they ever ask if someone has "smoked a joint" any more than they'd ask if someone had ever been drunk. They do ask if one has a drinking problem or has abused drugs.

Ginsburg's use of pot during the 1970's predated his government service and was then only infrequent occurrences, so it never occurred to him to volunteer word of it. What happened was that the press talked to some people who knew him while he was teaching at Harvard and who may not have been entirely sympathetic. When Ginsburg was faced with it he promptly acknowledged it, called it a mistake he regretted and he should never have done it. I'm sure there are a great many of his generation who feel the same way. Withdrawing his name from the process was entirely his doing.

Nancy sends her love and, again, our thanks to you.

Best regards.

Sincerely,

Ron

Mr. Alan Brown
APO New York

November 23, 1987

Dear Mr. Kruidenier:

Thank you for your October 16 letter. It has only just reached me, hence this late reply. You mentioned other letters. I'm afraid, in the flood of mail that comes to the Executive Branch, much of it gets buried out there in the bureaucracy. In the future, if you should write, put the number 16690 on the front of the envelope. That will get your letter directly to me.

I'm most grateful for your support, and particularly so with regard to line item veto. I've been preaching that ever since I've been here. Perhaps you know that Governors in 43 states have that. I had it as Governor of California. It truly would be of the greatest help in balancing the budget.

Let me tell you why the attack must be on the Congress itself and not on certain individuals—although I'm tempted many times to single out a few. The law requires the President to submit to Congress each year a budget for the coming year. Congress is then supposed to take that, change parts of it if they so desire and vote on it. Since I've been President, not one of my budget proposals has ever been considered by the Congress. They've termed each one "dead on arrival" and then packed all the appropriations into what they call a "Continuing Resolution." When this reaches me, I can't veto it without shutting the entire government down. See what line item veto could do to change that?

You are right on a great many things, including the Iran-Contra affair. As to your suggestions of things to do, I'll be doing them in this election year ahead. I do have one problem. I can go out making speeches (and I will), but much of the news media is on the other side. They will report that I made a speech and show it on TV for about half a minute, but not the part where I make the points you want to hear.

Well, again my thanks to you for your generous words and support.

Sincerely,

Ronald Reagan

Mr. Philip J. Kruidenier
Des Moines, Iowa

December 18, 1987

Dear Nackey:

Maybe we're even—I didn't enjoy reading those editorials [*The Union Leader,* December 3, 5, 1987] you didn't enjoy writing. Nackey, I'm still the R.R. I was, and the evil empire is still just that. I wasn't talking about you or people like you when I spoke of "inevitable war." I did have in mind a few individuals who probably aren't aware or conscious of their feeling about inevitable war. Maybe I didn't make myself clear, but I was talking about those individuals giving up on any effort to influence history and accepting permanent hatred and enmity as the only future for the two greatest superpowers. The probability of disaster is too great to accept that without making an effort.

We haven't weakened the western defense at all, quite the contrary. They are removing four warheads for every one we are taking out. But, more important, we still have thousands of tactical warheads on line that even us up with their conventional weapon superiority. We won't bargain those away until and unless they agree to a reduction of conventional weapons. Incidentally, their S.S. 20's were targeted on every important city and seaport in Europe. Ports we'd need to reinforce our allies.

Nackey, on the budget problems, I'm aware that the Democrats have tagged me as responsible for the deficits, but I counted on people like you to know the President can't spend a dime. We haven't had a budget since I've been here. Yes, the law says I must present a budget every January. And every January the Congress throws my budget away and passes a "continuing resolution" with all the appropriations in that one resolution. If I veto, the government shuts down.

Yes, I've asked for increases in defense spending. Rebuilding our national security was a must. Even Carter had projected a five-year military buildup to begin in 1982. Well, the Congress cut my defense budgets by $125 billion. But, at the same time, they added $250 billion to my domestic budgets in those "continuing resolutions."

The problem is that for almost 50 years the House of Representatives has been solid Democrat except for four years—two in Truman's Administration and two during Ike's.

Happy Holidays!

Sincerely,

Ron

Mrs. William Loeb
Manchester, New Hampshire

Roy Moseley, a British author, had earlier written a biography of movie actress Merle Oberon.

WASHINGTON

December 21, 1987

Dear Mr. Moseley:

I have just received your letter, and thank you for your generous words. You were most kind, and both Nancy and I are truly grateful.

We are pleased to learn you are doing a book on Cary Grant. We did not know of his heroism in World War II, but that's explainable. Cary was (off screen) modest and quite unassuming. He was definitely not the character he played so well on screen. We were great admirers of both Cary Grants and felt the warmest friendship for him as a person. As for the on-screen Cary, I used to proclaim to all who would listen that he should receive an Academy Award for never having done a poor, or even routine, performance.

We are both grateful that he was one of the Medal winners in the Kennedy Center Honors Awards during our time here.

Before our marriage, Nancy was under contract to M.G.M. She did a screen test with Cary for a part in one of his pictures. The test narrowed down to her and another actress who was given the role. Nancy, of course, was disappointed. Cary took her to lunch at the studio cafeteria and very kindly talked away her disappointment and complimented her on her acting. He told her she did something many actors didn't know how to do. She listened to the other actor.

In later years, after we were married, Nancy was his dinner partner at a banquet. I believe I was toastmaster that night so we were all at the head table. It was shortly after the birth of Cary's daughter. He started to tell Nancy what this meant to him and he teared up. That was all Nancy needed to start her crying. There they were, facing the entire banquet crowd, and both in tears.

One last item, Cary did a picture with Grace Kelly in which he wore some crew-neck sweaters. I thought they were great. Nancy ran into him and told him how much we enjoyed the movie. She also told him how much I liked those sweaters. A day or two later a package arrived at our house; in it were two sweaters of the kind he'd worn in the picture. I still have them.

Well, I can only add that you are writing about a magnificent thespian, a true gentleman and a cherished friend. I wish you well.

Sincerely,

Ronald Reagan

Mr. Roy Moseley
Los Angeles, California

1988–1989

... this General Secretary [Gorbachev] with his
glasnost and perestroika has really moved the Russian
people. ... And I'm convinced he is sincere about
wanting to make a change. He'd have to be to take on
the bureaucracy the way he has.

·*Letter of June 7, 1988*·

CONSERVATIVES, including dedicated Reagan disciples, were troubled by the Intermediate Nuclear Forces (INF) treaty signed in December 1987. One wrote and asked him to avoid dancing to the Yalta waltz.* Trusting Reagan, Congress and the public supported this stunning agreement after he explained the advantages. The Senate approved the treaty, 93 to 5, on May 27, two days before Reagan's trip to Finland and then to the Soviet Union, where crowds lined the routes of his motorcade, cheer-

---

* Critics of President Franklin Roosevelt argued that he had surrendered too much territory and power to Soviet leader Josef Stalin at the Yalta Conference in 1945.

ing, smiling, and welcoming him to Moscow. At Moscow State University, where he addressed the students and faculty, the President praised the freedom inherent in political and economic competition. The prepared speech called for friendship between the Soviet public and Americans: "We may be allowed to hope that the marvelous sound of a new openness will keep rising, ringing through, leading to a new world of reconciliation, friendship and peace." The delighted audience gave the proud president a standing ovation.

Before leaving Moscow for London, Reagan, in a news conference at the U.S. ambassador's residence, blamed the Soviet human rights abuses on the "bureaucracy" and added there had been improvement for the respect of human rights in the Soviet Union under Gorbachev. Hundreds, later tens of thousands, of dissidents were allowed to emigrate to the United State and Israel. Reagan praised the Soviet leader as being the very first general secretary to agree to destroy Soviet weapons and the first not to call for a one-world communist state. Gorbachev, proud of his special relationship with Reagan, recognized the determination, the hopefulness, and the respect he and Reagan shared with each other. In Early December, two weeks after the ground-breaking ceremony at the Ronald Reagan Library in California, Reagan met Gorbachev in New York for a mini-summit. They would visit together twice more: in San Francisco in June and in Moscow in September 1990. By then it was certainly clear to Reagan that the "Evil Empire" did not have an evil leader.

During 1988, his last full year in office, President Reagan received 275 letters in his special correspondence file. In the final weeks before the January 1989 inauguration, he received 88 letters. Among his very last hand-written replies in 1989, he reminisced that he cast his first vote for FDR in 1932, just after he had graduated from Eureka College and found a job in that "terrible time of great unemployment." Next he wrote and defended a cost-of-living adjustment for members of Congress and other high-level federal government executives and judges. Although he had campaigned for reducing federal expenditures during his political career, the President also recognized the economic effects of inflation as well as the necessity for attracting and keeping talented persons in office.

Now, after eight years in office, the President could take pride in reducing the unemployment rate as well as the disastrous inflation the nation faced in 1980. But the federal budget receipts still did not meet outlays. A deficit of $155 billion in 1988 was the latest in the series of eight deficits since 1980. The national debt, $995 billion in 1981, had ballooned to more than $2.6 trillion. These were discouraging numbers, especially to orthodox Republicans. And for the first time since 1914, the United States became a debtor nation. Reagan's appeals to Congress, calling for a line item veto and a constitutional amendment to prevent these deficits remained unanswered.

In foreign policy, this president could recall the shift he made in the superpower relationship as the United States rebuilt its military power. He believed peace could come only through strength. He recognized the necessity of negotiating with superpower leaders, especially Mikhail Gorbachev, a creative leader who would bring reform to the Soviet Union. The Soviet threat declined in part during the 1980s because of the costly and bloody war in Afghanistan. Gorbachev called for a pullout of troops in February 1988. The economic strains of this brutal conflict along with Soviet attempts to match the Strategic Defense Initiative precipitated a collapse of the Soviet Union. Gorbachev called for political reforms, and these changes led to free elections in March 1989. Some months later the Berlin Wall came down, and the Communist Party's monopoly on power ended. By 1991 Reagan's "Evil Empire" had dissolved.

With his overall approval rating at 68 percent and his handling of Soviet relations endorsed by 88 percent of Americans, Reagan left the White House to the applause of his real American heroes. As he said eight years earlier in his first Inaugural Address, these heroes—the factory workers, the farmers, retail counter clerks, entrepreneurs, individuals and families who support charity, churches, education, and government—renewed and sustained national life. And for these Americans, President Reagan created thousands of handwritten letters, letters that reflected his wisdom, humor, compassion, and constant belief in the rights of the unborn. Moreover, his deeply held religious values permeated his optimism, his genuine respect for persons in the military, and his sensitivity to others, regardless of race, creed, or color.

January 6, 1988

Dear Mr. Tringali:

I have only just received your letter of December 12, hence this tardy reply.

I'm afraid some of the confused media reporting has led you to some mistaken conclusions about our relations with the Soviet Union. I assure you I hold to the words of Demosthenes 2,000 years ago in the Athenian marketplace when he said, "What sane man would let another man's words rather than his deeds proclaim who is at peace and who is at war with him?" The treaty we have just signed calls for the destruction of the medium-range nuclear missiles. The verification provisions are the most stringent ever signed in an arms reduction treaty. I assure you we'll carry them out.

My remarks about Gorbachev and Afghanistan were intended to simply point out that he was not in a position in the Soviet government to have played any part in the invasion of Afghanistan. Also to point out that he inherited a great embarrassment. After eight years the massive Soviet military machine has been unable to overcome a handful of freedom fighters who are outnumbered, and outgunned, hundreds to one.

General Secretary Gorbachev is the first leader in the history of the Soviet Union who has agreed to destroy weapons they already have. All the others have agreed only to limits on how many more they'll build. He is also the first leader who has not reaffirmed the Marxian concept of a one-world communist state. It will be interesting to see if he is still silent on that subject this June when he faces the Communist Party Congress.

As to the other important matters—human rights, regional conflicts, etc.— believe me, they were a major part of our agenda and will continue to be.

I hope this eases some of your concerns.

Sincerely,

Ronald Reagan

Mr. John J. Tringali
Mill Valley, California

[January 1988]

Dear Walter:

Happy 41st anniversary of your 39th birthday! I've been 39 years old 38 times now and still find it most enjoyable, especially when you consider the alternative.

Of course, it's also a time for looking back, taking a trip down memory lane. I'm doing that right now, and you'd be surprised how many of the happier times have to do with a gentleman named Walter Annenberg.

The first, or should I say the earliest, memory has to do with a somewhat homesick, lonely performer on a train between Philadelphia and New York. I was the lonely performer. Then a porter delivered an invitation from a gentleman in the Club Car. You were that gentleman. You asked me to join you, lovely Lee and your friends. For the rest of the ride I was anything but homesick and lonely.

The memories continue: visits in Philadelphia, then beautiful Sunnylands and, yes, Winfield House in London. And always a kind and thoughtful host, but, more important, a cherished friend.

Walter, there are no words to express how much Nancy and I treasure your friendship and the support you've given in our present occupation. During the holiday season when people say, "Happy New Year," we know it will be happy. We'll be with you and Lee in Sunnylands. Happy Birthday and God Bless You.

Sincerely,

Ron

The Honorable Walter Annenberg
"Sunnylands"
Rancho Mirage, California

January 7, 1988

Dear Mrs. Jones:

I, too, recall November 11, 1918, and it stays in my mind as the end of "The Great War"—World War I. I was just a lad in Monmouth, Illinois, watching the outburst and happiness in the downtown area where virtually everyone in the town had gathered.

I'd be most pleased to have the music to the poem, and thank you for sending the poem. I'm pleased to have it. If you do send the music, on the envelope write c/o Kathy Osborne. In that way the letter will reach me right away.

Again, my thanks.

Sincerely,

Ronald Reagan

Mrs. G. E. Jones
Morrilton, Arkansas

Peggy Say's brother, Terry Anderson, the Associated Press Bureau chief in Beirut, was taken captive in Lebanon by the Islamic Jihad in March 1985 and held until he was released in December 1991.

January 13, 1988

Dear Peggy:

I'm very tardy in acknowledging your Christmas greeting, but it has only recently reached my desk. I thank you and the Andersons for the beautiful card, and I assure you we are praying for your loved ones. We are also doing everything we can and exploring every avenue to bring about their release. Don't mistake silence for abandonment or lack of caring.

I know there are no words that can lighten the grief you all feel or make the pain of those in captivity easier for them to bear. Just please know their plight is of great importance to us. They are not forgotten, nor will they be.

Sincerely,

Ronald Reagan

Ms. Margaret Say
Batavia, New York

January 22, 1988

Dear Ruddy:

How nice to hear from you. We really enjoyed the goodies, and tell your mother thanks. I'm going to turn this place upside down until I find the book.* Sometimes the bureaucracy gets in the way.

Congratulations on your grades. I'm sorry I can't be of help on the science fair. I have to confess I didn't do very well in science when I was in school.

Yes, and congratulations on your bowling score. I did some bowling when I was your age, at the YMCA in Dixon, Illinois, but I never scored 134.

I don't have many answers to your questions about Gorbachev's family or his hobbies. We never got around to that kind of conversation, possibly because all our talk had to be through interpreters. You are right, it would be better if he could understand our language or, of course, if I could talk Russian.

Just between us (on another subject), I was rooting for the Redskins, even though in my job I'm not supposed to take sides. I think it's going to be quite a Super Bowl.

Good luck in your play about Martin Luther King, Jr. He was a great man.

My best to your mother.

Sincerely,

Ronald Reagan

Rudolph Lee Hines
Washington, D.C.

* Several months earlier, Ruddy's mother dropped off a book at the White House. It described California mountain ranges and what the Reagan ranch looked like in the 1800s.

February 1, 1988

Dear Bill:

Don't worry about the photographer, I've had him shot.

I still think we are on solid ground on the I.N.F. Treaty based on our verification provisions and on the fact that Gorby knows what our response to cheating would be—it's spelled Pershing.

Bill, hold your fire on Deaver. Our information is that some of the usual press editing of his answers in an interview were slanted. We'll have to wait until we see his book.

We are both excited about your new undertaking, and of course we will both be at liberty in the near future. Is there a juvenile character and an ingénue contemplated in your script—important roles of course? We'll be waiting for opening night and the movie version.

Nancy sends her love—so do I.

Sincerely,

Ron

Mr. William F. Buckley, Jr.
New York, New York

James Stewart served as a director of Frank B. Hall and Co., Inc., an insurance brokerage.

February 9, 1988

Dear Jimmie:

Thank you very much for your kind letter and generous words. I'm most grateful. Thank you, too, for sending me the copy of Paul Manheim's letter to the *Times*. Believe me, it will be the basis for some future (near future) statements of mine. His figures are accurate but, most important, they reveal the shortcomings of statistics. Disraeli once said, "there are lies, d—n lies and statistics." There is no question but that we all have been careless in our way of determining the unemployment rate. Is there serious unemployment in Washington when the Sunday *Washington Post* carries 62 full pages of help-wanted ads?

Well, again, my thanks and best regards.

Sincerely,

Ronald Reagan

Mr. James Stewart
New York, New York

Japan's former prime minister, Yasuhiro Nakasone, took great pride in his friendship with President Reagan. The photograph album which he sent commemorated this relationship dating back to May 1983 when the Prime Minister visited the White House.

February 11, 1988

Dear Yasu:

What a happy surprise! Your letter and the album* were delivered to me today, and Nancy and I haven't stopped going through it since it arrived. What happy memories it brings back. Memories of our effort in behalf of a better relationship between our two countries, but more important, memories of a wonderfully warm friendship that will be with us always.

Thank you for a gift we shall cherish. Nancy sends her love to Tsutako and you, and so do I.

Warmest regards,

Ron

The Honorable Yasuhiro Nakasone
Tokyo, Japan

* An album of photographs selected from an exhibition in Tokyo in mid-December, entitled "Ron & Yasu—in the Footsteps of the Japan—U.S. Leaders, 1982–1987."

February 15, 1988

Dear Father Sabatos:

I know I'm very late in answering your good letter of December 16, but sometimes it takes a while before mail reaches my desk. I have only just received your letter.

Let me assure you I'm in complete agreement with you on the matter of dealing with the Soviets. In our recent negotiations, I repeated several times an old Russian proverb until the General Secretary was tired of hearing it—"doveryai no proveryai." It translates, "trust but verify."

You are right that the Soviets would like to trade us out of completing the S.D.I. I finally convinced them it was not a bargaining chip. There is no way that I will give up on trying to find and develop a defense against nuclear missiles.

Again, my thanks to you and very best regards.

Sincerely,

Ronald Reagan

The Reverend Daniel C. Sabatos
Brooklyn, New York

February 15, 1988

Dear Dr. Broussard:

Thank you for your letter of January 20th. I'm glad you support our I.N.F. Treaty even though you have some reservations. I assure you, we won't give away the store. I respect Henry Kissinger and consider him a good friend but, in this instance, I do not believe he is fully informed.* A nuclear war cannot be won and must never be fought. In such a war between the two great powers, one has to ask if we ever launched those weapons at each other, where would the survivors live? Over 100 Soviet citizens are still unable to return to the homes in Chernobyl and that power plant accident was less than the effect of one single warhead.

But you are right that we must always deal from strength and insist on verification of every agreement. In my meetings with the General Secretary, I repeated several times a Russian proverb—"doveryai no proveryai"—trust but verify.

Again, thanks and best wishes.

Sincerely,

Ronald Reagan

Dr. Gerald E. Broussard
Oak Grove, Louisiana

* The correspondent noted that Kissinger, in a recent newsmagazine article, was reported as saying that a 50 percent reduction in U.S. missile force would make remaining land-based missiles and submarines more tempting targets for a preemptive first strike.

WASHINGTON

February 15, 1988

Dear Mr. Brooks:

I'm late in answering your letter of December 22, but it sometimes takes a while before mail reaches my desk. Thank you for that letter. I'm grateful to you for sharing with me because you strengthen my resolve.

I have asked the Governors of our fifty states to counsel together on their ideas as to what kind of reform of welfare we could come up with. My goal is to create a program that provides help to those who, through no fault of their own, cannot provide for themselves. But it should be a program that aims at making them independent of welfare as quickly as possible.

I'm afraid that we've fallen into a trap wherein a bureaucracy exists as long as it can perpetuate dependency, so its goal is not to free people from needing the bureaucracy's services.

Again, my thanks to you.

Sincerely,

Ronald Reagan

Mr. Richard E. Brooks
St. Peters, Missouri

WASHINGTON

February 19, 1988

Dear Mr. Smith:

Thank you very much for your letter of January 26, and my apology for being so late with my reply.

I and my Administration are wholeheartedly in agreement with you when you state that the battle for the unborn is a civil rights cause. On every front—through Constitutional amendment, through legislation, through new regulations on Title X and through consistent advocacy in the courts—we are taking every step in our power to end abortion. I give you my promise that these efforts will continue.

Again, my thanks for your letter, and for all that you are doing in this cause.

Sincerely,

Ronald Reagan

Mr. Donald S. Smith
Anaheim, California

February 22, 1988

Dear Mr. Healey:

Forgive the delay in answering your letter of December 21, but it has only just now reached my desk. I've found this is not unusual here in Washington, probably something to do with bureaucracy.

I appreciate this opportunity to straighten out some misperceptions that have resulted from political demagoguery and, yes, press hysteria. I have used my veto and have been overridden on several extravagant bills. But the main problem has been the replacement by congress of a legitimate budget bill with a continuing resolution. This has happened every year I've been here. It lumps all the spending measures in a resolution that must be passed or government is shut down. This is why I've tried to get a line-item veto such as I had when I was Governor of California. Now, however, maybe there is light at the end of the tunnel. Leaders in the Congress have gotten together and agreed they should send the President separate appropriation bills so the veto can be used without shutting down the government.

You mentioned Social Security. President Johnson got this "off budget" program into the budget to make the deficit look smaller. Social Security is paid out from a trust fund that cannot be used for anything else. The payments into that fund each year are thus counted as revenue; and since they amount to more than the Social Security, they reduce the apparent size of the deficit. It's a pen-and-ink trick and we'd be better off treating it, as once we did, as an "off budget" program. Mr. Healey, the truth is our deficits are structural, they are built into the system. There have only been eight single years in the last 57 when there was no deficit. Then when the war on poverty program was launched in the 60's, we saw the Federal budget in the 15 years from 1965 to 1980 increase to about five times what it was in '65. But the deficit increased to 38 times what it had been.

In six years of my Administration Congress reduced my defense budgets by $51 billion. Was this aimed at reducing the deficits? Hardly. In those same six years they added $123 billion to domestic spending. We have found programs where the overhead was $2 for every $1 delivered to the needy. Our defense spending was entirely justified. When I took office, half our military aircraft on any given day could not fly for lack of spare parts. The same situation prevailed with our Navy ships. They couldn't leave harbor.

Thank you for writing and giving me a chance to state our case.

Sincerely,

Ronald Reagan

Mr. John H. Healey
Midland, Texas

February 25, 1988

Dear Alan:

Thank you for your letter of February 8 and your report on the Spanish media. The Nicaraguan communist government has a very sophisticated disinformation network and it's worldwide. Here in our own country it has involved our media to a very great extent. Calling the Sandinistas a democratic government indicates how much they influence the media where you are—although I was pleased to read what you said about Jose Maria Carrascal and the Madrid daily *ABC.**

Well, again, thanks. We're continuing the fight and will stick with it. Nancy sends her best.

Sincerely,

Ron

Mr. Alan Brown
APO New York

* This Madrid reporter praised Reagan for his astute policies.

March 7, 1988

Dear Jean and Bill:

What a surprise and what a trip down memory lane. Yes, the painting is the view I had from that very spot,* and I've been living with memories since it arrived. Thank you both. There are no words to properly express my gratitude and my pleasure at having that lovely painting of a spot so dear to my heart. In just a few weeks we'll be hand-carrying it to the ranch. . . .

Let us know when you'll be in Washington. I'll hope we are on hand. I say that because there are a few things such as the Moscow summit pending with no exact dates set as yet. If we're here, you can bet you'll be in the Oval Office.

Again, a heartfelt thank you for "Lowell Park." Nancy joins me in every good wish and warm regard.

Sincerely,

Dutch

Mr. and Mrs. Bill Thompson
Dixon, Illinois

* Fran Swarbrick, a Dixon artist, painted the view at Lowell Park. Bill Thompson's grandfather built and was the first owner of the Ronald Reagan boyhood house.

March 14, 1988

Dear Friends [third-grade students]:

Thank you very much for your kind and very nice letters. I have read each one with great pleasure and am returning them with autographs attached. I am going to try in this letter to answer your questions.

First of all, while I was a member of the Democratic party for much of my life, I left that party and became a Republican when both parties underwent some fundamental changes. I ran for President as a Republican after serving two terms as the Republican Governor of California. I'm in the last year of my second term as President. The law limits the President to only two terms so I can't run again. Before all this I was in motion pictures.

We live in the White House, which is truly a mansion. Actually, our living quarters are on the second floor. They are very nice and most comfortable. The main floor has larger public rooms for the functions that go with being President. For example, there is a dining room with seating for more than 100 people. It is used for formal occasions such as when foreign rulers or heads of state come here on visits. Tourists visit these formal rooms on daily tours.

Yes, the White House has an outdoor swimming pool and a tennis court. The house itself is almost 200 years old.

You asked about automobiles. The government provides transportation for the President and First Lady. This happens to be a Cadillac limousine which has certain features like telephones, etc.

As to our personal life—yes, we have a ranch in California, and our favorite sport is horseback riding. We manage several trips a year to the ranch and enjoy riding daily while we are there.

Now let me tell you a little history about our country. Every country has what is called a Constitution. These are documents which spell out what the people can do. Our Constitution is 200 years old. It is different than all those other Constitutions in one very important way, and we can be very proud of that difference. In all the other Constitutions the governments tell the people what they are allowed to do. In ours, "We the People" tell the government what it can do, and it can only do those things which we the people allow it to do. That is the meaning of our freedom as a people.

Well, again, I thank you for your letters and for the nice things you had to say. If ever our paths do cross, I'll be very happy to see you.

Sincerely,

Ronald Reagan

Pupils of Mrs. Nix's Third Grade Class
Fort Worth, Texas

WASHINGTON

April 18, 1988

Dear Mr. Peaslee:

Thank you for your letter of February 2, and forgive my tardiness in answering; but it sometimes takes a while before mail reaches my desk.

I appreciate very much your generous words and your support and am glad to have an opportunity to speak to your concern about the "Reagan Revolution" and whether it was abandoned. Please don't think I'm trying to pass the buck, but I've never retreated from what we started in 1981 and, as an ex-President, I'll be speaking out in behalf of carrying on until the unfinished business is finished.

I can understand your not having all the information on what has taken place here in this "company town." When we launched our economic recovery program in 1981, as well as some long-needed social reforms, we had a majority in the Senate. The Democrats were in charge of the House of Representatives. But having the Senate meant having chairmen of all the Senate committees and control of those committees. We could not have achieved what we did if we hadn't had that one house for 6 years.

But now, we no longer have that advantage. The opposition party controls both the houses of Congress. I've had vetoes of pork barrel spending measures overturned, and our own programs buried in committee or simply killed on the floor. Billions of dollars have been cut from our defense budget, and some of our social programs, such as stopping runaway abortion, aren't given the light of day in the Congress.

Well, I'll stop here and thank you for letting me get this off my chest; but my goal in the years ahead is to make people aware of the need to give a Republican President a Republican Congress. In over half a century only one Republican President, in addition to my 6 years of one house, has had a Congress with both houses Republican; and that was Eisenhower for only 2 of his 8 years. [1953–1955].

Again, thanks.

Sincerely,

Ronald Reagan

Mr. William W. Peaslee
Erwin, North Carolina

Armand Deutsch arrived in Hollywood in 1947 and produced the movies The Magnificent Yankee *and* Saddle the Wind *in the 1950s. President Reagan appointed him vice chairman of the President's Committee on the Arts and Humanities in 1982.*

June 7, 1988

Dear Ardie:

It was great to get home [from Russia and England], and your letter made it even greater. Thank you for, as always, your generous words and wonderful way of raising my morale. We all felt good about the trip, and then I read your letter and went into high gear.

Ardie, this General Secretary with his glasnost and perestroika has really moved the Russian people. We couldn't believe their friendliness and warmth. I'm talking about the people in the street—not the world of officialdom. Wherever we went they were massed on the curb, waving, smiling and cheering. And I'm convinced he is sincere about wanting to make a change. He'd have to be to take on the bureaucracy the way he has.

Well, bless you both, and love from both of us.

Sincerely,

Ron

Mr. Armand S. Deutsch
Beverly Hills, California

June 7, 1988

Dear Ward:

Just a belated line now that I'm back from the summit and getting rid of jet lag.

Ward, I had to veto the trade bill, but right now, as I promised, a trade bill I think could be acceptable is being put together on the Hill. If it goes as I think it will, I'll be able to sign and will.

Ward, we've created 16 million new jobs in the last five years. We have the highest percentage of what is called our potential labor pool ever employed in our history, and we're continuing an expansion that is the longest we've ever known.

Our trading partners in the world are in virtually an opposite situation, and at our economic summits they repeatedly tell me their problems. Their problems are much like the legislation I just vetoed. Having been President of my union for six years, the Screen Actors Guild, I think I'm pretty pro-labor and believe plant closings, etc., belong in labor-management contracts, not in government regulations. Our best estimates of the effect of the bill I vetoed are [a] loss of more than half a million jobs.

Well, enough of that. I appreciate your concern and, as always, know you speak with my best interest in mind, and I'm grateful. Let me assure you I'm going to work my tail off to get George [Bush] elected.

Sincerely,

Ron

Mr. Ward L. Quaal
Chicago, Illinois

June 8, 1988

Dear Mr. Chase:

Word has reached me that you and I share something other than being products of the vintage year 1911. I preceded you by some months in that year, and now I learn that I've preceded you with regard to some plumbing problems.*

I thought it might be of some encouragement if I told you that all of my problems are long gone and I feel great. Please know I'm rooting for you and so is Nancy. You'll be in our thoughts and prayers.

We started life in the same year. We played football in the same era. We were in the military during the same war. There's no reason why we shouldn't have the same result with our plumbing repairs. God bless you.

Sincerely,

Ronald Reagan

Mr. Robert R. Chase
Bronxville, New York

* Medical problems of the prostate and the colon.

October 20, 1988

Dear Alan:

Well, at last! I thought maybe they'd kicked you out [of Spain] with the F16s and you were looking for a new base. But seriously—thank you for your most generous words about our stay here in the puzzle palace on the Potomac.

We leave with no regrets, many happy memories and, of course, a few wishes that some of our unfinished efforts could have been completed. But, all in all, we were happy here and now we look forward to life in California. Neither of us looks upon it as retirement. There are too many things yet to do.

Right now, and for the next few weeks, I am campaigning for George [Bush] as much as I can, without neglecting the job I have and that he seeks. I'm convinced his opponent [Michael Dukakis] would be a disaster.

Nancy sends her very best to you, as do I.

Sincerely,

Ronald Reagan

Mr. Alan Brown
APO, New York

November 21, 1988

Dear Phil:

Thank you for your very kind, warm letter. Your words were more than generous, and I'm most grateful.

You are so right about having the Lord's help. I know my prayers were heard, and sometimes I called on Him so often I worried that He might get tired of hearing from me. I have come to understand Abe Lincoln's words when he said, "I could not stand this job for 15 minutes if I did not believe I could call on the One who is wiser and stronger than all others."

Again, my thanks, and love to Jo.

Sincerely,

Ron

Mr. Phil Regan
Pasadena, California

Barry Goldwater served as a pilot in World War II, and later, the Air Force. From 1953 to 1965 and 1969 to 1987 he served in the U.S. Senate. His book, The Conscience of a Conservative, *in 1960 would lead to his selection as the Republican candidate for the U.S. presidency in 1964.*

November 21, 1988

Dear Barry:

Just received your nice letter, and I thank you for your generous words. They mean a lot to me.

As you can imagine, I'm looking at January 20 with mixed emotions. There is, of course, anticipation about getting back to California and the ranch, but then some regret because of things we didn't get done here.

I hope our paths will cross, and Nancy joins me in this. She sends her love, and from both of us warmest regards.

Again, thanks.

Sincerely,

Ron

The Honorable Barry Goldwater
Scottsdale, Arizona

November 21, 1988

Dear Ann:

I won't commiserate with you about your illness, knowing what it's leading up to.* I'll just share your joy. And I know we're both happy about the election.

This enclosed pin has to do with the election. In my campaign speeches for George I responded to the Democrat line, "Time for a change." I told the audiences, "we were the change, we started it 8 years ago." Then I was amazed on one of my later trips to discover people wearing this pin ["We are the Change" buttons].

Now, I'll get back to collecting things for the journey to California. It's quite a job. I can't believe what all we've collected in just 8 years.

We're both very happy for you and Gary. Give him our best regards.

Sincerely,

Ron

Mrs. Ann Shinaver
Fresno, California

* Baby expected in May.

January 17, 1989

Dear Elsa:

Sorry to be so late in answering your letter, but things have become pretty frantic back here, what with packing and all. Thank you for your generous words.

Elsa, let me give you some things about the pay raise which are not generally known. Under the law, pay raises for others—executive cabinet members and, most important, judges are all tied to the pay for Congress. It's all or no one, according to the law. Right now we are having an unprecedented number of judges returning to civilian life because of the pay situation. These are younger judges facing college costs for their children on a pay level that is lower than that of a junior clerk in a law firm.

But the most important thing is, this shouldn't really be called a "pay raise." It's a cost-of-living increase. Inflation since 1969 has made the comparison between 1969 salaries and today's a great reduction in purchasing power. Actually, the recommended increase still lacks about $6000 of equalizing the 1969 level in purchasing power.

Well, it's only a few days and we'll be back in California. We're looking forward to it.

Sincerely,

Ron

Ms. Elsa Sandstrom
La Jolla, California

WASHINGTON

January 17, 1989

Dear Ruth and Billy:

Probably before you get this we will have spoken to each other at the Inauguration. But then there might not be a chance for much conversation. So this is to thank you from the bottom of my heart for your letter of January 10. And more than that, to thank you for all that your friendship means to us.

Thank you for your prayers. I know they have been answered, and to steal Lincoln's words, I have had help from One who is stronger and wiser than all others.

Nancy and I want you both to know that a change in our geographical location must not lessen a relationship we treasure. Nancy sends her love, and so do I.

Sincerely,

Ron

The Reverend Billy Graham
Montreat, North Carolina

January 17, 1989

Dear Bill:

I'm late with this but didn't get it until my return from California. Since reading it, you've been in our prayers. We're happy to get the word from you that you are on the recovery road and will be coming to California. I'll be getting my mail at my new office [in] Los Angeles, California. . . .

It's four days 'til private citizenship again. We've been in a tornado of packing the accumulation of these years. It's a bittersweet time, with all the good-byes and such, but it's coupled with our love for our California home.

But now let me close with a big thank-you for that column. I should say those columns. I've been grateful and proud to have had your support over the years, and now this summing up that you did I will treasure.

Nancy sends her love, and from both of us, every good wish for your return to full health and vigor.

Sincerely,

Ron

Mr. William A. Rusher
New York, New York

J. Peter Grace served as chairman of the W. R. Grace and Company from 1945, when he was thirty-two years old. He later served as chair of the Catholic lay organization the Knights of Malta, which had almost three thousand members in the United States.

January 18, 1989

Dear Peter:

As I write this, remembering our conversation, you are probably in some far-off corner of the world. So I write with the expectation this will greet you on your arrival back in home port.

Thank you for your letter of January 9 and your generous words. More than that, though, thank you for all you've done in my behalf and, yes, for the nation's welfare. And thank you for the part you played in conferring that honor on me in New York with the Knights of Malta. I shall long remember that evening as truly one of the high spots in these eight years.

Now that I'm on my way to California, my office address is . . .

Again, thanks.

Sincerely,

Ron

The Honorable J. Peter Grace
Washington, D.C.

Acknowledgments

—

S EVERAL years ago, while researching at The Ronald Reagan
Presidential Library in Simi Valley, California, I asked a research
archivist about a reference in the manuscript collection to the
President's Handwriting File. I learned that this file of more than
3,500 letters contained President Reagan's handwritten replies to thousands of correspondents in the United States and certain foreign countries
between the years 1981 and 1989. My intensive research in five other presidential archives had uncovered few comparable files containing such a
vivid and personal record; none was as lively and optimistic. While reading through these Reagan letters, I sensed that here was a unique president
who conveyed a special warmth through his written words. At the White
House, Camp David, and Rancho del Cielo near Santa Barbara and
aboard Air Force One, the President penned careful paragraphs that
were sometimes instructive, often deeply grateful, at times (though rarely)
angry, and remarkably optimistic.

As I read through these thousands of pages of incoming letters together
with the President's thoughtful replies, I discovered that these handwrit-

ten documents sketched a portrait of a person rarely presented in the print media, on the college and university campuses, or in the inner cities. Threads of Reagan's optimism, decency, humanity, humor, anger, bluntness, loyalty, thrift, charity, and understanding became a tapestry of his presidential character. The letters that he wrote to residents from Dixon, his small hometown in Illinois, and also to friends who attended Eureka College with him were filled with nostalgic memories. Other letters to unemployed workers, newspaper and magazine columnists, Soviet leaders, Hollywood friends, sports figures, modest and wealthy benefactors, and ordinary citizens and young students described his visions and answered their questions. His deep pride in the military was shown in his letters to women and men serving in the armed forces. He valued their many sacrifices to keep America strong and safe. Warm and compassionate letters written to parents and families whose members had died in the service of the nation reflected a president filled with grief over the loss of life. Also a delight to read are his descriptive letters to a Washington, D.C., elementary school pen pal, Rudolph Hines. All his letters, written in a clear hand, portray his deep love and respect for the United States and his faith in a loving God. Moreover, they reveal the inner strength, determination, and courage of a talented leader.

Our son, Ralph A. Weber, the associate editor, also immediately recognized the uniqueness of President Reagan's handwritten letters. His wise judgment was invaluable during selection of the most interesting letters and in contributing to pivotal decisions in designing this project. He joined me in believing that these insightful Reagan letters should be shared with all Americans.

Researchers at the magnificent Reagan Library, some forty miles northwest of Los Angeles International Airport, receive generous and prompt assistance. I am deeply grateful for the friendship and encouragement given by R. Duke Blackwood, the Library's director. His enthusiasm and support added strength to this study. I am indebted to him and to the research archivists on his staff. In particular, I wish to acknowledge the assistance given by Cate Sewell, who promptly answered complicated questions and searched numerous files with patience and skill.

When I first began this research three years ago, Dennis Daellenbach at the Library provided good insights on Reagan manuscript sources.

Mary Brown, Diane Barrie, Kelly Barton, Greg Cumming, Sherrie Fletcher, Shelly Jacobs, Lisa Jones, Meghan Lee, Jennifer Sternaman, and audiovisual specialist Josh Tenenbaum all proved to be supportive and gracious in providing archival materials and other research data. These bright, dedicated, and very knowledgeable persons make the library research room a welcome place and solve many complex problems in historical research.

President Reagan's White House staff members, Anne Higgins and Kathy Osborne, answered my many questions about the correspondence process; and their dedication and gentleness reflected, I am sure, the president they served. Joanne Drake, chief of staff for the Oval Office of Ronald Reagan, and Gary Stern, the general counsel for the National Archives, provided special support for this project.

I wish to thank my literary agent, Leona P. Schecter, for her initial and continuing enthusiasm: She recognized the distinct value of publishing Reagan's handwritten letters and found a fine editor, Adam Bellow, to endorse this venture. My friend at Boston College, Professor Thomas H. Hachey, provided helpful counsel during the research process. I am also grateful to Mr. and Mrs. Gordon C. Luce and Mrs. Mary Jane Wiesler in San Diego for their recollections of President and Mrs. Reagan; their insightful comments gave me a special perspective on Ronald Reagan as governor and president. My wife and I were fortunate to be invited by our friend, Dr. Harvey Snider, to carry on research and writing at his lovely home in Point Loma during our several research visits to Southern California.

Our friends, Dr. L. A. and Carlotta Anderson in Pahrump, Nevada, kindly shared their home and the library in that city during an early phase of this project. The Point Loma Library together with the Milwaukee Public Library and the Brookfield Public Library proved especially rich in background materials on the Reagan presidency. I am deeply grateful for research support at the Marquette University Memorial Library: staff members, Adam Bond, Christy Fellner, Mary Frenn, John Jentz, Molly Larkin, and Julie O'Keeffe, found answers to a variety of economic and political queries with promptness and expertise.

For her extraordinary fine work in typing the manuscript, I thank Diane Paszkiewicz; her precision and expert computer skills brought the manuscript to timely completion.

Once again my wife, Rosemarie, assisted me in research at this presidential library. Now, thirteen books later, she still continues with enthusiasm and limitless support for these scholarly adventures. Her thoughtful questions and wise observations together with her efficient copy machine expertise enhanced this project. We are both grateful to our children, Mary, Elizabeth, Ralph A., Anne, Catherine, Neil, Therese, Thomas, and Andrew along with their spouses and children for understanding the demands of research and writing. The blessings of family keep everything else in its proper perspective.